ZARELA'S VERACRUZ

ZARELA MARTÍNEZ

WITH ANNE MENDELSON

HOUGHTON MIFFLIN COMPANY   BOSTON   NEW YORK   2001

Zarela's
Veracruz

For information about permission to reproduce selections
from this book, write to Permissions, Houghton Mifflin Company,
215 Park Avenue South, New York, New York 10003.

Visit our Web site: www.houghtonmifflinbooks.com.

Library of Congress Cataloging-in-Publication Data

Martínez, Zarela.
    Zarela's Veracruz / Zarela Martínez with Anne Mendelson.
        p.   cm.
    Includes index.
    ISBN 0-618-00713-X
        1. Cookery, Mexican.   2. Cookery — Mexico — Veracruz-Llave
(State)   3. Veracruz-Llave (Mexico : State) — Social life and customs.
I. Mendelson, Anne.   II. Title.
        †x716.M4 M378   2001
        641.5972'62—dc21   2001026402

Book design by Anne Chalmers
Cover photograph by Laurie Smith
Prop styling by Edouard Prulhière
Food styling by Wes Martin
Dress for Zarela Martínez by Lela Rose
Map by Rodica Prato

Printed in the United States of America
RRD/WILL   10 9 8 7 6 5 4 3 2 1

To my mother,

AÍDA GABILONDO DESOUCHES,

my guide through life,

and to my children,

who bring me joy and make me proud

It gave birth to Mexico's first great civilization. It witnessed Mexico's first encounters with white people from Spain and black people from Africa. It is shadowed by the country's highest peak and claims most of Mexico's oil deposits. It contains the world's northernmost tropical rain forest and boasts the nation's highest per capita income and most diversified agriculture. It is Mexico's perennial tourist hot spot—for Mexicans. I don't say that it has Mexico's best food, for that honor can be disputed by several regions. I do think it has the country's most surprising, imaginative, and seductive food.

I INVITE YOU
to travel with me through Veracruz state
and learn why pre-Hispanic mythology
placed the blessed afterlife in
this beautiful spot.

— ZARELA MARTÍNEZ

ACKNOWLEDGMENTS

"*Gracias por tomarme en cuenta*" (Thank you for taking me into account). I was to hear this phrase countless times during the making of this book. For me, it sums up the generosity of the people of Veracruz.

This book might never have been written if it were not for Martín Ruíz Camino, who was director of tourism for the state of Oaxaca when my book *The Food and Life of Oaxaca* was published in 1997. He suggested that I also explore Veracruz and introduced me to his counterpart there, Luis Eduardo Ros. Mr. Ros enthusiastically placed all the resources of his state at my disposal and provided me with a very knowledgeable guide, Carlos Baizabal, who accompanied me on countless research trips from one end of the state to the other. The result is this book and a companion public television series, *¡Zarela! La Cocina Veracruzana*, produced by WMHT in Schenectady, New York.

Both projects came to a happy conclusion with the support of Veracruz's governor, Miguel Alemán Velasco; the secretary for economic development, Everardo Sousa Landa; the present director of tourism, Mauricio Guillaumín Croda; and his assistant, Ivonne Voor-duin. Maria Esther Hernández Palacios Mirón, formerly of the Instituto Veracruzano de Cultura, was very helpful, as were Raul Pazzi Sequera of the Casa de la Cultura in Pánuco and Maestra Ernestina Guerrero of the Escuela de Bachilleres in Tantoyuca. In Tlacotalpan, Mayor Hilario Villegas Sosa, city historian Humberto Aguirre Tinoco, José Luis González, and Rafael Figueroa Alavés and his son Rafael opened many doors and answered many questions. In Huatusco, Don Rafael Guillaumín and his family solved many problems and offered gracious hospitality. The Castro-Garnica family of Panadería La Fama in Coscomatepac taught me about breads, and Don Ángel Solís brought tears to my eyes with his songs. María Teresa Contreras and Benito Escalera were my inspiration in Catemaco. Dora Elena Careaga told me much about Afro-Cuban influences in the food of Veracruz. In Papantla, Victor and Gloria Vallejo, Heriberto Larios Rivera, Cesar Arellano Valencia, and Maestro Teodoro Cano were marvels of organization and professionalism. In Xico, Amado Manuel Izaguirre Virués kindled wonderful sparks of cultural insight.

La Asociación de Hoteleros de Veracruz provided lodging for me and the WMHT crew in member hotels. I must especially thank the Hotel Lois in the port of Veracruz, Carlos and Ana María Rubio of Hotel el Palmar in Costa Esmeralda, the Hotel el Tajín in Tuxpan, and Los Cocuyos in Huatusco for their repeated hospitality.

MANY RESTAURATEURS fed me (and the crew), let me into their kitchens, and shared invaluable recipes. I am particularly indebted to Tomasita Meléndez Hernández of Las Brisas del Mar in Boca del Río; Raquel Torres Cerdán of La Churrería del Recuerdo in Xalapa; the staff of Salto de Xala in Xalapa; Carmina Gutiérrez Pontón of La Fuente in Orizaba; Bertha Bernal de Ríos in Córdoba; Mary Carmen Peredo of El Mesón Xiqueño in Xico; Débora Íñiguez de Vives and her son Carlos of Doña Lala in Tlacotalpan; Irma Ramón Romero and Dora Hernández of La Viuda in Alvarado; Elena Gutiérrez de Careaga of Santiago's Club in Tamiahua; Elia Pretelín Moreno of Restorán Julita in Catemaco; and Vicente and Esperanza Bonilla of Casa Bonilla in Coatepec.

Home cooks were also very generous with their time and information; their contributions are recognized in numerous individual

recipes. I'd like to single out María del Carmen Virués de Izaguirre and Enriqueta Izaguirre de Virués of Xico, Inés Pavón Contreras of San Andrés Tuxtla, Santa María de Guadalupe Armenta Guzmán of Los Naranjos, and Marta Gómez Atzín and members of the local INSEN chapter in Papantla.

My daughter, Marissa Sánchez, along with Vera Rudzwick, Costas Haralapopoulos, Winston Cole, Gary Jacobson, Edward Bonuso, and other members of the staff at my restaurant, Zarela, in New York City, kept things running smoothly during my frequent absences. Richard Pinto of Empire Purveyors translated Mexican meat-cutting terminology for me. Ann-Michele Andrews solved multiple mysteries of sweets and pastries, and my mother, Aída Gabilondo Desouches, my son Aarón Sánchez, and Ylario Fernández and Ada Valencia tested many recipes. My son Rodrigo Sánchez offered valuable suggestions and cheered me on at every step.

I AM GRATEFUL for the opportunity to work with the dedicated and talented staff at WMHT, including Donn Rogosin, for initially approving the project; producer Stephen Honeybill; his assistant, Barbara Lawton, who graciously provided the travel photographs for this book; cameraman Michael Melitta; and sound technician Nicole Arseneault. On our first scouting trip, Victor Agustín Benítez shared with us his knowledge of Veracruzan food and culture.

For the beautiful pictures of the food, very special thanks to photographer Laurie Smith (my *comadre*); Ada Valencia, who prepared the food; Wes Martin, who styled it; and prop stylist Edouard Prul-hière. Many thanks also to Lela Rose and her staff for designing the dress that appears in the cover photograph; stylist Jean Powers, for putting the whole look together; and Richard Stein, for hairstyling. I can't forget the contribution of decorator-artist Rebecca Graves.

My deepest appreciation goes to my fearless agent, Jane Dystel; my wonderful editor, Rux Martin, and her assistant, Lori Galvin-Frost; my brilliant collaborator and friend, Anne Mendelson; and anyone else who had a hand in helping to make this book what it is.

— Zarela Martínez

CONTENTS

PREFACE

I NEVER EXPECTED to find myself writing a book about Veracruz. It is true that I traveled there briefly more than fifteen years ago and ate very well. But somehow I had mentally pigeonholed Veracruz as the state of Big Oil, unrelated to the things I most treasured in the cultural mosaic of Mexico.

I've always been drawn to those places that speak most powerfully of the pre Hispanic past and a spirit never wholly broken by the conquerors. When my travels took me to the state of Oaxaca, I sensed the great dignity and courage of its peoples in their jealously preserved, often austere cuisine. Their inward richness in the face of outward poverty and struggle was something that made me proud to be a Mexican.

To fall equally in love with Veracruz, I had to stop measuring it against what it was not — especially Oaxaca, its neighbor and complete opposite, which was the subject of my previous book. That Veracruz is the wealthiest state in Mexico was probably more of a strike against it than an advantage to me. I knew that it is also the most popular tourist destination for Mexicans traveling in Mexico; perhaps I thought that therefore it must be touristy. Whatever the reason, I always had polite excuses when my Mexican friends urged me to return there. But at last I let myself be talked into an extended visit, and another, and another . . . Shall I tell you what transformed my attitude? The food, yes, but more than that — it was the poetry.

Now, I had actually met a poet on my very first visit to the great port city of Veracruz, in 1985: the late, beloved Paco Píldora (Francisco Rivera Ávila), whose verse columns on the city scene ran in the local newspapers for about fifty years. I remembered him long and fondly, but I had nothing but the city with which to link him in my mind until I began traveling in the hinterlands of Veracruz state. Then I found a world where poets are officially designated to honor their towns by composing verses for civic occasions, where young men (not necessarily intellectuals, and often workingmen) love to hear these important symbols of the community declaim their works aloud, where long-dead local poets live in the hearts of ordinary citizens, where a small-town bakery may have its story immortalized in verse, and where a restaurant owner may be prouder of her poetry than of her cooking.

My EPIPHANY, I think, was my first encounter with Amado Manuel Izaguirre Virués, the city poet and *cronista* (official chronicler) of Xico in the north-central highlands. I was asking about the fiesta of the town's patron saint, Mary Magdalene, when suddenly I realized that Amado's voice had taken on the cadence of verse. This was not a poem he'd composed before but a spontaneous, natural rhythmic evocation of the aura of incense and fireworks, baking and cooking:

> *Es cuando Xico huele*
> *a incienso y pólvora,*
> *a mole y champurrado,*
> *a pan blanco y capéos . . .*

(It's when Xico has the scent of incense and gunpowder, of *mole* and hot chocolate, of fine bread and frying fish . . .)

As he spoke, I felt intoxicated, not only with the heady perfumes of the fiesta but with Amado's love of the Spanish language. I had not fathomed how deep this love runs in Veracruzan culture. It is the key to something essential about the state, just as the seventeen indigenous languages of Oaxaca and the many thousands of people there who are proud to speak no Spanish at all are a key to something in the Oaxacan character.

I don't want to oversimplify. Like the rest of Mexico, Oaxaca and Veracruz are *mestizo* cultures, a mix of Old World and New World.

But they face in different directions, both on the map and in their inner orientation. Oaxaca looks outward toward the Pacific and never completely made its peace with the Spanish invaders; Veracruz faces the east, where the conquerors came from, and willingly accepted them.

I **FEEL** that I have now embraced two incredibly different but complementary sides of the Mexican heritage. The contrasts are plain in the food. In many parts of Oaxaca, village cooking displays some of the purest survivals of pre-Hispanic traditions in all Mexico. In Veracruz, in contrast, you are struck by the emphasis on olive oil, butter, sherry, capers, Mediterranean herbs, Moorish spice palettes, citrus fruits, sesame seeds, rice, almonds, olives, raisins, and even the local version of manchego cheese. That's not the whole story, by a long shot. Through Veracruz, I also came to appreciate Mexico's links with Africa and Cuba. But if Veracruzan food were a poem, every line would be shot through with Spanish references. I am grateful for having had the chance to understand this aspect of my native land.

TAMAULIPAS

LUIS POTOSÍ

Tampico

NORTH

Lake Tamiahua

Tamiahua

HIDALGO

Tuxpan River   Tuxpan

Poza Rica

El Tajín   Papantla

Costa Esmeralda

PUEBLA   Nautla

NORTH-CENTRAL HIGHLANDS   HONEY

Naolinco

Perote   Villa Rica
Xico   Xalapa   Zempoala
Cofre de   Coatepec   La Antigua
Perote

Citlaltépetl   SOUTH-CENTRAL HIGHLANDS

Huatusco   Veracruz City
Coscomatepec   Boca del Río
Córdoba

Orizaba   Fortín   Hernán Cortés
de las Flores   SOTAVENTO   Alvarado

Tlacotalpan   Tuxtlas Mountains
Papaloapan River   Santiago   Catemaco
Tuxtla   Lake Catemaco
Otatitlán   San Andrés
Tuxtla

Coatzacoalcos
San Lorenzo   Minatitlán

FAR   TABASCO
SOUTHEAST

OAXACA

Coatzacoalcos River   ISTHMUS OF TEHUANTEPEC

CHIAPAS

UNITED STATES

GULF OF MEXICO

Mexico City   Veracruz

PACIFIC OCEAN

GULF OF

MEXICO

WHERE IT ALL BEGAN, AND HOW

O N T H E M A P, Veracruz is a string bean of a state, squeezed between the mountainous backbone of Mexico to the west and the Gulf coastline to the east. When people talk about the central Gulf coast of Mexico, they are referring to the rich and verdant tropical lands of Veracruz state, with a little chunk of Tamaulipas to the north and Tabasco to the south.

Seldom can you get from one place to another in a straight line, because steep slopes and major waterways are almost everywhere. This alone would give the different parts of the state a strong regionality, even if Veracruz did not happen to border on seven other Mexican states to the north, west, and south, each of which casts its influence on the adjoining area. Locals recognize five or six different regions in Veracruz, but in almost all of them, there is a further division between the far-reaching uplands and the narrow plains of the coast.

In our national memory, Veracruz has never lived down its reputation as the place that signaled the beginning of the end for Moctezuma's empire. One spring day in 1519, a band of Spaniards

ZARELA'S VERACRUZ

led by Hernán Cortés landed on an island facing what is now the harborside of Veracruz city and began to prepare for their march inland to the Aztec capital. No one elsewhere in Mexico has ever let Veracruz forget that the local inhabitants hospitably welcomed the invaders and even fed them well, with the mistaken idea that they were benevolent allies against the resented Aztecs. In honor of the day — it was Good Friday, April 21 — Cortés named the place La Villa Rica de la Vera Cruz, "the rich town of the True Cross."

Veracruz city actually wandered around for some years as the invaders tried to find a spot sheltered from vicious winds and free of deadly diseases. But by 1599, they returned to the spot facing Cortés's original landing place and built the city that would become in some respects the most important settlement of New Spain.

*T*o APPRECIATE the role of Veracruz and the character it developed, you must realize that the city was the sole gateway between the east coast and Mexico City, the capital that Cortés founded on the ruins of Moctezuma's Tenochtitlán. It was also the only gateway to the route from the Atlantic to the Pacific Ocean. The Spanish crown, trying to squelch unauthorized trafficking of goods between New Spain and other European countries, made the port city the beneficiary of a strict trade monopoly. All provisions (including food) coming from the mother country or Cuba to the colony had to pass through the burgeoning town. So did the gold, silver, and other products leaving the New World for Spain. Veracruz also handled anything being transported overland to or from the official west coast port of Mexico, the nearly uninhabited Acapulco.

Veracruz grew at a gradual pace, hampered by perilous north winds, outbreaks of yellow fever, and several generations of English and other pirates lurking as close as they dared to the official shipping point for Mexican silver. It developed a strong Caribbean orientation, grounded in the pre-Cortés era, when Havana had been the great Spanish outpost in the New World. Communication was at least as reliable with the old headquarters as with the new capital, Mexico City. Even today Havana and Veracruz consider themselves sister cities. Modern visitors to the state, like me, are often surprised and later enchanted by the traditions of improvised poetry, music, and dance that came to Veracruz — with many changes in the process — through the Spanish and African communities of Cuba. Food is another example, and maybe the most fascinating, of the same complex heritage.

ZARELA'S VERACRUZ

The province of Veracruz originally consisted of the lands lying along the principal routes to Mexico City. Eventually it stretched northwest and southeast along the Caribbean coast for nearly 450 miles, from the Pánuco and Tamesí rivers in the north to the Tonalá River in the south. The state's western border is no more than fifty or sixty miles inland at most points. This narrow belt of territory happens to encompass some of Mexico's finest natural farmland. The invaders rapidly discovered that they had an ideal location for both Spanish crops and tropical products that they were already raising in Cuba, especially sugarcane and coffee.

VERACRUZAN COOKING still vividly reflects the colony's early development. It was to this slender strip of land that Spanish friars intent on converting the heathen first came with seeds and cuttings from the plants that they knew: wheat, rice, almonds, grapes, and lettuce; peach, orange, and lime trees; herbs, including cilantro and chives; and European garden vegetables, such as chard and cabbage. Because the province had cool hills as well as steamy lowlands, the colonists were able to grow both tropical and temperate-zone crops while establishing successful ranches for livestock brought from Spain. (Veracruz is still one of Mexico's most prosperous producers of hogs, sheep, and both beef and dairy cattle.)

Similarly, this area was the scene of the Spaniards' earliest encounters with the great culinary building blocks of New Spain: corn, beans, and squashes for basic nourishment; chiles and pumpkin seeds for flavoring and thickening; turkeys, the major domestic animal; and vegetables and fruits such as tomatoes, tomatillos, avocados, and sapotes. Interested and receptive, the invaders gradually took to a blend of traditions. But the particular fusion that occurred in Veracruz is not identical to anything you may have tasted in other parts of Mexico. As seen by restaurant-goers, Veracruzan food may seem to share some overall features of Mexican cuisine, but it is set apart by the strength of the Spanish influence and by a factor that came as a total revelation to me when I began exploring the state: a powerful African legacy.

I began to grasp the place of Africa in the Veracruzan kitchen when I realized that for many centuries sugarcane was the most profitable crop of the region. (Today it is second only to corn, and in months when the cane fields are being burned to clear the stalks of leaves and debris before harvesting, nearly the whole state seems to smell of smoke.) The fields were worked at first by Indian slaves;

Cortés himself forced them into growing sugar when he founded a plantation in the southern part of the province. But they died off in such numbers that the Spanish, congratulating themselves on their merciful behavior, spared the survivors and began importing Africans instead. The reasoning was that African people were used to fierce tropical climates and that they were good for four times as much work as the *indígenas* (native people).

*V*ERACRUZ PROVINCE became a major player in the malignant slaves/sugar/rum trade system operating between Africa, the Caribbean, and Europe. This is why the state today so often recalls the atmosphere of the islands. Unlike African Americans in the United States, the large black and mixed-race population of Veracruz has little interest in black identity or the search for African roots. It is only very recently that people have begun talking of such things. But nearly everywhere you look, you find a broad spectrum of Veracruzan dishes that have near relatives in all the Caribbean plantation territories.

There are, for example, the starchy foods that the islanders collectively call *viandas*, including not only New World root vegetables like yuca, the somewhat similar malanga, and sweet potatoes, but the plantain-banana tribe brought from Africa via the Canary Islands. There are the dense, meaty varieties of winter squash and pumpkins that apparently made their way from Central and South America to Africa in the early days of the slave trade and then journeyed back to the West Indies. There are peanuts, which did the same thing and are more imaginatively used in cooking along the central Gulf coast than in any other region of Mexico.

As a cook, I feel an incredible thrill in seeing these relationships. I have always been fascinated by the process of culinary and cultural *mestizaje* (commingling) between indigenous peoples and Spaniards in Mexico. But I did not know that I would find an even richer, more flavorful three-way *mestizaje* still flourishing in the part of Mexico first claimed by Cortés. As you explore the recipes in this book, I hope you will be kindled by the same excitement I felt when I traveled in Veracruz, seeing and tasting the momentous historical encounters that are still written in the faces of its people and in its food.

PLACES AND PEOPLE

A TOUR OF VERACRUZ

CITY OF VERACRUZ

AND SOTAVENTO

$\mathcal{E}$L PUERTO (the port), as the city is called to distinguish it from Veracruz state, is not one of Mexico's most beautiful cities. Visitors from abroad remember it for other reasons, such as the constant comings and goings of fishing boats, immense cargo ships from the ends of the earth, and naval vessels (it is home base for the Mexican navy and the national naval academy). Mexican visitors remember it as the site of the nation's most popular Carnival Week celebration.

There is more hurry and bustle here than in most parts of Mexico, and the locals have a reputation as the friendliest, most fun-loving, and brashest people in the country. They speak Spanish with the pungent accent of Cuba and proudly call themselves *jarochos*, which used to mean something like "rude SOBs." But for a Veracruzan, *jarocho* is a name with an intoxicating sense of romance. It is also claimed by the residents of Sotavento, the tropical heartland region of which the port city is the unofficial capital. (Some people call all citizens of Veracruz state *jarochos*, but that's probably stretching the term.) To be a *jarocho* or *jarocha* is to share in a vibrant culture rooted in Spanish, African, and indigenous Mexican contributions, though the third is somewhat less striking than the first two. Especially in the smaller cities of Sotavento, the *jarocho* legacy sings aloud in the local music, dance, clothes, poetry, and food.

*M*OST VISITORS will be starting from Veracruz city, which at first looks like nothing but sprawl and traffic. But even here you begin to sense something heady and seductive, a quality that draws Mexicans in droves during Carnival Week every year. You find it most fully in the portico-lined town square, or *zócalo*, the Plaza de Armas, with the graceful colonial city administration building on one side and the Cathedral of Our Lady of the Assumption on the other. Come here on a clear, mild evening, and if you've hit the right day of the week, the naval band will be accompanying a bevy of white-clad couples moving through the small, precise, delicately sensuous steps of *danzón*, a symbol of the romantic Veracruzan tradition. *Danzón* is an offshoot of the *habanera*, which came here generations ago from Cuba. It is in the Veracruzan blood, and I have fallen in love with it so deeply that I chose the name Danzón for my second New York restaurant.

I have never found the port city an ideal place to explore Veracruzan cuisine at its best, but it does have a few culinary traditions as beloved as *danzón*. One is the *ostionerías*, the inexpensive "oysteries" selling oysters and other shellfish just off the boats that ply the coast. "The simpler, the better" is the watchword here; the *ostionerías* stick to a few well-known styles, especially *cocteles* (cocktails) of one super-fresh shellfish variety or a combination, flavored with condiments such as Worcestershire sauce, catsup, and even orange soda. (Only gringos are dismayed by such seasonings; Mexicans consider them totally Mexican.)

The other experience that shouldn't be missed is breakfast at La Parroquia. This famous and atmospheric porticoed café used to stand near the corner of the Plaza de Armas in the shade of the modest cathedral (hence the café's name, which means "the parish church"). It was everything a Mexican or Cuban or Spanish café ought to be in song and legend: a political forum, a salon for artistic interchanges, a center for power breakfasts, a home away from home for half the city. It also had the best coffee I have tasted in Veracruz, which considers itself Mexico's premier coffee-growing state. This is where I introduced myself more than fifteen years ago to a keen-featured, white-haired gentleman presiding over what was obviously his regular table: Francisco Rivera Ávila, who had been chronicling Veracruzan affairs in verse since the 1940s under the pen name Paco Píldora. I sat entranced while he tried to convey to me the gist of the Veracruzan love affair with extemporaneous rhyme. With effortless skill, he showed how *jarochos* play the popular rhyming game called *bomba* and illustrated the most famous Veracruzan form of all, the ten-line stanzas (*décimas*) in which he had written a witty, passionate, polemical history of Veracruz, starting with the conquest. It was Don Paco who gave me my first glimpse of the cultural and emotional ties between Cuba, the direct source of the Andalusian-derived rhyme-game tradition, and Veracruz.

*P*ACO PÍLDORA was gone when I went back, and La Parroquia had split into two rival entities, headed by unreconciled descendants of the previous owner. One heir got the lovely original site of the café, now called Los Portales. The other, Felipe Fernández Caballos, took the magnificent old Italian espresso machines and the name La Parroquia to new premises, which I thought were totally colorless and disappointing — until I heard the first clink of a spoon on a glass.

That brought it all back. The famous *café lechero* (coffee with milk) at La Parroquia was always served in glasses, not cups. The waiter, holding a big old-fashioned spouted kettle high in each hand above the glass, would pour a shot of strong coffee from one and a foaming Niagara of rich milk from the other. When the customer was ready for a refill, he would signal by tapping a spoon on the glass. This custom originated, or so I've read, in honor of a trolley conductor whose route took him past the old Parroquia and who would ring the bell as the car approached to tell the waiters to have his coffee ready. The day he died, the proprietor supplied the usual signal at the regular time by clinking a spoon on a glass. All the customers followed suit, in memory of the deceased. Be that as it may, the music of spoons on glasses and the sounds of political discussion now fill the new place as they did the old. And the coffee, blended and roasted by Felipe and his brother Ángel, is as good as ever, blended with milk from the brothers' own herd of cows.

If it is your first morning in Mexico, this is the place to start learning that breakfast may be the best meal of the day. The fresh rolls are particularly excellent, but it would be a crime not to explore the imaginative egg dishes, scrambled or fried in a dozen different ways, or cooked as Spanish-style omelets (*tortillas*). The one dish you are sure to find nowhere else is La Parroquia's special omelet, served in a bowl swimming in rich turkey broth (see the recipe on page 227).

The rest of Sotavento runs along the coast southeast of the port city, then turns inland along one of Veracruz's greatest rivers, the Papaloapan. One of its culinary, if not scenic, highlights is Boca del Río, a southern suburb of the port at the mouth of the Jamapa River. When I first visited the area, it was a sleepy, straggling collection of shacks and flimsy adobe houses. I went back in the nineties to find Boca del Río in the middle of a real estate boom. It is now a sea of huge high-rise hotels, condominiums, and shopping centers stretching as far as the eye can see. The biggest mall boasts a Japanese restaurant and a Dim Sum King, which I guess goes to show that Boca del Río really is now very cosmopolitan. Luckily, one thing hasn't changed: the best seafood in the area can still be found here.

I MUST DIGRESS to tell you what may be the most important thing about Veracruzan food: its absolute glory is fish and shellfish — anything that swims. The seafood alone would be reason enough to visit Veracruz state — almost any part of it — even if it had no other attractions. Look at a map and you will understand. The state boasts not one water habitat but many, some of them almost unique in the world. The mountains in the west send down innumerable clear, rushing, waterfall-filled streams to the Gulf of Mexico. Some are steep and swift almost all the way down to the sea. (These have had a lot to do with the region's economic wealth, for they supplied the power that allowed Veracruz to become a major manufacturing state.) Others broaden out into deltas and estuaries, with differing amounts of saltwater and freshwater, depending on the tides and the seasons. There are also magnificent lakes, especially in the far north and south. The 450-mile-long Gulf coast of Veracruz is broken up here and there by amazing tidal swamps, reefs, bays, and lagoons, most of them teeming with shellfish. As a result of all this, the state is a paradise for lovers of fish and shellfish of all kinds, from trout to water snails to lobster-like *langostinos*. The question of which area has "the best" is not easy to answer, for so many have the best in their own way.

Which brings us back to Boca del Río. Past the crowd of high rises, you come to a district of quiet streets and sea breezes. Here happy crowds devour the favorite seafood dishes of the state — wonderful soup-stews, fresh fish fillets stuffed with seafood mélanges, shrimp stir-fried with garlic, seafood-filled coconut halves, red snapper *a la veracruzana* — at such well-loved places as Riviera Pardiños, Las Brisas del Mar, Restaurant Acuario, and El Varadero. Fish is brought here from the whole coast and the estuaries of the Jamapa as well as from the principal river of Sotavento, the mighty Papaloapan — "River of Butterflies" in Nahuatl, the language of the Aztecs.

$\mathcal{M}$OST OF SOTAVENTO lies in a lush, steamy plain along the lower Papaloapan basin. It is the heart of *jarocho* country. Some people say that the exuberant and irreverent citizens of Alvarado, a major fishing center strategically located between the river and a fertile lagoon, are the ultimate *jarochos*. The town is full of riverbank *pescaderías* (restaurants devoted to the catch) serving fantastically fresh fish and succulent shrimp from the lagoon.

But my favorite example of the culture, and, I think, the loveliest town in Veracruz, is Tlacotalpan, about an hour's drive farther west. Tlacotalpan, "the Pearl of the Papaloapan," was the farthest up the river that ships coming from the coast in earlier times could navigate. The beautiful little city grew rich as a trading center before railroads and highways replaced rivers as the major shipping routes of Veracruz. It sank into decline in the mid–twentieth century but is now enjoying a revival as a cultural center. People come here from all over Mexico on February 2, the date of the major town fiesta, La Candelaria (Candlemas Day). I have never seen the famed running of the bulls (ferried over the river for the occasion from the cattle ranches that surround Tlacotalpan) or the decorated barge that takes the splendidly clad statue of the town's patron saint, the Virgin of the Candelaria, down the river to calm the waters, but that is one of my ambitions.

To get the full effect of Tlacotalpan's beauty, you should first see it from the river, which is joined here by a large tributary and is enormous even when it isn't flooded (which happens often — hence the importance of the Candelaria ceremony). No one is building high-rise condos in this tranquil backwater! The tallest things you see on the skyline are the palm trees that rise above the Cathedral of San Cristóbal and an array of old colonial houses painted in tropical-looking pastel colors with striking contrasts.

*T*LACOTALPAN HAS WORKED HARD to preserve a side of Sotavento that is half lost or disappearing elsewhere. In its heyday, it was a place of style and importance. Its glories were exports of tropical woods, rubber, cotton, and beautiful furniture, imports of European luxuries, the gorgeous little nineteenth-century Netzalhualcóyotl opera house (the only one in Sotavento); and a wonderful tradition called the fandango. Of these, the fandango is still going strong, and so are some of the local crafts that make it what it is.

I could say that a fandango is a dance, but it's really a whole arts festival. The inspirations are Spanish and Afro-Cuban. Though fandangos are also celebrated in Alvarado and other Sotaventan towns, those of Tlacotalpan are the most elaborate. The dance is performed on a resonating platform called a *tarima*, said to have come into use when colonial masters forbade the Africans to play their drums. It is accompanied by a harp and two forms of small guitar, the *jarana* and the *requinto*. The dancers stamp out a series of intricate rhythms on the *tarima* while either they or the instrumentalists keep up a dialogue of verses, usually the beloved *décimas* that Sotaventans learn to invent in childhood. The subject can be anything from love to local personalities and events, and the *decimistas* pick up and cap each other's rhymes with daring, often bawdy wit. Sometimes the women dance in exquisite costumes with wide snowy underskirts of *deshilado*, a lacy drawnwork made by pulling the threads from white cotton cloth into patterns called *rejillas*.

The Tlacotalpan fandangos are living history, not only because of the performers' magnetism but because other skills are carefully kept up. A local champion of the *deshilado* tradition, María Antonia Guzmán de Ramos, has fostered a revival of the art and founded a thriving crafts gallery, the Casa Artesanal, whose offerings include fandango costumes, tablecloths, and other beautiful *deshilado* creations. The *jaranas* are lovingly crafted in workshops, as is the traditional furniture of the region. The eighty-one-year-old official town poet, Don Guillermo Cházaro Lagos, is still helping the younger generation acquire the art of inventing *décimas*. Meanwhile, the town historian, Don Humberto Aguirre Tinoco, keeps Tlacotalpan's continuity with the past before the public eye through both learned and popular books and essays. No place in Mexico better merits the honor bestowed on Tlacotalpan in 1998, when it was chosen as a UNESCO World Heritage of Humanity Site.

As for the food, I think the recipes I took away from Tlacotalpan — for example, Leticia Alavés's almond-based confections and the glorious sweet potato–enriched *garnachas* (savory tartlets with a vibrant array of toppings) made by Rosa María Castro Chisanto — speak for themselves.

The fertile plain of the Papaloapan continues inland from Tlacotalpan almost to the border of Oaxaca state, full of sugarcane and rice fields as well as livestock ranches. This is an important center of the Mexican sugar-refining industry, though by no means the prettiest part of the river basin. One moving chapter in the state's turbulent religious and racial history is memorialized in the sleepy riverside hamlet of Otatitlán. In pre-Hispanic times, this spot was associated with Yacatecuhli, the patron god of merchants, traditionally depicted with black skin. The church that the conquerors built here was dominated by the Black Christ over the altar, a powerful jet-black image that the indigenous people and African slaves came for miles to worship. It was torn down and decapitated during the violent antireligious outbreaks of the so-called *cristeros* in 1921. But the devout worshipers of Otatitlán rescued the headless trunk and took it back to the sanctuary. A new head was carved to replace the old one, though the original miraculously reappeared many years later and is now housed in a glass case in the church. Today the cult of the Black Christ is stronger than ever in Veracruz and neighboring states.

XALAPA AND THE NORTH-CENTRAL HIGHLANDS

*H*EAD WEST AND NORTH from the port city and you quickly enter a different climate and mind-set from the sweltering southern plain of Sotavento with its vivid *jarocho* culture. The ground rises as you travel, and in less than two hours you are in cool, green hill country that tends to be swathed in clouds. So persistent is the highland *chipichipi* (misty rain) that the state capital, Xalapa, has not been able to build its own airport; you must drive from the Veracruz airport, some sixty-five miles away.

The steep terrain cuts off pockets of the central highlands from nearby areas, so that little divisions matter a lot. People speak of the *centro norte* and the *centro sur*, though the two areas are close neighbors except for the mountains. Xalapa, or Jalapa (today people almost invariably spell it with an X), is the hub of the "north center." It lies along a pre-Hispanic route that Cortés followed to the Aztec capital. For the average visitor from the United States, its main claim to fame will be the jalapeño (Xalapan) chile. Indeed, this is the most beloved and useful chile of all Veracruz, employed either fresh or smoke-dried in an amazing range of dishes. But nowadays it isn't commercially grown within twenty miles of the city. And there's a lot more to Xalapa than a chile, however noble. Even a few days in the city's civilized and gracious ambiance make a visitor understand its reputation as the Athens of Veracruz.

XALAPA IS A COLLEGE TOWN, home to the University of Veracruz and other major schools. The state government offices are here, along with a jewel of a museum, the Museo de Antropología de Xalapa, which is a wonderful place to start learning about the many peoples who have lived in Veracruz since the time of the Olmecs, Mexico's most ancient civilization. A first-class center of ecological studies, the Clavijero Botanical Garden, will help you appreciate the region's plant wealth. Beyond these attractions, Xalapa has a low-keyed charm, a harmonious marriage of the colonial and the ultra-modern.

The city was important even before Cortés, since it was always a convenient resting stage between the coast and the capital. When the Spanish arrived, most of them tried to spend as little time as possible exposed to the torrid climate and deadly tropical fevers of the port city. Anybody who was anybody settled near Xalapa for most of the year. It was no provincial hamlet but a cosmopolitan town that regularly hosted Mexico's largest Spanish trade fair. Here tradespeople displayed and bid on goods from the farthest ends of the empire, from Chinese silks and porcelains to the silver and gold work of New Spain. After Spain withdrew from Mexico, Xalapa still managed to prosper. It became a large manufacturing center, especially for textile mills powered by the many rushing streams of the region.

ZARELA'S VERACRUZ

The natural wealth of the area is as astonishing as the vistas are breathtaking — that is, when it's not raining. Xalapa and the neighboring hill towns are perched between the semiarid ground just inland from the coastal plain and a complex part of Mexico's backbone, the Sierra Madre Oriental. Because foreigners going to and from Mexico City usually had to pass through Xalapa, travelers over the centuries have left many accounts, sometimes with charming drawings or pictures to match, of the mountainous panoramas to the north, south, and west of the city. The most awe-inspiring peaks are Cofre de Perote, crowned with a "coffer" (a chest-like volcanic rock formation), and, far to the west, the nation's highest mountain, the incomparable snowcapped Citlaltépctl — Mexico's answer to Fuji.

The forests of the lower hills, where the vegetation of the *tierras calientes* ("hot lands") starts yielding to oak and pine trees and the weather is misty or rainy most of the year, are prime hunting grounds for orchid lovers. But they also shelter so many other kinds of flowers that Xalapa is sometimes called the City of Flowers because of the trade in these lovely plants. The woodlands also harbor an amazing range of wild greens and mushrooms, which figure prominently in the cuisine of Xalapa and the surrounding towns, as do some of the flowers. Then there are the fruit groves. All around Xalapa are magnificent orchards of both tropical fruits (bananas, mangos, sapotes) and the ones brought by the friars from Spain (apples, pears, plums, peaches). In fact, just about anything that grows in Mexico will grow in the Xalapa region.

COFFEE, HOWEVER, IS the biggest cash crop. The terrain is high enough to grow fine strains of *Coffea arabica*, the aristocrat of coffees, and the constant clouds and mists provide ideal climatic conditions. The state pins great hopes on further expansion of its already sizable presence on world coffee markets.

The biggest local center for coffee growing is the town of Coatepec. The shiny evergreen leaves of coffee bushes glisten on hillsides all around this hub, and experimental plantings at all stages of growth line the roads at the important research station of Parque de Café de Las Ánimas. Most of the major local *fincas* (growing estates) and *beneficios* (facilities for treating and roasting the harvested coffee) are concentrated around Coatepec, but since the best beans are exported, this doesn't necessarily translate into getting a decent cup of coffee in otherwise excellent restaurants!

Throughout the hills, there is a strong Spanish heritage; many people look like Andalusians or Castilians, and Mediterranean flavorings are deeply ingrained here. At the same time, chiles and corn and all the foundations of Mexico's *mestizo* cooking are as central here as they are elsewhere in the nation. On top of all this, each town has its individual claim to kitchen immortality.

The hill-country cooking is full of delicacy and inventiveness. You find unbelievably fresh fish and shrimp from the coast, along with trout and freshwater *langostinos* from the mountain streams. People cook a great deal with flowers, especially the fragrant white *flor de izote* (yucca) and the brilliant scarlet blossoms of a tree called *gasparito* or *colorín (Erythrina americana)*, which are used in omelets and fritters. These catch your eye from twenty feet off at the market, displayed in pinecone-like clusters with tube-shaped flowers sticking out like flame-colored quills.

Stuffed jalapeños — *chiles xalapeños rellenos* — are a local obsession. The fillings are savory or sweet-savory, with chopped meat, chicken, fruits, and vegetables, or even canned tuna. The chiles are either fresh or smoke-dried; the latter are called *chipotles* or, in the case of a specially prized thin-skinned variety, *moritas*. Any of these chiles can also be prepared without stuffing, but *chiles xalapeños rellenos* are universally agreed to be one of the great highland-area dishes (although people make them all over the state).

XALAPA is a city of very good food, but I don't know that it has a distinctive cooking style separate from that of the surrounding communities. I have fond memories of meals in Xalapa, not because of startling, recherché touches but because of skillful and solid preparation. I've never enjoyed any version of fish *a la veracruzana* better than the straightforward one served at La Sopa restaurant. This is a modest hangout in one of the lovely old alleys of the city, frequented by students, government workers from the nearby Palacio Municipal, and anyone who appreciates good food. One of the city's finest restaurants is La Churrería del Recuerdo, a "supper place" (*cenaduría*) specializing in the kind of informal fare that is served between the *comida*, a late lunch that is the main meal, and breakfast the next morning. This pattern may be falling afoul of modern inter-

national business schedules in some parts of Mexico, but I don't think Xalapans are about to give up their favorite *cenaduría* dishes.

La Churrería del Recuerdo is remarkable both because of its excellent food and because the owner, Raquel Torres Cerdán, combines the roles of gifted cook and trained anthropologist. People flock to this convivial spot to eat the *churros* for which it's named (strips of deep-fried dough rolled in sugar, eaten dipped in hot chocolate or coffee), the corn snacks, and the unusual but homey dishes that draw on older traditions of Veracruzan cooking. I have had wonderful tamales there (including, believe it or not, strawberry tamales wrapped in corn leaves), an excellent salad of *nopalitos* (cactus paddles), and the famous *pambazos*. For those who have never encountered *pambazos*, they are among the world's best hot sandwiches, lovely little flour-dusted rolls with savory fillings such as beans, cheese, and crumbled *longaniza* sausage (see page 246).

All the towns around Xalapa have more or less the same cooking style, but in every one you find something that lingers in memory or a particular specialty that every citizen swears is unique to this dot on the map. In Coatepec, at Casa Bonilla restaurant, the home of what may be Veracruz's best *tapaditas* (small fried masa cakes shaped around a filling), I was astonished to hear that the elusive secret of the *langostinos* in chipotle chile sauce was the leaf of the allspice tree. I'd heard of this before — allspice is native to the American tropics, and the dried berries are one of Veracruz's important export crops — but this was the only place I found people cooking with allspice leaf.

𝒩EARBY PEROTE'S claim to fame is that it is the wheat-growing capital of a state that doesn't grow vast amounts of wheat. Naturally enough, it has become renowned for baking. Its great specialty is a family of sweet rolls called *cocoles*, made in many different variations on the rhomboid shape that gives *cocol* its name. Perote's close neighbor, Naolinco, which may have the most dramatically sweeping view in the whole state, is a honeybee center and produces all kinds of inventively shaped sweets as charming to look at as they are delicious. These two towns are both famed for the art of sausage making, or charcuterie, brought here long ago from Spain, but there is an intriguing difference. In Naolinco, most of the charcuterie (they call it *tocinería*) is of fresh pork — *longaniza* and chorizo sausages, great pork cracklings, and headcheese (*queso de puerco*). The color and seasoning come mainly from Mexican red chile. In Perote, the Spanish influence remains almost unadulterated. The pork products here are mostly cured, including a fine *jamón serrano* (Spanish-style mountain ham) and sausages like those you might find in parts of Catalonia (*butifarras*) or the Basque country (*chistorras*). The spice in the chorizo is Spanish paprika.

My favorite of all the towns around Xalapa is Xico (short for Xicochimalco). This may be because of the lovely colonial architecture, brightly painted walls, and sparkling clean cobbled streets. Or perhaps it is because I was introduced to Xico by the city poet and chronicler, Amado Manuel Izaguirre Virués, whose beautiful evocations of the place and its traditions gave me sudden insight into Veracruz's sense of itself.

XICO is almost inseparable from the Virués and Izaguirre families, whose history I've heard brought to life by Amado and his indomitable mother, Doña María del Carmen Virués de Izaguirre. Sitting in their formal living room with its heavy red velvet draperies and high-backed chairs, I felt that I was entering another world as they told yarns of long-ago Xico characters, like the cousin who achieved the perfect temperature for her very best stew by ordering the maid to stir it for hours over a single lighted coal and periodically inspecting the girl's arm for redness to see if the dish was done.

From what I heard and observed, the members of the Virués and Izaguirre families were individualists, civic activists, and good cooks. They arrived from Spain in the nineteenth century and soon became prominent citizens of Xico. Even today, town officeholders are likely to be Viruéses or Izaguirres. The families have always been associated with one of Xico's proudest specialties, the celebrated liqueurs. These are made everywhere in the region, but the general consensus is that Xico is the main headquarters for *licores*. Doña Carmen is one of the foremost makers, and an array of bottles in all shades from cerise to chartreuse stands in state on a table in her living room, next to the family *recetario* (handwritten recipe book).

I wish I could give directions in this book for making *licores* in the style of Xico, but unfortunately they require professional equipment, which makes them impractical for home experiments. But I take comfort in the fact that the one dish most passionately linked with Xico can be brilliantly re-created in our kitchens: *mole xiqueño*, or *mole de Xico* (page 326).

The *mole* of Xico is the fruitiest of the great Mexican *moles*, almost like a super-rich mixed-fruit jam or satiny marmalade that also has elements of nut butter and a sensuous chile sauce. It is usually dished up in copious amounts with poached or braised meat or chicken. Connoisseurs of the famous *mole poblano* may detect similarities, and the citizens of Xico will readily agree that many influences wandered across the state border from neighboring Puebla, the source of *mole poblano*. But Xico's version is a triumph in its own right. It is usually reserved for special occasions. For instance, its perfume fills the air every July at the celebration of Mary Magdalene, Xico's patron saint. I was privileged to witness one of these events, and though I've been attending Mexican fiestas since I was a small child, I felt that I was experiencing something new.

WHAT I EXPECT TO SEE at a fiesta is an explosive release of pressure — a delirious, almost shocking contrast to the highly structured everyday world of Mexico, where even simple shop transactions call for displays of formal respect. But from my first glimpse of Xico's preparations for the week-long celebration, I beheld a combination of joint purpose and grace, a whole community coming together to choreograph something joyous but ordered. No detail was left unattended. When I got there, people were sweeping already tidy streets and painting already resplendent houses. The excellent town bakers had been hard at work since before daylight, turning out hundreds of fragrant loaves and rolls. Willing hands everywhere were nailing up welcome signs and stringing colored paper decorations.

As at many other Mexican fiestas, people here dress the saint's statue in a new costume that must cost a king's ransom and carry her through the streets while setting off *toritos*, papier-mâché figures of bulls rigged with firecrackers. (This is a prelude to the running of the real bulls through the Xico streets a few days later.) What I'd never seen anywhere else was the astonishing designs of colored sawdust that carpeted the main street for the six blocks leading to the church. Each block had a different picture, executed by that block's residents — men, women, and children working as a team. All this for the "beautiful saint" and her procession, which wipes out every picture!

The next morning, the street was as clean as if it had been swept by elves. The citizens of Xico were now pitching in for the next stage of fiesta week: carrying an extraordinary arch of pure white cactus flowers, gathered by a small committee of men chosen for the honor, to the door of the church. That sight, for me, epitomized how the members of the community transform themselves into one heart and one soul.

THE SOUTH-CENTRAL HIGHLANDS

*F*ROM THE *centro norte* to the *centro sur* of Veracruz state is a long, circuitous trip, at least if you think going by a navigable road is a good idea. The two highland areas grew up in somewhat parallel ways, though communication between them was never easy. They do have much in common, starting with the fact that they both lie along old colonial routes from the coast to Mexico City, but there are things that set the south-central highlands apart.

In this area, the brutally exploited slaves who were brought from Africa to grow sugarcane and raise cattle rose up against their Spanish masters with special fury. By the late sixteenth century, many had escaped into the hills, where they lived by their wits for generations. These runaway blacks — *cimarrones*, in Spanish — were joined by rebel Indians and *mestizos* and made frequent raids on the great Spanish estates. They also continually ambushed and robbed convoys carrying provisions or treasure along the Mexico City road. One of the leaders, an African prince named Yanga, negotiated so successfully with the Spanish troops sent to suppress him that in 1609 the Mexican viceroy granted him and his followers liberty, with enough land to establish an independent settlement just off the highway. The village, San Lorenzo de los Negros, or simply La Villa de Yanga, was the first free black settlement in the New World.

This gesture did not improve conditions for the slaves, however, or stop other *cimarrones* from continuing their attacks in the region. In 1618, a committee of Spanish settlers petitioned the viceroy, Diego Fernández de Córdoba, for the right to establish a garrison to keep peace in the neighborhood. The founders, the so-called Thirty

Knights *(Los Treinta Caballeros)*, named their town Córdoba in the viceroy's honor.

A few miles farther west along the road, other groups fearful of marauding *cimarrones* established a little fort, called Fortín, and a larger one nestled close to the southern slopes of Pico de Orizaba, as the Spanish called Mount Citlaltépetl. Named Orizaba for the mountain, the more important outpost grew into one of Veracruz's major commercial centers.

It has been centuries now since the rebel blacks were assimilated, if not totally merged, into general Veracruzan society, though people with African features still predominate in some hamlets. Today, Yanga village is the site of a Carnival celebration dedicated to the memory of Yanga that has become a potent symbol of the Third Root *(Tercera Raíz)* — the modern name for the African presence in a nation that used to be defined only in terms of Mexican and Spanish roots. At Carnival time, people come here from all over Veracruz, wearing African-motif costumes, and the lighter-skinned revelers paint themselves black or don fierce black masks.

Fortín has meanwhile become Fortín de las Flores, a placid and unfort-like town filled with tropical flower nurseries. It has a quiet hotel that boasts a swimming pool filled with snowy, fragrant gardenias.

*C*ÓRDOBA AND ORIZABA are now the twin hubs of manufacturing in the area, thanks to hydropower from the many mountain streams that carve dramatic canyons, waterfalls, and even underground rivers through the landscape. It rains a lot here, which cuts off the incredible views of Citlaltépetl on most days and has earned Orizaba the nickname *La Pluviosilla* (little rainy one). But the constant soakings are also the reason that so many crops thrive in the uplands. Sugarcane and cattle ranching are still vitally important, but the region also produces other crops, such as rice, sesame, tobacco, and the many fruits that find their way into an exquisite array of candied fruits at Dulcería Don Pedro in Córdoba — figs, prunes, melon rind, coconut in hollowed-out lime shells. Coffee has become so important that the name of the Córdoba baseball team is Los Cafeteros de Córdoba.

Córdoba and Orizaba are not as picturesque as Tlacotalpan or as culturally diverse as Xalapa. Rather, they offer unplanned, thought-provoking encounters with other centuries. For Mexicans, both cities

are fraught with historical associations. Córdoba — officially, Heroic Córdoba — is where the last Spanish viceroy, Juan O'Donojú, and the representative of the insurgents, General Agustín Iturbide, met on August 24, 1821, to sign the momentous treaty that ceded independence to New Spain and cleared the way for the creation of a free Mexico three years later. Orizaba saw some of the crucial battles of the wars with France and the United States. A big factory town, it was also a major early center of the Mexican labor union movement and played a prominent role in the events leading to the Mexican Revolution. But the two towns wear their history lightly, without letting it distract too much attention from the present.

I could spend weeks eating in Orizaba. For me, this city has the most varied gastronomic scene of any place in the *centro sur*. There is the brewery, Orizaba's largest employer (and the local headquarters of Mexico's largest brewing company, Cervicería Cuauhtémoc Moctezuma), which turns out some of the best labels of the parent corporation — Dos Equis, Bohemia, and Superior, among others. There are the street carts and little stalls that open up on corners in the evening, offering some of the most interesting snacks and supper dishes in the state. The most famed are the *garnachas orizabeñas*, fresh corn tortillas spread with either red or green salsa and topped with potato and shredded meat. Orizaba is also the best place in Veracruz to look for dishes using good garden vegetables, something that most Mexican restaurants painfully lack. The spot that appears to feature vegetable dishes most regularly is La Fuente, the restaurant of the Hotel Pluviosilla. This is no accident, for Carmina Gutiérrez Pontón, whose family owns the hotel, is busy trying to give pride of place on the menu to traditional, not necessarily glamorous dishes that people first tasted in their mother's or grandmother's kitchen. She also tries to make room on the menu for local herbs and greens.

*T*HE ORIZABAN CULT of the chayote was an eye-opener for me. Other Veracruzans refer to the citizens of Orizaba as *chayoteros* (chayote eaters), and it is said that an Orizaban cook would have no trouble constructing a dinner in which every course featured some part of the plant. I marveled at the sight of the chayotes growing in fields and gardens all around Orizaba, their leafy, sinuous vines making a green roof over trellis frames and their fruit hanging like knobby pears.

The elegant and authoritative Doña Aminta Osorio, an ardent local champion of chayotes, spent a good part of an afternoon telling me what makes them special here. In the first place, people grow not just the pale green ones that we're used to but a whole range of cultivars, with fruit as large as papayas or as small as cocktail avocados, ivory-colored or jade or deep green, round or pear-shaped, smooth-skinned or covered in dense spines. Each kind has its own nuances of flavor and texture.

Moreover, Doña Aminta told me, no one in Orizaba would be content to eat just the fruit. People gather the leaves to cook as a green and save the almond-like pits to roast. Above all, they cook the *chayotextles*, or tuberous roots. These are like the most delicious potatoes you have ever tasted, but crisper and nuttier than any potato. *Chayotextle* takes to any treatment you'd use for other starchy vegetables. It is lovely sliced and batter-fried, mashed with seasonings, or turned into croquettes. What on earth is wrong with the people who raise chayotes in this country, that they simply let the best part of the plant go to waste?

*D*RIVING NORTH from the Córdoba-Fortín-Orizaba road, you come into the richest and greenest part of coffee country, carved out of dense forests in the beautiful eastern foothills of Mount Citlaltépetl. The lovely towns of Coscomatepec and Huatusco, perched on the verdant slopes, date back to outposts of the Aztecs. Huatusco — or, more precisely, a corner of the township headed by Huatusco — is the site of a nearly forgotten experiment named the Colonia Manuel González. The project was started by the government of Italy, which was desperately trying to relocate starving peasants, and that of Mexico, which had decided that it needed foreign-born laborers to make its agriculture competitive with that of the "more advanced" western nations. Starting around 1880, the Manuel González colony was one of the largest of several planned communities in Mexico to which emigrants from the Veneto and the Tyrolean Alps were transplanted to become workers on the corn, sugar, and coffee estates. Within a few generations the Italians had been assimilated and dispersed throughout Mexico. Surprisingly, I did find some remaining touches of their cuisine. People still make an Italian *minestra* (with Veracruzan black beans), the town bakery continues to produce Italian bread, and there's even a local version of mortadella.

The south-central highlands share a general culinary style, with some of the same features as that of the Xalapa area. Traveling in these parts, I found every community quick to announce that it was the cradle of some delicacy. Huatusco boasts that it originated a unique kind of chile-seasoned sesame paste (generally with other seeds and nuts added to the mixture) called *tlatonile*. And Córdoba considers itself the true home of the mint julep. No, you're not hallucinating — I said mint julep, although here it's spelled *menyul* and contains a medley of ingredients unknown anywhere in the old Kentucky home.

I HAVE SAVED my best memories of these highlands until last. One is of being serenaded by the resident poet of La Fama bakery in Coscomatepec, Ángel Solís Mata. La Fama would be a wonderful place even if it didn't have a resident poet. It has been around for some seventy-five years, and the heirs of the original founder (including his ninety-seven-year-old daughter-in-law, who comes to the shop every day of the week) welcome you as if you were a long-lost member of the family. La Fama offers a dizzying selection of differently shaped breads, rolls, and pastries in various styles, all boasting names like *doncellas* (damsels), *huesos* (bones), and *maderistas* (a political label circa 1910, referring to supporters of the reformer president Francisco Madero). I find their *cocoles* even better than the more celebrated ones of Perote (for the recipe, see page 334).

The courtly Don Ángel is undoubtedly the most surprising member of the sales staff. He is a mostly retired jack-of-all-trades who celebrates every occasion at La Fama in verse. When I first walked into the bakery, asking questions about the bread, he presented me with several of his poems, including a philosophical rumination on the parts we all play on the stage of this life. But after I told him who I was and why I was there, he proceeded to make up a song in my honor and sing it to me on the spot! It had Spanish lyrics about me and my mission, to the tune of "Singin' in the Rain." Don Ángel didn't leave it at that. The next time I went to Coscomatepec, he was ready with another serenade — this time to the tune of "New York, New York."

The other indelible memory that I took with me from these parts was a scene in the town square of Córdoba, where older people come every week to revel in *danzón* and schoolchildren to learn it, accom-

panied by recorded sound tracks. One foggy, chilly evening just after dusk, I saw among the dancers a father bending with infinite tenderness over an eighteen- or twenty-month-old toddler warmly dressed in a purple sweatshirt, gently guiding her through the beautiful steps.

PAPANTLA AND THE NORTH

GOING NORTH from the city of Veracruz along the hot, humid coastal plain, you find a completely different mixture of people and history from those in Sotavento and the central highlands. One reason is that the indigenous peoples who were living in many parts of Veracruz when Cortés arrived were swiftly crowded out of the better agricultural areas and left to survive in just a few corners of the present-day state. Two of these groups, the Totonacs and the Huastecs, are still considerable presences in the north. At the same time, the northern coastline is the home of two enormous sources of wealth that do not go easily together: fish and petroleum. The oil drilling that began around the Gulf coast close to the turn of the twentieth century changed Mexico's history and brought a great deal of foreign capital into the country before the oil reserves were nationalized in 1938. The balance is fragile, but so far the marine environment has been kept productive.

The coastal route northward begins with some of Veracruz's most famous historic sites — what the guidebooks call "Cortés's first footsteps." Here are the places where, through his interpreters, he offered the bewildered Totonac leaders a combination of bluster, sanctimonious Christian rhetoric, and conspiratorial promises of aid against the hated Aztecs.

The trail leads through a few miles of modern urban sprawl to Cortés's ruined settlement near the mouth of La Antigua River. This was the second location where the Spanish tried to establish a port city in the sixteenth century, but they abandoned it and returned to their 1519 landing site. Today a tiny fishing hamlet crowds right up to the historical monument of La Antigua (short for La Villa Antigua, or "the Old Town"). We got there on a touristless weekday, and the place was almost eerily peaceful. Someone's laundry was drying on the massive roofless walls of an old administrative building now dubbed La Casa de Cortés, with great willows and *ceibas* (kapok trees) silently shading the deserted structure.

About six miles farther north are the ruins of the great Totonac city of Zempoala, or Cempoala, which Spanish reconnoitering parties first thought was made of silver. (It turned out to be a brilliantly reflective white plaster.) Some pivotal events of the conquest took place here — not only Cortés's meeting with El Cacique Gordo (the Fat Chief, the enormously obese local ruler), but his violent destruction of the sacred Totonac temple images and his defeat of a Cuban expedition that was sent to arrest him after the authorities in Havana decided that he was a loose cannon. The small modern town of Zempoala stands a mile or two from the deserted city, and I confess that when I am in the neighborhood, I usually head not for the historic site but for Daría Muñoz's splendid seafood place, Restaurant Daría.

A few miles farther on, Cortés came to Quiahuiztlán, a fortress-like Totonac town dramatically set on a towering basalt cliff above a navigable inlet. He decided to found his settlement by this harbor. Although the Spaniards ended up abandoning the site for La Antigua within a few years, it still bears the name Villa Rica, signifying that it was the first home of the "rich town" of Veracruz. Here also, Cortés began his Mexican career of double-dealing, telling one story to an alliance of Totonac chiefs who had met to discuss the situation and another to a party of Aztec tribute collectors who happened to show up in Quiahuiztlán right after the Spaniards arrived.

CONTINUING INTO THE NORTH country (as Cortés did not, at least on that first march), you skirt many tidal swamps and creeks — prime fishing spots — and pass through many green stretches of cattle pastures and citrus groves. At the mouth of the Bobos River lies the little fishing town of Nautla, where parties of French colonists began arriving during the early years of Mexican independence. (France had great hopes of moving in to fill the vacuum it expected to see when the Spanish finally left for good in 1825.) A few miles inland from Nautla, they founded the river settlements of Jicaltepec and San Rafael and began growing several tropical crops while trying to decipher the secrets of Veracruz's most precious and elusive native plant, vanilla.

Vanilla culture has almost completely vanished from the old French settlements, though it still survives a little farther away. Not many people speak French today, and there are few traces of French influence on the local cooking. But the descendants of the original settlers are responsible for the concentration of good cheese making in this part of the Bobos River Valley.

*T*HE COASTLINE north of Nautla has some of the few beaches in Veracruz that are suitable for recreation. The state government touts the area as the Costa Esmeralda and would like to develop the beaches into serious tourist attractions, but so far the Costa Esmeralda has not been "discovered" in a big way. Between the road and the oceanfront, you are more likely to see zebu-type milk cows than beachniks under the palm trees.

Prosperity in the area is concentrated some twenty-five miles inland, in the vigorous but very nonpicturesque oil town of Poza Rica. Just east of this noisy, swift-paced center lies the heart of the modern vanilla industry: the hill town of Papantla, a name virtually synonymous with true Mexican vanilla. Papantla is not a pretty town, but it is deeply tied to the old Totonac culture. Before so much of the jungle was carved away, it was a center of rubber production and supplied a lot of allspice.

Allspice definitely plays second fiddle to vanilla in the pantheon of New World flavorings, but it is a crop of some importance around here. The region produces about four thousand tons per year. The Spanish, who found allspice growing on the islands as well as the mainland, prematurely christened it *pimienta*, or *pimienta gorda*, in the belief that the dried berries were large, fleshy peppercorns. For Europeans, it seemed to combine the fragrances of pepper, cloves, cinnamon, and nutmeg, and it could be brought back to Spain more quickly and cheaply than any of these spices from the distant East Indies.

Allspice is tricky to grow successfully, but it is easy compared to vanilla. The plant is a climbing tropical orchid that, when just the right conditions for pollination exist, will produce a long, skinny pod (in Spanish, *vainilla*, or "little sheath") filled with tiny seeds. For centuries before the Spanish came, the Totonac people had been quietly gathering the unscented green pods and using a special sun-drying technique to cause them to develop the most sublime, unique fragrance.

Once Europeans smelled that perfume, entrepreneurs everywhere longed to transplant vanilla around the globe and start producing it on an industrial scale. It took more than two hundred years for this to happen, but at last, in the 1830s, some clever research in Belgium and Réunion led to a breakthrough: the development of a hand-pollination method that could replace the natural conditions in the Papantla jungle. The Mexican monopoly on this rare, expensive spice was broken. Today the state's vanilla production is limited to a small area near Papantla, where a few dedicated growers continue to hope that the complexity and depth of Veracruzan vanilla will attract a following among knowledgeable gourmets.

*I*N PAPANTLA, we visited the farm of Victor Vallejo, a leading vanilla grower, and the *beneficio* of Heriberto Larios Rivera, who has been growing and shipping vanilla for many years. The ticklish hand-pollination has to be done for each blossom during one three- or four-hour window of opportunity very early on the single day that that flower opens. It is usually done by women and children, because smaller hands are better at reaching into the intricately shaped flowers.

The beans mature on the vines for about nine months before they are picked. Then they are laid out in the sun and "sweated" in blankets or closed containers, to start the process of fermentation. For two or three months they are dried in the sun, which gradually reduces their moisture content by about 80 percent. By the end of this process, the beans are a glossy brownish black, and enzymatic action has caused the natural vanillin — the substance that gives vanilla most of its fragrance — to crystallize on the surface. Inside the pod, the thousands of tiny seeds have shrunk to almost invisible specks.

The beans are sorted for quality and tied into plump, sleek bundles for shipping. But a certain number of pods find their way into the fanciful creations that delight visitors walking into Papantla-area crafts shops and the Mercado Hidalgo, just off the town square: vanilla beans plaited into black braids, flower shapes, crucifixes, chalices, Egyptian ankhs, crowns, and animal figurines. These are

charming and make great sachets, but I would stick to plain vanilla beans for cooking.

Pods that are split or broken during processing are steeped in grain alcohol to produce vanilla extract or made into a vanilla liqueur sold in Papantla as Xanath (the Totonac word for "flower"). Around Papantla, the most reliable name to look for is Orlando Gaya, a company in the nearby town of Gutiérrez Zamora, which is an old and trustworthy processor of true Papantla vanilla.

TODAY THE TOTONAC PEOPLE are seldom involved in vanilla production except as plantation workers. But they are an emphatic presence in Papantla and a large area extending westward from Nautla into the mountains of Veracruz and neighboring Puebla. This is only a fraction of the territory the Totonacs occupied when Cortés arrived.

Here and there small groups of Totonacs live in rural villages, surviving by age-old methods of subsistence farming and practicing a religion that incorporates both Christian and pre-Hispanic elements. But more people work and live in the towns and cities. The Totonac men characteristically dress in white muslin, with a long-sleeved smock worn over loose pants gathered at the ankle. The women still practice some hand weaving and embroidery, which is remarkable in Veracruz, where indigenous crafts barely exist and the few village artesanías are often more Spanish than anything else. (It is just another of the ways in which Veracruz is the opposite of Oaxaca.)

The food of the Totonacapan region still has a very distinctive character. The local corn kitchen is exceptionally varied and sophisticated, with many more kinds of tamales than any other part of Veracruz. People draw on a wide range of wild fruits. Hearts of palm, similar to those from "swamp cabbage" in Florida, are a major delicacy, cooked in many different ways, while the rest of the tree is used to create everything from hats to brooms to thatch. The fruits are eaten like grapes. Another palm, the coyol, furnishes a fruit like a tiny, subtly flavored coconut. Mint is a favorite flavoring in all kinds of savory dishes. (Interestingly, you don't find people cooking much with either vanilla or allspice, which are basically cash crops for export.) Tiny wild chiles the size of chiltepines are highly prized in sauces. Black beans and pumpkin seeds are eaten just about every day — sometimes together, as in the famous Totonac dish called frijoles en achulchut (page 287).

*V*IRTUALLY EVERYONE who visits Papantla has a chance to see what is probably the most renowned symbol of Totonac culture, the spectacular dance called the *voladores* (fliers). It is an invocation to the gods of the elements, though there is no consensus on what all the details mean.

In Papantla, it is regularly performed next to the church (on the day I was there, actually during Sunday mass). The backdrop is a towering pole like a ninety-foot maypole, with footholds leading to a tiny platform on top. Four dancers and one musician (sometimes two) carrying a drum and a pipe climb up the footholds. The musician, casually balanced on the platform, plays both instruments while the dancers secure themselves to very fragile-looking ropes that are twisted around the pole so they will unwind in precise synchrony. Aligning themselves with the four cardinal points of the compass, the dancers launch themselves in breathtaking unison backward into empty space — heads down, arms dangling, as much at ease as diving fish. The ropes gradually play out as they "fly" down, each circling the pole thirteen times. (Thirteen and fifty-two — four times thirteen — were numbers universally sacred to the pre-Hispanic civilizations and served as the basic units of all their calendars.) Just as the dancers complete the last circle and it seems that they must crash into the ground, they suddenly right themselves, in time to land on their feet.

These spine-tingling performances take place in several towns of the Totonacapan. They are also a regular feature at the ancient monument of El Tajín, Veracruz's greatest archeological site. If you visit only one pre-Hispanic ruin in the state, this should be it.

*E*L TAJÍN is located about seven miles west of Papantla. No one knows its original name or exactly who built it, but it is thought to represent the apogee of what scholars call classic Veracruz civilization. Today the Totonacs call it Tajín after a storm god, but many archaeologists believe that their civilization came long after the decline of this remarkable center. So far about 170 separate stone buildings have been unearthed in the hilly green jungle, and many more still have to be explored, in an area of only a few square miles. This must have been one of the most densely populated cities of ancient Mexico. Probably most of it was built between A.D. 600 and 900.

El Tajín was abandoned after about 1150 and gradually reclaimed by the jungle. There is no consensus on why, or on whether or not the

Totonacs are the descendants of the people who built it. It is their belief that the place was sacred to the spirit of the *huracán* (hurricane), which is all too well known in these parts. The buildings give you an eerie feeling of being in a real city, one in which all the residents are under a spell of invisibility while time travelers from another century walk around with cameras and guidebooks.

$\mathcal{T}$HE PAPANTLA REGION actually marks a very fuzzy boundary between the territories of the Totonacs and those of the other major northern indigenous people of Veracruz, the Huastecs. The Totonacapan blurs into the Huasteca without official boundaries, and sometimes it's a judgment call as to whether some custom or culinary tradition belongs to one or the other. The one thing that's certain is that there is more ethnic diversity in the Huasteca than in the Totonacapan. The area begins a little north of the Costa Esmeralda on the Gulf coast and Poza Rica thirty miles inland. It goes quite a distance beyond Veracruz's northern and western borders, into San Luis Potosí and Tamaulipas states.

The Huastecs must have been completely unrelated to the Totonacs, because their language belongs to the Maya family far to the south; it's as if a group speaking a Romance language turned up between Poland and Germany. They lived in a crossroads region that underwent some bewildering ethnic shake-ups even before Cortés arrived and got more confusing afterward. In colonial Mexico, the Totonacapan kept more of its old cultural and racial identity than the Huasteca. Perhaps this is because the Totonacs tried to be Cortés's allies when he landed in 1519. But when he came back three years later to secure the northern parts of the region for Spain, the Huastecs resisted him bitterly. Following in the ruthless footsteps of the Aztecs, who had displaced various peoples less than a century before the Europeans landed, the Spaniards punished the uncooperative Huastecs by sending many of them to work as slaves on the islands. The former Huastec lands ended up with a strange scattering of refugee peoples and once dominant Nahuas (Aztecs). It is thought that somewhere between 100,000 and 150,000 Huastec speakers still live in the multistate Huasteca. Some of the women wear the traditional embroidered cape, the *quechquémel*. But most Huastec people in Veracruz blend almost indistinguishably into the *mestizo* world.

The main resource of this area in the far Veracruzan north is oil, which was first discovered around 1900 near Tampico, just across

the state border in Tamaulipas. Subsequent exploration revealed vast onshore and offshore deposits, mostly in the so-called Faja de Oro (Gold Belt) of Veracruz. The discovery rewrote Mexican history, bringing wealth to this part of the Huasteca and creating some extremely grungy-looking towns. But the countryside is still surprisingly green and uncluttered, devoted to cattle ranches and fruit plantations.

Going north from the Costa Esmeralda toward Tamaulipas, you traverse more of the steamy coastal plain and keep coming to richer and richer fishing waters. Fishing was the greatest treasure of the region before oil. The two manage to coexist without too much difficulty in the oil port of Tuxpan, on the Tuxpan River. It isn't much to look at (although there are some breathtaking sunsets), but Tuxpan is home to a lot of good seafood. People of African descent were the economic backbone of many towns like this when they were purely fishing communities, and they keep the knowledge of fishing very much alive. The atmosphere of the old fishing towns in the north is often much like that of Sotavento, and there are shared traditions like the fandango (known as *huapango* in the Huasteca, and based on a distinctive musical tradition called the *son huasteco*).

NORTH of the Tuxpan River lies a series of sandbars and lagoons, culminating in Veracruz's largest saltwater lagoon, Lake Tamiahua. Stretching more than a hundred miles from the town of Tamiahua to the state border at the mouth of the Pánuco River, it is an ideal environment for several important kinds of shellfish. The quality of the shrimp — sweet, succulent, and utterly fresh — is a revelation to anyone from this country, where nearly all shrimp have been frozen. The crabs grow to great size in the lagoon shallows, but the oysters are tiny, about the size of walnuts.

Ostionerías in the port city and all over the state serve these wonderful little nuggets of delicate flavor, painstakingly raised and harvested by the fishing cooperatives of Lake Tamiahua. It's a demanding process that involves locating the spat (larval oysters), putting down poles hung with oyster-shell collars for them to attach themselves to, and then, after they reach a certain size, transferring them to semipermanent beds to finish growing.

Unfortunately, they are a pleasure hard to duplicate in this country, because our oysters are much bigger. The only close equivalent

would be Olympia oysters from the Pacific Northwest, which are terribly expensive even there and almost impossible to buy elsewhere. The oysters of Lake Tamiahua are so affordable and plentiful that recipes often call for more than a hundred. Substituting cut-up larger oysters is really no solution (any more than substituting cut-up nectarines for cherries would be), because in omelet fillings, cocktails, and seafood mélanges, the tiny oysters retain their shape and keep their flavor locked in until you bite into them.

When I think of the north of Veracruz, I think of many surprising junctures between romance and reality, past and present. Tamiahua is a stark example, with its massive state-of-the-art oil facilities and its stubbornly old-fashioned fishing industry. Over the waters of the lagoon, you see simple fence-like lines of stakes and nets called *charangas*, with men here and there poling skiffs — a kind of small-scale fishing that has almost completely vanished from the United States. This is part of what I taste when I eat Tamiahua oysters at a Veracruzan seafood bar. No wonder it can't be duplicated here. But if all the prized foods on earth could be reproduced anywhere at will, local cuisines would no longer be local.

CATEMACO AND THE FAR SOUTHEAST

A **LEGEND KNOWN** to many pre-Hispanic cultures held that the god Quetzalcoatl, the Feathered Serpent, departed eastward over the water from a place near Coatzacoalcos on the southern Gulf coast and that he would return someday from the sea. You might not think of gods and legends when you visit Coatzacoalcos today. History and mythology buffs know that the southeastern third of Veracruz, from the Papaloapan River to the border with Tabasco state, takes you farther into the distant past of Mexico than any other part of the state — indeed, of the nation. But I also have to say that it takes you far into a

raucous, fast-paced, traffic-jammed present, because some of the biggest Mexican oil wells and refineries lie near Coatzacoalcos. Mexicans never mind these crashing juxtapositions.

The past that I mentioned is the lost world of the Olmecs, the "mother culture" of all Mesoamerican civilizations. It is frustrating to realize how little trace of them can be found today in their first heartland, the Coatzacoalcos River Valley, or at the later settlement at Tres Zapotes, west of the Tuxtlas Mountains. About all that's left to see now are one or two of the sixteen known multiton basalt heads carved by the Olmecs, sitting half forgotten in a town plaza or a tiny museum. I hope that someday the great Coatzacoalcos Valley ruin of San Lorenzo (page 36) will be restored as impressively as the Totonac sites of El Tajín and Zempoala farther north. The area deserves to be remembered for achievements other than petroleum refining, because once you know of the Olmec presence, it's hard not to look at the steamy green southern landscapes of southern Veracruz and think, "This is where it all began."

ONLY ABOUT 120 miles separate Coatzacoalcos on the Gulf side of the narrow Isthmus of Tehuantepec from the Oaxacan town of Juchitán on the Pacific side. The isthmian people were subjugated along with the rest of Mexico by the Aztec empire not long before Cortés arrived. The Aztecs and the Spanish had an easier time conquering the peoples of the southeast isthmus than the indomitable Oaxacans, perhaps because this part of Veracruz lacks the many inaccessible mountain retreats of Oaxaca. The Populacas were driven from the best lands, and most of them ended up in a few corners of the Tuxtlas Mountains. As in so many areas of Veracruz, their place was taken by black slaves, and the culture came to have a strong Afro-Cuban slant. You can still see traces of it in the frequent use of root vegetables like yuca and malanga.

The old Olmec haunts formed a rich agricultural region for the conquerors, thanks to the many streams that plunge toward the Gulf from the mountains between Oaxaca and Veracruz, then subside into alluvial flatlands. But this area did not have the strategic importance of Xalapa or the Córdoba-Orizaba axis, so the torrid, swampy southeastern lowlands enjoyed several centuries of rural isolation and obscurity, quietly providing very fine fishing and yielding the usual Veracruzan mixture of old and new crops (except for coffee, which could not take the fierce heat).

All that changed at the turn of the twentieth century. Like the Poza Rica and Tamiahua areas of northern Veracruz, the Coatzacoalcos River Basin and nearby coast became a world-class source of black gold. The pace of oil development has perhaps been even more overwhelming than in the north. Pipelines, highways, railroads, and refineries punctuate green deltas and former jungle. The farms and fisheries are still there, but even though you can eat well enough in grubby Coatzacoalcos or in Minatitlán, the twin oil city a few miles to the south, cuisine is the last thing that would bring anyone to the area.

Luckily, there is another dimension to the southeast. To experience it, you must visit the magical region of Los Tuxtlas, about fifty miles west-northwest of the oil scene. Los Tuxtlas crystallizes the natural beauty of Veracruz and also provides a fascinating window into its cuisine.

Los Tuxtlas is generally understood to mean the towns of Santiago Tuxtla, San Andrés Tuxtla, and Catemaco. They are situated close to the Gulf coast, about equidistant from the southern border of Veracruz and the edge of the Sotavento region on the banks of the Papaloapan River. This area is unique in terms of Mexico's natural history. It ought to be just another stretch of flat coastal plain, but many geological ages ago, an isolated cluster of volcanoes thrust themselves up here, nowhere near any of the major mountain chains of Mexico. The Tuxtlas Mountains are dormant now (or have been since the largest, San Martín, blew its top in 1793), but just by being there, they create a unique range of microclimates. The climate is refreshingly different from that of the rest of the sultry southern lowlands. (On a winter morning, you can actually see your breath in the clear air.)

Alexander von Humboldt called Los Tuxtlas "the Switzerland of Veracruz," and the label has stuck. According to the anthropologist Fernando Bustamante Rábago, in pre-Hispanic belief the region was a happy realm ruled by Tlaloc, the rain god — an Elysian home for the souls of the departed. (In defense of this theory, I can tell you that Tlaloc rains on parts of Los Tuxtlas more than three hundred days of the year.)

BECAUSE of the volcanic soil, the land is amazingly fertile even by Veracruzan standards. This is the northern extremity of what used to be vast tropical rain forests stretching to modern-day Yucatán and Guatemala. The point where the forest meets the Tuxtlas Mountains is also where tropical and temperate flora and fauna converge, creating habitats as diverse as they are fragile. The beautiful fragments that remain amount to less than 10 percent of the original Tuxtlas rain forest.

Hernán Cortés himself made the first — though certainly not the last — decision to exploit the rich soil for a cash crop, and founded a sugarcane plantation and processing center that was enormous by contemporary standards. More drastic assaults on this rare environment followed when cotton growers clustered in the Tuxtlas area. Then, late in the nineteenth century, King Tobacco replaced King Sugar. Foreign entrepreneurs, many from Holland and Germany, came here to grow tobacco (and often to manufacture cigars) for the European market. Thousands of acres were carved into plantations. Tobacco is still the dominant crop, one that Tuxtlans considered their bread and butter throughout most of the twentieth century. As you drive toward San Andrés, the smell of harvested tobacco drying in thatched barns is everywhere.

A lucrative lumber industry sprang up while the tobacco fields were being cleared. Entrepreneurs began planting agribusiness-sized mango and citrus groves. Cattle ranches spread out over denuded mountains; today the dairy producers are among the happiest promoters of the Switzerland image. It's hard to imagine that less than sixty years ago, the artist and archaeologist Miguel Covarrubias, looking at these mountains from his plane seat, could write, "The slopes were covered with jungle that from the air looked like tightly packed broccoli."

Even in its present reduced state, though, the Tuxtlas region is a thing of delight. The three principal towns are good jumping-off places for exploration rather than magnets in their own right. The largest, San Andrés, is a busy little city looking toward now-peaceful San Martín. It is known in Mexico as a center for manufacturing cigars, yet another skill brought from Havana. A few miles farther west, the largest known Olmec stone head sits opposite the city hall and a little museum in the town plaza of Santiago, the smallest and prettiest of Los Tuxtlas. Several miles southeast of San Andrés is Catemaco, a lakeside resort and fishing town that is the biggest tourist draw of the trio.

$\mathcal{T}$HE TERRAIN on which the three Tuxtlas sit is an area of fantastic diversity. There are noble volcanic peaks as high as 5,200 feet and sheltered green valleys. The different forest habitats still harbor (though sometimes in sadly reduced numbers) cougars, ocelots, jaguarundis, deer, howler monkeys, coatimundis, kinkajous, anteaters, agoutis, peccaries, and tapirs. They are also a butterfly lover's paradise. And the water habitats are just as amazing, or even more so. They range from plunging gorges and dramatic waterfalls to freshwater lakes in old volcanic craters and the fertile coastal region of Sontecomapan, where freshwater streams meet Gulf currents and tidal swamps.

The largest and most beautiful of all the crater lakes is the one at Catemaco, about seventy-five square miles in area. At dawn, Lake Catemaco is an extraordinary sight, a misty mirror framed by the barely emerging silhouettes of a dozen former volcanoes. In fact, the lake has been one of the galvanizing issues that have brought together many Tuxtlans (and friends of the region) in an ambitious preservation campaign.

María Teresa Contreras — "Tere" to all and sundry — is a prime mover and shaker in these efforts. She and her husband, Armando, are the owners of La Panga, a popular lakeside bar and restaurant in Catemaco. Everyone in environmental circles turns up at La Panga. Thanks to a lot of dedicated work, an estimated 3 percent of the regional forest has already been reclaimed.

Thanks to Tere and her family, I was able to sail past the lake's mangrove swamps, gaze into the eyes of a baby monkey on the Isle of Monkeys (where a team of biological researchers is studying a colony of red macaques from Thailand), and marvel at great flocks of waterfowl — a fraction of the estimated 560 species that live in the Tuxtlas area or visit during migration. I also had the privilege of visiting an important ecological buffer-zone project, the Ejido (communal farm) Adolfo López Mateos. Here amid lofty green mountain slopes, a community of Indians, aided by environmental scientists from the nearby Los Tuxtlas Biosphere Reserve, have created a combination of nature preserve and sustainable-agriculture farm. Visitors are escorted to a magnificent waterfall along a winding nature trail rich in both native species and other plants suitable for small-scale mixed tropical farming — coffee, plantains, several kinds of citrus trees, and yuca, among others.

*T*HE PRIDE AND JOY of the Catemaco-area kitchen is fish. Some local fish exist nowhere else, and others don't taste the same elsewhere. Knowledgeable diners from all over Veracruz (and farther away) crowd into informal thatched-roof eateries and simple hotel restaurants to devour the water snails (*tegogolos*) of Lake Catemaco, a *minilla* (hash) of the local freshwater eel, a little fish the size of a sardine called *pepesca*, still tinier fish such as *tepotes* and *topotes* (eaten

THE MOTHER CULTURE

$\mathcal{N}$EARLY A THOUSAND YEARS before Alexander the Great, Veracruz was home to a magnificent city of the first Mesoamerican civilization, the Olmecs. The Olmec people probably appeared along the central Gulf coast between 1500 and 1300 B.C. Their history before that is a blank — even their name for themselves is unknown. ("Olmec" is a modern label borrowed by archaeologists from early postconquest accounts of a "People of Rubber" in southeastern Mexico.) By about 1300 B.C., the Olmecs were living in the Coatzacoalcos River Valley and had developed a distinctive art style. Close to an obscure present-day village named San Lorenzo Tenochtitlán, they founded a ceremonial building complex on a tremendous raised earthen platform. I'm sorry to say that the site is nothing much to look at today, partly because it was deliberately destroyed and buried in ancient times and partly because the most spectacular sculptures were taken to museums elsewhere. But it was a revelation for archaeologists fifty or sixty years ago.

$\mathcal{T}$HE MOST ASTONISHING discovery was a series of colossal stone heads, the largest about nine feet high and weighing some thirty tons, with strange, brooding, broad-nosed and thick-lipped faces that early discoverers described as African. (Scholars today almost universally discount any such racial connection.) They wear curious caplike helmets that remind visitors from the United States of old-fashioned football helmets. We can guess how mighty a city San Lorenzo must have been not only from the powerful artistic effect but also from the fact that the volcanic stone for the great heads originated in the Tuxtlas Mountains, some fifty miles away, and was sculpted without the use of metal tools.

We know that the Olmecs grew corn and the other standard Mexican crops on a prosperous scale, fished the fertile rivers and coasts of the far south, and traded with distant regions. We know that their glyphic writing system and some features of their culture, such as the ceremonial ball game, various religious beliefs, and probably the calendar system, were prototypes used by later civilizations — for example, the Mayan — in other areas of Mesoamerica. We know that they worshiped the fiercest beast of the coastal jungle, the jaguar, and left hundreds of enigmatic, skillfully carved jade, serpentine, and basalt figurines with hybrid jaguar/human features, pointing to a deeply important cult of the "were-jaguar" (a cat equivalent of the werewolf).

But it's both tantalizing and frustrating to realize how much more we do not know about this great people: where they came from, what language they spoke, the source of their wealth and power, and, above all, why their capital, San Lorenzo, was suddenly, violently overthrown around 900 B.C. The marks of fury are still on many of the great heads, which were defaced before being thrown down along with the rest of the city, to be swallowed by the earth for nearly three millennia.

THE SAME FATE overtook a second, somewhat later Olmec city, La Venta, on a swampy island in the Tonalá River Delta, a mile or so over the border between Tabasco and Veracruz. A third, much lesser city, Tres Zapotes, slightly west of Los Tuxtlas, apparently was settled by the Olmecs close to the time when La Venta was mercilessly destroyed, around 300 B.C. Tres Zapotes was luckier than its predecessors. It seems to have lasted through the final decline of Olmec culture, around the start of the Common Era, and was occupied by several later civilizations on up to A.D. 1000 or 1200. But like San Lorenzo, it's an out-of-the-way and disappointing sight for visitors, a few miles from a meager museum displaying one gigantic stone head — the first uncovered in modern times — and various other remnants that haven't been removed to museums in Xalapa or Mexico City.

Today the best places to view the heritage of the Olmecs are, unfortunately, not the places where these people lived. You really get a sense of the Olmecs' majesty and mystery in the National Museum of Anthropology in Mexico City and the splendid Veracruz state anthropological museum in Xalapa (see page 12). I urge you to visit these great collections and wonder, along with me, how and why the towering, solemn stone faces and uncanny jaguar-people materialized on Veracruzan soil at the dawn of Mexican civilization.

fried crisp, like whitebait), and a clan of succulent white-fleshed freshwater fish called *mojarras*. Other kinds come in daily from the nearby lagoon of Sontecomapan, with its mixture of different saline conditions and resulting cornucopia of fish and shellfish.

People here disdain cooking these treasures with rich, complex sauces. They prefer to set off the freshness of the catch with a few simple, classic flavor combinations, such as *chile limón* (chile and lime juice with a little salt), *chile pastor* (chile-lime sauce with fresh onion), and *tachogobi* (a wonderful sauce made from tiny local tomatoes, which seems like the essence of tomato flavor).

The region is known for other specialties as well. There is a famous tradition of wood-smoked foods: everyone knows the pork version called *carne de chango* ("monkey meat" — see page 243), but people smoke poultry and fish by the same method. Tuxtlans are passionate about a mighty beef stew called *tatabiguiyayo*, traditionally made for village celebrations, when a whole cow is butchered, and they cherish a kind of tortilla known as "pinched" (*pellizcada*) because of the pleated folds of the surface. But the fact remains that fish and shellfish are the soul of the cuisine.

The citizens of Los Tuxtlas know that the fortunes of their region are the fortunes of its precious natural resources. They have magic on their side, in a very special sense. The region is a nationally known center for the arts of *curanderos* (shamans), *brujos* (sorcerers, or folk healers), and other masters of age-old medical spiritual practices such as the *temezcal* (ritual steam bath). All the healers and witch doctors depend on a wide array of medicinal herbs and plants, many of them (like the fish of Lake Catemaco) tied to some unique ecological niche. Without the forest, the *brujos* and *curanderos* know they would lose the physical materials of their art. So you can add enchanters to the list of allies who are fighting to reclaim one of the world's most magical places.

*I*F I HAD TO CHOOSE only one site in Veracruz for a prospective visitor to see, it would undoubtedly be Catemaco. No spot tugs more strongly at my heart. There are days in New York — dreary Thursdays with icy streets and a long backlog of e-mail — when I say to myself that I ought to go and live by Lake Catemaco. I'm not really thinking of taking the plunge — not now. But I know that it would be balm to my soul.

LIVELY BUT ACCESSIBLE: THE COOKING OF VERACRUZ

$\mathcal{T}$HE FOOD of Veracruz is one of the most accessible regional cuisines, appreciated even by people who think they don't like Mexican food. If you *do* have a passion for far-flung Mexican kitchen adventure, you'll find much in Veracruz to stimulate (and gratify) your curiosity. But the strong Spanish and Afro-Caribbean roots of the Veracruzan kitchen make for a remarkable range of different culinary choices. I find that some cooks gravitate at once to dishes with the Mediterranean notes of olives, raisins, and almonds, while others are surprised and delighted to encounter something as African as peanuts.

You can go a long way in investigating several major facets of the cuisine using only ingredients that you're likely to have on hand already. If you want to explore dishes that bear a strong pre-Hispanic stamp, you'll have to make the acquaintance of certain important chiles and aromatic herbs, but the crucial ingredients will not be as obscure or numerous as in some other Mexican regional cuisines.

EQUIPMENT

To **cook** from this book, you don't have to run around acquiring special equipment that you'll never use for any other purpose. Any kitchen stocked with an array of well-made saucepans, skillets, knives, mixing bowls, and ordinary implements can handle the recipes in this book. These are the most important for day-in, day-out use:

- A small, a medium, and a large heavy skillet.

- A griddle or griddle substitute, like a large cast-iron skillet, for roasting vegetables.

- Heavy-gauge pots and Dutch ovens in several sizes. (My favorite are the inexpensive cast-aluminum Dutch ovens sold here in Latin American markets.)

- Pyrex baking dishes in several sizes (square or rectangular are most useful).

- Wooden spoons (several).

- A large heavy mortar and pestle (not absolutely necessary for most things, but this gives the best texture for some kinds of grinding and pureeing; the ideal kind is a Mexican volcanic stone *molcajete*).

- A heavy-duty blender as well as a food processor; in the recipes, you will see that these have different, complementary uses. A mini-processor is also useful.

- One or two medium-mesh sieves, for refining blended or processed sauce mixtures.

- An electric coffee or spice grinder.

- A heavy-duty electric mixer.

- An inexpensive cast-aluminum tortilla press (sold in Latin markets or through mail-order).

INGREDIENTS

Herbs

Veracruzan cooks use a remarkable range of both Mediterranean and New World herbs, usually fresh. In fact, I was startled by the lavish use of fresh herbs until I realized that often they are meant to add a bit of bulk as well as a lot of flavor.

AVOCADO LEAVES: Fresh or dried avocado leaves add a delicate anise-like touch to many sauces in Veracruz. People also use them powdered *(polvo de aguacate)*; look for both whole (we can only get the dried ones here) and powdered forms in Latin markets.

BASIL: Oddly enough, basil is used in modern versions of pre-Hispanic purification rites by shamans and *curanderos* (folk healers), but never in cooking.

BAY LEAVES: These are used liberally, much as in Spanish cooking.

CILANTRO: Originally a Spanish herb, cilantro is indispensable in Veracruzan — as in all Mexican — cooking. It may be sold as "fresh coriander" or "Chinese parsley."

EPAZOTE: This herb is almost as important as cilantro in Veracruzan cooking. I realize that not everyone has access to fresh epazote, even though it is a common seasonal roadside weed in many parts of the United States. The dried herb is all right for some uses, but it doesn't work at all in sauces that are essentially purees based on fresh greens. In such cases, I vote to go with "fresh" and "green" rather than "epazote," and add a large amount of cilantro to supply the necessary body.

HOJA SANTA: This is the one major Veracruzan ingredient in this book that I used in the knowledge that it is very difficult for home cooks in this country to find, at least fresh. A few years ago, I would have said not "very difficult" but "impossible." Since then, suppliers have begun selling *hoja santa* in this country, mostly for restaurateurs. (It can easily be grown in many areas and actually grows wild in Texas.) You can order it now by mail — but, unfortunately, generally in quantities too large to be practical (there is usually a $1/2$-pound minimum) unless you use it liberally all the time, as cooks do in Veracruz. I feel justified in including it, however, because the situation is changing rapidly as cooks here get to know about *hoja santa*. I am confident that in a year or two it will be sold fresh by specialty grocers and farmers' markets in large cities.

When you taste it, you will see what all the fuss is about. *Hoja santa* is the leaf of a bush (*Piper auritum* or *P. sanctum*) in the same genus as pepper. The broad, heart-shaped leaves may be as big as large cabbage leaves and have a dark green surface so tender and beautiful that you just want to caress them. *Hoja santa* has a strong anise-like perfume — but more herby than anise — that I find addictive. We use it constantly in my restaurants, and I cannot imagine ever being without it.

The dried leaf is available in this country in any Mexican grocery. The quality varies widely. Sometimes it is quite aromatic, sometimes no better than crumbling newsprint. Good dried *hoja santa* can replace the fresh — up to a point. It will not do where the body and juiciness of the fresh leaf are important. At home, I have sometimes substituted fresh tarragon in purees, with not strictly authentic but pretty good results.

MARJORAM: Marjoram, a near cousin of Mediterranean oregano, is used regularly.

MINT: Fresh mint is one of the major savory herbs, especially in the cuisine of the Huastec and Totonac areas.

OREGANO: Mediterranean oregano (the true *Origanum vulgare*) is as popular in Veracruz as the unrelated but very similar-tasting Mexican oregano (*Lippia graveolens*), which dominates in most parts of Mexico. Mexican oregano is sold (under the McCormick label) in many supermarkets. There are also other local herbs that are called oregano because the flavor is very close.

PARSLEY: Mexicans generally use the flat-leafed kind often sold as "Italian parsley" in the United States. It is one of the classic Veracruzan *hierbas de guisar* (stewing herbs, for braised dishes).

THYME: Plentiful use of fresh thyme, often together with one of the oreganos, is a hallmark of Veracruzan cooking. I've indicated where the dried herb is an acceptable substitute.

Spices

Veracruzan cooks are as sparing with spices as they are generous with herbs. I am often surprised to realize that some flavorful dishes contain no spices at all except chile. When I ask about this, the usual refrain is, "We never use spices, because they give you indigestion." The seasonings they *do* use are so deeply satisfying that you don't sense anything missing. These are the most important members of the simple Veracruzan spice palette.

ACHIOTE: You have eaten achiote (the dried seeds of a Caribbean tropical shrub) a million times without knowing it. It is the source of annatto, one of the world's most popular and useful food dyes. Annatto extracts are used to color butter, margarine, and all kinds of yellow and orange cheeses. But only in Central America and the Caribbean do people really cook with the small, hard brick-red seeds. They are ground and steeped in water or oil (or sometimes rendered lard) to dissolve the colorful coating or made into a paste to add to sauces. South of Veracruz state, especially in Yucatán, achiote is used in many kinds of complex spice pastes. In Veracruz, however, achiote paste is generally made without added seasonings. The flavor is hard to describe — mild, but with a distinctive earthy quality that doesn't come through until it's cooked with other foods.

I approximate the achiote paste of Veracruz by grinding the seeds (¼–½ cup) as fine as possible in an electric coffee or spice grinder and mixing them with just enough water to form a paste.

Work in batches of 2–3 tablespoons at a time. Watch out, and wear an apron when doing this, because the mixture will stain anything it touches a violent reddish orange.

Commercial achiote paste, sold in many Latin markets, usually has seasonings more suitable to other regional Mexican cuisines. However, I sometimes use it for convenience.

ALLSPICE: Though allspice is native to the region and you see the trees growing wild in many parts of Veracruz, it is little used by local cooks. People seem to think of it as a cash crop for export, not something for everyday domestic use — though they do cook with the (unfortunately unexported) evergreen leaves.

ANISEED: This is used frequently as both a sweet and a savory flavoring. I have wondered if it found a popular place in Veracruz because of its resemblance to the fragrance of the native avocado leaf and *hoja santa*.

CANELA: This is the Spanish word for true cinnamon, *Cinnamomum zeylanicum*, also called Ceylon cinnamon or soft-stick cinnamon. It is *not* the same thing as the common hard stick cinnamon sold here, *C. cassia*, which is crude and strong-smelling. To make sure that people don't automatically reach for the wrong spice, I always call for *canela*. Hide your ordinary cinnamon where you can't pick it up by mistake while cooking anything from this book. *Canela* is flaky and soft enough so you can break off the edges with your fingers, and its subtle flavor blends into other seasonings without sticking out like a sore thumb. It is soft enough to grind in a blender. Ordinary cinnamon will break the blades.

Unfortunately, some Spanish-language packages cheerfully label cassia *canela*. You can recognize real *canela* by its fragile, flaky appearance.

I do not buy *canela* preground. Like all dried spices, it tastes best when freshly ground, using an electric coffee or spice grinder or a mortar and pestle.

CUMIN: Next to pepper, this is the most used of the Old World spices in Veracruz. It is added, in restrained amounts, to many meat dishes and may be a culinary echo of Moorish seasonings in Spain. Cumin combined with coriander seed seems to be a hallmark of Afromestizo cooking in Veracruz. Be sure to grind it fresh, preferably after toasting it in a small heavy skillet over medium-low heat, stirring occasionally, for 2–3 minutes.

PEPPER: This is the Old World spice that shows up most often in savory dishes. People generally use black pepper in discreet amounts, but there is one notable exception: the seafood dishes called *a la pimienta*, where a big dose of pepper goes into a quick panfry or simmer with onion and/or garlic and minced green chile. Rarely, white pepper is used in a Veracruzan dish for its color and slightly subtler flavor. Never buy preground pepper; in these recipes, "ground pepper" always means fresh from the pepper mill.

VANILLA: Although it is the state's most glamorous food export, this is used only sparingly in Veracruzan cooking. When you find vanilla called for in a recipe, try to use genuine Mexican vanilla beans. The Papantla area of Veracruz was the original home of the plant. Vanilla was later transplanted to other shores, but it still achieves its finest flavor in the region of origin.

Vanilla extracts are subject to some sleazy manipulation of language. Always be sure to buy pure vanilla extract (preferably Mexican, from the area of Papantla and Gutiérrez Zamora), and religiously avoid anything that says "vanillin." This is an artificial simulation of just one of the important flavors in true vanilla. Mexican vanilla bean and vanilla extract are available by mail-order (see page 366).

Chiles

Mexicans use chiles not just for heat but for the interplay between heat and many other possible nuances of chile flavor — herbaceous freshness, floweriness, fruitiness, wininess, smokiness, or a combination. Two things strike me about Veracruzan chile cuisine: the frequent use of tiny wild (or wild-type) hot chiles, and the centrality of jalapeños. The other chiles grown in the state are supporting rather than star players. Fresh and dried forms of the tiny hot chiles and jalapeños are equally popular.

FRESH CHILES

CHILTEPÍN: If you live in the Southwest, you've probably seen chiltepines growing on backyard or roadside bushes. They are thought to be close to the ancestral form of chiles (*Capsicum annuum*, var. *aviculare*) from which nearly all the Mexican hot peppers were developed. They can be as round as peas, oval, or skinny and pointed. All have a murderous sting, but some have more complex flavor than others.

In Veracruz, varieties of these chiles grow everywhere. If you have access to a Southwestern "pepperbush," you can gather a handful. Or use the tiny green chiles often sold in Southeast Asian markets. They are also popular when pickled in brine and served as a hotter-than-hell table condiment.

HABANERO: This innocuous-looking little number is not only the hottest chile of the world kitchen but also one of the sweetest and most aromatic. Its popularity in Veracruz is a link with the cooking of the Afro-Caribbean and the Yucatán Peninsula (it's thought to have come from Cuba, and people in the West Indies cook enthusiastically with this or the close relative called Scotch bonnet pepper). Habaneros belong to a different species (*Capsicum chinense*) from most Mexican chile peppers. They are about the size of a small walnut in the shell, have a funny crumpled shape, and can be bought either green or in a spectrum of yellow-orange-crimson-purple shades. The ripe yellow, orange, and red ones have the most developed flavor. Look for plump, bright, unwithered chiles. Antiheat precautions (see page 48) are especially important in handling habaneros.

JALAPEÑO: Everywhere in the state, jalapeños are grown and used more liberally than any other chile variety. The fresh ones are of beautiful quality, plump and crisp-fleshed, with a delicious fresh chile flavor as well as lively heat. They are almost invariably used green, though they're acceptable when ripe red. The tiny tan streaks on the skin of many jalapeños are no defect; they're just part of its nature. I find the commercially grown jalapeños in this country strangely variable in the degree of heat and often dull-flavored, limp, and tired-looking. Try comparison-shopping until you find a reliable supplier. Large jalapeños are particularly prized for stuffing.

POBLANO: This is the mildest of the Mexican hot chiles. The biggest ones are as large as a small green bell pepper. They are dark green (sometimes almost purplish) and have a distinctive triangular shape narrowing to a point. Poblanos are popular here, as everywhere in Mexico, for stuffing or for use as *rajas* (long strips).

SERRANO: If jalapeños don't look too good in your local market, you might try substituting an equal weight of the very similar serranos. Though smaller and proportionally slimmer than jalapeños, these pungent bullet-shaped chiles (best used green) are completely interchangeable with fresh jalapeños in sauces and braised dishes.

TO GRIDDLE-ROAST FRESH CHILES: See page 58.

DRIED CHILES

Any fresh chile takes on different culinary nuances when dried. Some develop a concentrated sweetness and complexity that jumps out at you in cooked sauces or braising juices. Others have their original identity simplified and reinforced. The most suitable types for the traditional sun-drying or oven-drying methods are the tiny wild-type chiles (often toasted and ground to a powder for seasoning) and larger ones with only a thin or medium-thick layer of flesh.

The larger dried chiles are generally reconstituted by soaking and griddle-drying (see page 50); in this form, they give not only flavor but body to pureed sauces. The minute wild-type varieties are seldom soaked, though they may be briefly boiled.

Local names are a serious puzzle in Veracruz. Everywhere I traveled, I found cooks happily referring to any popular native variety as *chile seco* (dried chile), as if it were the only known kind of dried chile. When I use the term *chile seco* as it was given to me in the recipe titles, I've tried to indicate in the translation just which chile is meant.

A NOTE ABOUT PURCHASING DRIED CHILES: Don't be tempted to load up on large quantities. They usually harbor small insects that aren't a problem if the chiles are used quickly but get to be a nuisance if you keep a big supply on hand all the time.

ANCHO: The reddish-black ancho, made by drying poblanos, is the most useful of the dried Mexican chiles, the one that gives the cleanest and most versatile basic chile flavor to a sauce, along with moderate heat. It has a very wrinkled surface and a broad shape (hence the name, which means broad). Anchos are among the most widely available chiles in this country.

ARBOL: A fairly small, pointed, thin-skinned dried chile, with a bright reddish orange color and a very sharp but pleasant heat. I sometimes substitute it for Veracruzan comapas. The árbol (tree) chile is widely available in this country.

ZARELA'S VERACRUZ

Precautions for Handling Chiles

THE HEAT-PRODUCING SUBSTANCE in all chiles is capsaicin, which can make your skin burn and cause agony if you inadvertently rub your eyes after touching them. If you're new to working with them, it's prudent to treat all spicy chiles as potential firebombs (though later you'll find that some are hardly irritating at all). The hottest parts are the veins and seeds inside; sometimes they're removed to moderate the sting. Try to touch the interior of hot chiles as little as possible; thin disposable plastic gloves are a big help. Wash your hands thoroughly after handling chiles.

CHILTEPÍN (DRIED): In most parts of the United States, tiny hot chiles are sold only in dried form, under various names such as *chile piquín*, "bird chile," or "birdseed chile."

CHIPOTLE: When ripened and smoke-dried, the jalapeño becomes the chipotle chile. These are used in every part of Mexico, but Veracruzans are particularly zealous about the art of smoking chipotles. The aim is to develop not just hotness and smokiness but also rich, nuanced flavor. There are two principal types of chipotles. One resembles the chipotles commercially sold in the United States, mouse-brown with a dull leathery finish and a wrinkled surface. Distributors here may call it *chile ahumada* (smoked chile) or *chipotle meco* (*meco* can refer to things with mottled or spotty markings). These chiles become meaty and intensely flavored when reconstituted by soaking in water. The smokiness is pronounced but not harsh.

The second major Veracruzan chipotle variety is slightly smaller and thinner-skinned, with a smoother surface and a dark purple-red hue. In Veracruz, they are generally called *moritas* ("blackberries," for the color). Morita-type and the common meco-type chipotles are interchangeable up to a point, but moritas are almost always preferable. They have a wonderful fruity-flowery quality that brightens any dish they're used in. They are starting to be imported into this country, and when chipotles are called for in Veracruzan dishes, I recommend searching for the morita variety. In Veracruz, both often go under the catchall name *chile seco*.

Canned chipotle chiles in adobo (a spicy red sauce) are a completely different product. These are not interchangeable with regular chipotles of either the meco or the morita type. In order to ward off mistakes, I generally call for the regular ones as "dried (*not* canned) chipotle chiles."

COMAPA: My favorite of the Veracruzan tiny wild-type chiles is the comapa, which dries to the size of a large dried chiltepín but has a characteristic shape, a bit like a small top. Like others of this general type, it may be sold as just *chile seco* (dried chile) in some parts of the state, but it has a personality all its own. It is a thin-skinned, fragrant dried chile with a bright orange-red color and a vivacious fruitiness. The comapa chile, which is always used for *salsa macha* (page 310), is not yet available in this country. I am sure that it will be imported within the next couple of years, but, meanwhile, I have worked out the recipes using large dried chiltepines, árbol chiles, or other readily available substitutes. This is not an ideal solution, because comapa chiles have more flavor and less heat than the substitutes: I have consequently had to reduce the proportion of chiles in order not to overwhelm the other flavors.

GUAJILLO: Long, thin, smooth-skinned, and usually brick-red, guajillos ("little pod" chiles) can be moderately to blazingly hot. Veracruzans, like other Mexicans, find that they complement the less fiery ancho and often combine the two in sauces. In Pánuco, in the north of the state, it's called *chile cascabel* (rattle or jingle chile), for the noise the seeds make when you shake it. Elsewhere in the state, the name *cascabel* denotes a shiny, thick-skinned, almost globular dried chile, also fairly hot. Guajillos are widely available in this country.

MULATO (MULATTO): A type of ancho chile made from a particularly dark-skinned, heart-shaped poblano variety. It is often combined with guajillos and/or regular anchos. Mulatos are widely available in this country.

Preparing Dried Chiles for Cooking

꠸꠸꠸

UNTIL I watched Veracruzan cooks at work, I would have said that a good Mexican cook regularly griddle-dries or toasts dried chiles (that is, puts the lightly rinsed chiles on a hot griddle just long enough to evaporate the moisture and make them fragrant). This is followed by soaking them for (usually) 15–20 minutes in hot water. But, surprisingly, I found no unanimity at all on these points in Veracruz. Many people throw dried chiles right into a sauce or soup with no griddle-cooking or soaking. Or they will toast them (especially the tiny wild-type chiles) and grind them to a seasoning powder rather than soaking and grinding them to a paste with other ingredients, the more orthodox Mexican method. And sometimes a cook threw me a curve. The gifted Lupita Armenta Guzmán (whom you will meet through several wonderful recipes) insisted that toasted chiles taste best when soaked in hot homemade stock rather than water. Now she has *me* doing it!

In the end, I followed the idiosyncrasies of the individual cooks in handling dried chiles. I am, however, giving the general griddle-drying method here for easy reference.

To GRIDDLE-DRY LARGE DRIED CHILES: For large chiles (anchos, guajillos, mulatos) and medium-small ones, lightly rinse under cold running water and shake off the excess. Heat a heavy griddle or cast-iron skillet over medium-high heat until a drop of water evaporates instantly. Place the chiles on the griddle, being sure not to crowd them. (You can always work in more than one batch.) Heat the chiles, turning occasionally with kitchen tongs, just until the moisture that clings to them has evaporated and you smell their toasted fragrance. They *must not scorch,* or the entire dish will be bitter. Allow 20–25 seconds for thin-skinned chiles like guajillos, 30–35 seconds for anchos and mulatos. Lift them out into a bowl as they are done, cover generously with boiling water, and let stand for 15–20 minutes. Drain thoroughly before proceeding. (The soaking makes them pliable and brings out the meaty quality of the flesh under the skin.)

To TOAST SMALL DRIED CHILES: Wild-type chiles (chiltepines and dried serranos) are handled somewhat differently. Set a small heavy skillet over the lowest possible setting and let it warm until hot to the touch. Add the chiles, *without rinsing.* Let them toast gently, shaking the pan and stirring frequently, for 15–20 minutes, or until nicely toasted but not scorched. They will rustle dully at first when stirred, then make a higher-pitched sound. When done, they should be brittle, crumbly, and slightly (not deeply) darkened, with a hint of a sheen. Chiles of this type are not soaked after toasting but are usually crumbled or ground when slightly cooled, with or without the seeds (follow the directions in individual recipes).

PASILLA (LITTLE RAISIN): A long, thin dried chile, prized for its intense dark color and ability to harmonize with other flavors in dried chile combinations (for example, in *moles*).

SERRANO (DRIED): This small thin-skinned orange-red chile is *not* a dried version of the fresh serrano that we know in the United States. The Veracruzan dried serrano is a bright-flavored chile, quite hot, but with a delightful floral quality. Though not meaty, it is one of the most flavorful dried chiles. It is not yet commonly available in this country; I usually substitute either árbol chiles or the small, flat, orange-toned dried chiles often sold in Chinese markets.

Masa and *Nixtamal*

Remember these two words well, for they are almost the soul of Mexican cooking.

MASA is just the Spanish word for dough, but to any Mexican it means, first and foremost, the moist corn dough for tortillas, tamales, and small dumplings. Before being ground, the corn is dried and turned into **NIXTAMAL** — hominy-like kernels that have swelled and acquired a new savor by soaking in an alkali solution (*cal*).

What exactly does nixtamalizing do to corn? I won't try to describe the chemistry, but it softens the walls of the kernels enough so that they can be separated from the interior. Softened and enlarged by the *cal* solution, the skinless kernels have a taste and aroma like no other food on earth — a delicately nutty quality combined with something almost chalky or mineral-like.

In scattered parts of Veracruz, traditionalists still make their own *nixtamal* and grind it on the same kind of stone *metates* (platform mortars) that people were using even before the Aztecs. More often, cooks buy *nixtamal* or ground masa from local *tortillerías* (small mills or artisanal-scale factories that make their own masa for tortillas and other corn products). Many turn to the instant-masa products from large manufacturers — prepared masa that is completely desiccated, then ground into a kind of flour.

In the United States, this instantized powdered masa is usually known as **MASA HARINA**, or masa flour. Masa Harina is actually a trademark name for the version made by the Quaker Oats Company, but it is one of those brand names like Thermos or Kleenex that have been adopted by almost everybody. Several commercial brands are widely sold in both Mexico and the United States, the best known being Quaker and — my usual preference — Maseca.

I gladly use masa harina for simple purposes: for everyday tortillas, little soup dumplings (*bolitas*), and most of the corn-based snacks and street dishes collectively called *antojitos*. (Never try to use cornmeal instead.) Masa harina's strong point is not just convenience but nonperishability. It will keep for weeks or months if stored in a cool dry place with precautions against insects, while fresh *nixtamal* or masa will usually go bad after two or three days, even if refrigerated.

Fresh masa and *nixtamal* are much more widely available in this country than many people realize. In the last fifteen years or so, Mexican enclaves have appeared in large and midsize cities almost everywhere in the United States. These communities always sprout a tortilla factory (or several rival ones) that makes *nixtamal* and grinds it. (Masa usually comes in both a standard fine grind for tortillas and a coarser grind for tamales.) Generally, these factories will sell their masa by the pound to retail customers. You must plan on using it within a day or two or freezing it, for it sours very quickly. A good mail-order source that supplies fresh or frozen masa by overnight express is María and Ricardo's Tortilla Factory in Massachusetts (see page 366).

Capers, Olives, Pickled Jalapeños, and Vinegar

Brined ingredients contribute a distinctive but not harsh combination of salt, acid, and an indefinable something in dishes with strong Spanish roots. In Veracruz, the process of culinary *mestizaje* (commingling) resulted in another wonderful brined addition to the larder: pickled jalapeños and other hot chiles. Cooks can delicately temper the degree of sourness by also adding some kind of vinegar. All these components have a slightly different effect — floral-briny, olive-briny, hot-briny, lightly tart. Sometimes the pickling juices from capers or other brined ingredients are added to the mix, sometimes not.

CAPERS: I find that large caper buds (about the size of a blueberry) have more of the exciting floral quality than small ones.

OLIVES: The green olives used in Mexico are always of the mild Spanish manzanilla type, sometimes stuffed with pimiento strips. Do not

experiment with more "sophisticated," astringent olives, which would only ruin the mellow flavors of Veracruzan cooking.

PICKLED JALAPEÑOS: Home-pickled or commercially pickled jalapeños lend a special vividness to some dishes built on fundamentally Spanish flavors. People sometimes like to tone down the bite of jalapeños that are to be pickled or marinated. They do this by adding sugar to the cooking water, sometimes with a little instant coffee as well. The chiles are simmered in the solution and then allowed to cool in it. When my recipes call for pickled jalapeños, any commercial Mexican brand can be used. U.S. brands, except for Goya, are too harsh and metallic.

VINEGAR: Vinegar in Veracruz is often homemade, adding a unique artisanal imprint to some dishes. Most of it is made from pineapples. The state is one of the world's premier pineapple-growing areas, so people know the growing season without even thinking about it. They wait until pineapples are dead ripe and sugar-sweet in April, then hang one in a muslin bag over a bowl to catch the juices that are released as the inside ferments and dissolves into vinegar. (I'm told that the optimum room temperature for this is about 78°F.) Or they save the cores and trimmings from pineapples and ferment them in a bowl with a little *piloncillo* (brown loaf sugar). When they use commercial vinegar, it is almost invariably cider vinegar, often slightly diluted with water; it is important that any vinegar should be mild rather than penetrating.

I have become addicted to a completely inauthentic but also completely delicious vinegar that has the gentleness of a good pineapple vinegar but is otherwise not related. It is the mild herbed Kressi brand wine vinegar from Switzerland, which I mention in a few recipes that strike me as especially suited to the pleasant bouquet of the product.

Bottled and Packaged Flavors

When I first began cooking in New York and trying to communicate my knowledge of Mexican food, I used to be bewildered by the blanket prejudice against anything containing a bouillon cube or a dash of Worcestershire sauce. I would hear Yankees telling *me* that that stuff wasn't Mexican, and it took all the courage I could muster to say, "Well, pardon me!" I still find myself making defensive statements

every time I use such ingredients in a recipe, as if to prove that I'm not a junk-food addict. Now, however, I do have a little more perspective on the issue.

Mexicans really do cook frequently with Maggi sauce, Worcestershire sauce (*salsa inglesa*), soy sauce, and powdered chicken stock base or bouillon cubes. There is no stigma attached to these ingredients. They are as carefully considered and measured out as any other seasoning. What I think the misguided purists are reacting to is a chapter in the cooking history of the United States, not Mexico. During much of the twentieth century, cans and bottles replaced cooking from scratch for millions of households in this country. As a result, many people came to use reconstituted cubes or powders as a substitute for soup, bottled sauce as a substitute for one made from fresh ingredients. This was not and is not the Mexican way. People do not pretend that mixing powdered chicken stock base with water makes a stock. But the chicken base may be used — in small amounts — along with other seasonings in a complexly flavored sauce. In other words, the bottled or packaged products are not shortcut excuses for something else. They are legitimate elements in a balance of flavors.

Cubes and stock bases may contain monosodium glutamate; if you have to avoid these, either skip the recipe or omit them and compensate with a little extra salt. Otherwise, do not look down on Maggi sauce or stock base, and do not try replacing them with fancy ingredients like balsamic vinegar or *glace de viande*. That stuff REALLY isn't Mexican.

Vegetables and Fruits

AVOCADOS: Until I go back to Mexico, I always forget how versatile and varied avocados can be. In this country, it's remarkable to find more than two or three different kinds in a store. At the market in Orizaba or Xalapa, I see some specimens the size of a large strawberry, others as big as a midsize mango. They may be light- or dark-skinned, smooth or rough, short or long, round or bottlenecked, and so forth. The flavor and texture also can vary, from very buttery and rich to a bit lighter and faintly tart. But what doesn't vary is that these are all unctuous Mexican-type avocados, a completely different strain from the hulking, watery, fibrous West Indian kind sold in Caribbean markets. In this country, look for the cultivars called Hass (smallish, with dark pebbled skin) or Fuerte (slightly larger and greener). Buy avocados a little on the firm side and give them 1–3 days to ripen at room temperature — once ripe, they can be refrigerated, but it does not preserve them at their best. Remember that the leaf of the Mexican avocado is a valuable aromatic herb (see page 41).

CALABAZA: There are more kinds of New World pumpkins than botanists know how to classify. The kind traditionally prized by Africans on both sides of the Atlantic is an enormous green-skinned pumpkin with deep orange flesh firm enough to earn it a place among the Afro-Cuban *viandas* (starchy tubers). It has to be bought sliced by the pound in West Indian or Latin markets. Otherwise, substitute the smaller Japanese kabocha squash. In Veracruz, people of African descent love to cook chunks of calabaza in braised dishes such as Pork with Mashed Pumpkin (page 253).

CHAYOTE: In Orizaba, I realized that this unique member of the squash-and-gourd family is one of those wonder plants whose every part is edible — the fruit, the pit, the vine, the delectable potato-like root. In the United States, the only part that is eaten is the pear-shaped fruit, which is usually not as firm and nutty as Mexican chayotes. Also, we have a choice of only one or two very similar varieties, while in Veracruz, one chayote may differ radically from another.

Chayotes are a nuisance to peel both because the skin can be deeply grooved and because the flesh exudes a sticky juice that coats your fingers like an unwanted glove. It helps a little bit to cut off the ends and rub the skin of the tips against the cut surfaces. In order to get the last remnants of skin out of those annoying grooves, I prefer to peel them with a small sharp knife rather than a vegetable peeler. Rinse your hands afterwards — the juice can be irritating. (Some cooks prefer to do the peeling under cool running water.) Cut the chayotes in half lengthwise and remove the "almond," as Mexicans call the pit. People sometimes cook them along with the flesh because they are too delicious to discard.

CITRUS FRUIT: Veracruz is citrus country. Most of what is grown are Valencia-type sweet oranges for export or processing. Fresh sweet orange juice is a delicious addition to some Veracruzan marinades and braised dishes. The sour or bitter orange (*naranja agria*), with a more sprightly flavor for cooking purposes, is grown on a smaller scale. Most important for cooking are the several types of *limones* (limes). The large green Persian lime sold in the United States is a good substitute (though slightly tarter and less fragrant) for the riper yellow-green lime most often used in Veracruzan cooking. Our limes gain some depth of flavor if allowed to sit at room temperature for several days. (Lemons are no substitute at all, so do not attempt to use them.)

Lime juice is the ideal foil for all kinds of Veracruzan dishes. My recipes often call for a garnish of lime wedges — but if you want a more authentic touch, slice off a lengthwise oval section $^3/_4$–1 inch thick from the side of a lime, then rotate the fruit and make three more lengthwise slices, leaving just a skeletal center with four rect-angular sides. These oval sections are easier to squeeze over food than wedges and look delightfully Mexican.

CORN: For fresh corn on or off the cob (*elotes, granos de elote*), I must tell you that no Veracruzan cook would put up with the products of the United States. Everyone here, it seems, wants fresh corn to be so full of sugar that you can't taste anything else. The term "sweet corn" is all too accurate, especially for the most recently developed "mira-cle" strains. With this sweetness comes an unwanted extra, a tough fibrous skin on the kernels that creates a most unpleasant texture when you try to grind or puree it.

Mexican corn kernels are starchy and filling, not sweet, and the skin is more delicate. In some cases, the fresh corn in this country is acceptable — just barely — if you do some looking for an old-fash-ioned *unimproved* variety like Golden Bantam or Silver Queen. What I most often use to avoid that awful fibrous texture is frozen shoepeg corn. It can sometimes be found fresh as Country Gentleman.

HEARTS OF PALM (*PALMITOS*): In the Totonac and Huasteca areas of Veracruz, people use the tender inner flesh from shoots of *Sambal palmetto* and some similar palm species as a delicious, endlessly use-ful vegetable. It is wonderful braised or pan-cooked by itself, sim-mered in a soup, pureed for a dip-like *ensalada* (salad), and in many other guises. Floridians may be able to find it fresh under the unat-tractive name of "swamp cabbage." I have heard reports of fresh hearts of palm sometimes being available in large cities in the United States, but most of us have to rely on canned hearts of palm, im-ported from several Latin American countries. They happen to be one of the best and least canned-tasting of canned products, once the brine is drained. My pantry always holds a few cans in reserve, and I have converted I don't know how many of my friends to the love of *palmitos*. But please note that every processor seems to put them up in a different-sized can or jar. Do the necessary arithmetic according to the amount given in the recipe, and don't worry if you end up with a few ounces more or less.

ONIONS AND THEIR TRIBE: One of the first things that struck me about Veracruzan cooking was that, on the whole, people use onion and garlic delicately rather than extravagantly to season food. I often encountered recipes calling for half of a small onion — and although "small onion" means something the size of a lime, not a pearl onion, it's still clear that restraint is the watchword. There are times when I deliberately increased the original amount to compensate for the dullness of other crucial ingredients as supplied by factory farms here. The onion or garlic, however, should always sing rather than shout.

When a Mexican cooks says *cebolla*, you can bet that she means a *white* onion. People consider them juicier and cleaner-flavored than the yellow onions generally used in this country. It's also important to realize that they are not stored as long as ours. The freshness is as crucial as it would be with green garden vegetables. The closest you can come to the freshest Mexican onions is to look for an Italian market or farmers' market that sells smooth white onions still attached to the green stalk, with no papery outer skin. Some markets call them bulb onions, but there is no one standard name.

Veracruzan recipes sometimes call for red onion by name, *cebolla morada*. Scallions are frequently used, including a thin purplish kind (*cebollín morado*). At the markets, I often saw shallots (not all that common in most of Mexico), curious scallion-like wild onions called *chanacates*, and others I haven't been able to identify. Flat-leafed chives are popular — in fact, almost mandatory in herb bouquets for braised dishes. Garlic is ubiquitous, but it, like onion, is used sooner after harvesting than in the United States and has a sweeter, more subtle flavor. Look for thin-skinned varieties with small pinkish cloves.

You will see that many of my stock and sauce recipes call for adding onion and garlic unpeeled; they are usually discarded after they have given up their flavor. This is standard Veracruzan practice. Cooks believe that a lot of the richness lies in the skin; hence the custom of leaving it on for some cooking purposes.

FOR DIRECTIONS ON GRIDDLE-ROASTING ONIONS AND GARLIC: See page 58.

ZARELA'S VERACRUZ

Griddle-Roasting Vegetables

(Fresh Chiles, Garlic and Onions, and Tomatoes)

THIS TECHNIQUE is one of the most important in the Mexican kitchen. It is the secret of intense, developed flavors in tomatoes, onions, garlic, and fresh chiles. Omit this step, and you will have sabotaged the final dish by failing to concentrate the natural sugars of the ingredients. Roasting is accomplished by direct contact with the hot surface of a heavy griddle or skillet.

I have used both cast-aluminum and cast-iron skillets, and both are good. So are the nonstick equivalents, as long as they are heavy-gauge metal and have a durable heat-resistant surface, not a flimsy nonstick finish that will disintegrate with the fourth or fifth workout it gets. (Ask whether it will stand up to 45 minutes over medium heat.) Cast-iron ware is probably the easiest to find. The true Mexican clay *comal* (griddle) is not a practical option for most of us — even if you can find one in a Mexican neighborhood grocery, it will have a fairly short life before it cracks.

All griddle-roasting works more or less the same way. You let the empty dry skillet or griddle stand over low to medium-high (never really high) heat until a drop of water sizzles the second that it hits the surface. Add the chosen ingredient (trying not to crowd the griddle — you can always do two or more batches) and cook, turning frequently with kitchen tongs or two long-handled spatulas, until the skin is either blistered and charred or somewhat darkened, depending on which vegetable you're using. The skin is like a cooking envelope that delivers modulated heat to the inside of the chiles, garlic, etc., letting it soften and caramelize. Onions and garlic become sweet, tomatoes more tomatoey, chiles more rounded and rich.

Each vegetable demands a slightly different timing or degree of heat. I suggest that you practice with all of them until you recognize the sizzle-on-contact moment, learn to turn things easily, and develop a feel for the right stage of doneness. The usual guidelines follow:

$\mathcal{F}$RESH CHILES: Medium-high heat for 5–7 minutes, depending on their size. When they are blistered and black all over, place in a plastic or brown paper bag for about 5 minutes to help loosen the skin. When cool enough to handle, peel and scrape off the skin with a small sharp knife, not worrying about getting every last blackened bit. To remove the seeds (necessary in some but not all recipes), first cut off and discard the stems with the attached white core, then slit them lengthwise and scrape out the remaining seeds. For extra heat, leave the membranes intact; for milder heat, cut and scrape them away. In some cases I've indicated a slightly different procedure.

$\mathcal{T}$OMATOES: Medium heat for 10–15 minutes for small or medium tomatoes, 15–20 minutes for large ones. They should be started stem end down, which helps keep in the juices. Turn frequently. When they are blistered and blackened all over, set aside in a bowl to catch the juices, until cool enough to handle. Peel off the charred skin, not worrying about getting every bit. The flavorful juices should be added to the dish along with the tomato pulp.

$\mathcal{G}$ARLIC AND ONIONS (always leave unpeeled): Medium-low heat, allowing 8 minutes for garlic cloves, 15–20 minutes for small onions, 20–25 minutes for medium onions. All should be turned frequently. Large onions should be halved crosswise and roasted for about 20 minutes; turn frequently and don't worry about the charring of the cut surfaces. Set aside the roasted vegetables until cool enough to handle, then peel over a bowl to save any juices. Scrape away the blackened surface of halved onions.

PLANTAIN: Plantains are the same species as bananas but come from strains grown for starch more than sugar. They are inedible when raw. Once the fruit reaches full size, it can be eaten (cooked) at any stage of ripeness. Don't be disconcerted by the sight of a completely green plantain, a yellow one with ominous-looking dark blotches, or even one that is grungy black all over. They can look awful to the untrained eye and still be perfectly good. When very green, they are thoroughly mealy and starchy, without a hint of sweetness. A few days later, they are blotchy yellow and semiripe and will cook to a slightly mellower consistency. When they are black and dead ripe, they are nearly as sweet and soft as bananas. Just be sure to select them at a uniform stage if you are cooking several.

Plantains are great in different fried forms. But the original way of preparing them — still one of the best — was boiled and mashed. This is how they were cooked in West Africa before they came to the New World. Even now some form of mashed plantains is common to all the Afro-Caribbean cultures. You will find that the green ones are intensely starchy and therefore taste best when eaten very hot. (The texture becomes too dense on cooling.)

All plantains are more difficult to peel than bananas, but the green ones are the worst. Start by cutting off the tips with a very sharp knife. You can leave the plantain in one piece or cut it crosswise into several chunks. Make one or two lengthwise incisions through the skin from end to end; with the knife tip and your fingers, work away the skin a little at a time until you can remove the whole thing from the flesh. Some people say that they are easier to peel if you leave them to soak in boiling water for about 10 minutes after removing the tips and making the lengthwise cuts. Once peeled, they should be covered with cold water. Be sure to blot completely dry if you are deep-frying them. Plantains can also be peeled after cooking, as I do in Seasoned Mashed Plantains (page 276).

SWEET POTATO: Originally from South America, this became a favorite vegetable throughout the Spanish Caribbean. In Veracruzan markets, sweet potatoes come in several colors, including a startling purple, deep orange, pale orange-yellow, and nearly white. (This last is often called by the Cuban name of *boniato* instead of the regular Mexican term, *camote*.) They can be simply boiled and mashed like yuca.

TOMATILLOS: What a difference a few years can make! When I was working on my first book, the only way many people could buy tomatillos in this country was canned, and I felt obliged to give directions for making tomatillo sauce with the canned ones, no matter how much I loathed them. Now fresh tomatillos are a familiar sight even in supermarkets. This elegant little fruit, *tomate verde* or *tomate de cáscara* in Mexico, is used in sauces where a mild, subtle tartness is called for. One of my most joyful discoveries in Veracruz was the wonderful pairing that tomatillos make with avocado in an uncooked green sauce (see *salsa verde con aguacate*, page 308). It is a most refreshing change from guacamole, with the lightly acid tomatillos tempering the richness of the avocado.

TOMATOES: Mexico is tomato heaven — there is no other word for it. The plant bears there year-round, and in the hot sun, the fruit develops the most intense flavor. That accounts for the most important difference between the typical Veracruzan sauces as made there or here. The simplest creations are magic when real tomatoes are at the heart of them. But the tomatoes available in the United States are pallid-flavored most of the year (including the bright red imported ones sold at fancy prices). Even local tomatoes in season can taste waterlogged rather than juicy. This is one reason that I often season dishes more abundantly than my Veracruzan friends or add an extra step of frying ingredients — it helps compensate for that missing dimension of tomato flavor.

The main types used in Veracruz are globe tomatoes, plum tomatoes (*tomates guajillos*), and a tiny kind called *tomate de milpa* or *tomate citlali*, sometimes sold here at farmers' markets as "currant tomatoes." **Globe tomatoes** (not as huge as the most overgrown beefsteaks and other giants) are the all-purpose tomato. **Plum tomatoes** are used when a dish requires meatiness and flavor without an excess of juice. **Currant tomatoes** are considered particularly exquisite. Their sharp sweetness is the secret of *tachogobi* (page 316), the famous coarse-textured tomato sauce served with fish around Lake Catemaco.

For best results here, shop with an eagle eye and try to find globe or plum tomatoes that are dead ripe, just about overripe. You can usually substitute one for the other in recipes if the total weight is the same, though when I call for "tomatoes" in a recipe, I'm generally thinking of globe tomatoes. Sample the kinds sold at local farmers' markets in season, and by all means substitute yellow or orange tomatoes for red if you find a batch with better flavor. For currant tomatoes, which are hard to find in most places, use the very small

cherry tomatoes imported from Mexico or the sweet and delicious grape tomatoes.

Never skip the step of griddle-roasting tomatoes (see page 58) when a recipe calls for it. It is one of the greatest secrets of true Mexican flavor.

YUCA (ALSO CALLED MANIOC OR CASSAVA): This is the most important native tuber of eastern Central America and the northeast coast of South America — as important as the potato on the Pacific side. Unlike potatoes, yuca won't grow outside the tropics. Also unlike potatoes, it has very large starch granules that make it waxy and almost translucent when cooked (it is the source of tapioca). As a result, when it is piping hot, it has a densely starchy quality that its fans find irresistible, but it becomes unpleasantly heavy and gluey on cooling.

Latin markets in the United States carry the brown-skinned yuca roots, which look a bit like small deformed baseball bats, about 9–12 inches long. The skin is usually waxed, theoretically to retard spoilage. They are notoriously hard to store in good condition, and wax or no wax, even experienced shoppers may end up having to throw away a lot of spoiled bits from what looked like a sound root. For this reason, it's always wise to buy more than a recipe calls for. Or do as Cuban cooks in this country do and buy frozen yuca, which is of consistent quality and also saves you the trouble of peeling the roots.

Yuca roots have both a bark-like outer skin and a thicker under-skin that you will see when you cut into the pure white flesh. Both must be peeled away before cooking with a very sharp small knife; some people find it easier to do this with the root cut crosswise into 3-to-4-inch lengths. Cut away any discolored areas. Place the peeled chunks in cold water as soon as they are done, to keep them from discoloring. There is also a stringy cord running down the center that should be removed either before or after cooking (easy to do if you halve the root or the pieces lengthwise). The reward for all this effort is in the eating. If you love super-starchy foods, your idea of heaven may be hot boiled yuca — or some of the other tropical tubers that are adored throughout the Afro-Caribbean, such as the native malanga and its adopted look-alike from the South Pacific, taro. Like yuca and green plantains, these have a glorious stick-to-the-ribs quality when hot (like potatoes that have become super-potatoes) but get depressingly gluey on cooling.

Dried Beans

In all my travels in Veracruz, I think I have been served pinto beans just once (in the exquisite *frijoles refritos en mantequilla* of La Viuda restaurant in Alvarado; see page 285). Otherwise, "beans" always means black beans. Large black beans are even sold in the market as *frijoles veracruzanos* in other Mexican regions. Beans are nearly inseparable from any Mexican meal, but they are even more important in Veracruz because they are used so often as a filling for *antojitos* (snacks) or tamales.

No Mexican cook would ever soak dried beans before cooking. You simply put them in the pot and cook them in water with an onion, some epazote (see page 41), and (later in the cooking) a little salt. When they're done, they're done, and people don't worry about beans taking more time (if they're old and somewhat dry) or less (if they're fresher). You then eat them gloriously soupy — in a bowl, or perhaps ladled over rice. For everyday beans, no one in Mexico would ever cook away or drain off all the liquid. They are drained only if they will be served in another form, such as refried beans.

I follow the classic Mexican approach for basic cooked beans. But if they are to receive further cooking as a filling in some other dish, I use the somewhat unorthodox procedure of soaking and just slightly undercooking them (see Semicooked Black Beans, page 284). I think it allows better control of the finished texture.

Rice

The Spanish saw the lush tropical climate and many swamps of Veracruz as an opportunity to grow lucrative crops not suited to most of Spain. Rice was one of their earliest and most successful experiments. Just as the Levantine provinces of Spain are its only rice-producing area, Veracruz remains the only state of Mexico to grow rice on a large commercial scale. Perhaps this is also a link with the state's African heritage, for the slaves brought their own rice-growing tradition from Africa to the New World plantations. Today rice is the basis of a dish that is almost synonymous with Veracruzan cuisine at its finest, *arroz a la tumbada* (page 175), a kind of cross between a soupy seafood paella and a risotto.

Like other Mexicans, Veracruzans are sticklers for rinsing rice before cooking. Place it in a sieve or colander and rinse under cold running water until the water runs clear. Rinsing makes the grains less gummy and more distinctly separate after cooking. Always remember to leave time for this step whether you use long-grain rice (the usual preference in Veracruz) or my own personal favorite, the medium-grain Spanish Valencia.

Nuts, Seeds, and Raisins

At the time of the Conquest, a long Moorish-Spanish tradition of cooking with almonds and sesame seeds met a long Mesoamerican tradition of cooking with pumpkin and other seeds. The Portuguese are thought to have brought peanuts from Brazil to West Africa, and from there, they were taken to the Caribbean islands and the Gulf coast of Mexico with the slave trade. The slaves may also have helped popularize sesame in Veracruz, because it was an important African crop.

The most important nuts and seeds in Veracruzan cooking are peanuts, pumpkin seeds, sesame seeds, and almonds.

ALMONDS, PECANS, AND PINE NUTS: Toast these nuts in a 350°F oven, stirring occasionally, about 10 minutes for whole nuts and 8–10 minutes for slivered almonds. (I use my toaster oven.) In confections based on ground almonds, I like to start with slivered blanched almonds. They grind more evenly than whole almonds when you are doing a large batch in the food processor.

PEANUTS: Veracruzan cooks often buy peanuts raw in the shell and roast them on a griddle over low heat or in a low oven. I usually omit this step, because I don't see any great advantage over the flavor of commercial roasted peanuts.

PUMPKIN AND SESAME SEEDS: On the other hand, I do like to toast pumpkin seeds before using, in a dry, heavy skillet set over medium-low heat. Use hulled pumpkin seeds and toast, stirring occasionally and shaking the skillet, until they are slightly browned and starting to pop, usually 3–4 minutes. Quickly scrape them out into a bowl before they can scorch. I treat sesame seeds the same way, except that they may take a minute or so longer to become light golden (they will not pop). Watch carefully, because if scorched, either pumpkin or sesame seeds will turn the whole dish bitter.

RAISINS: These are an essential part of the Spanish repertoire of basic flavors that came to Veracruz along with capers, olives, and almonds. They add sweetness and intensity without being cloying. Those sold in Veracruz are usually less gummy than our packaged raisins. Use the dark raisins, which are thought to have more flavor than the golden kind.

Cooking Fats

Spanish cooks have traditionally loved to mix different cooking fats, and they brought their eclectic preferences with them to Veracruz. To this day, butter and olive oil are more popular in Veracruz than in other parts of the country. Nowhere else have I eaten refried beans made with butter. And nowhere else have I seen such lavish use of olive oil (especially to cook seafood) or such reliance on mixtures of oil with lard or rendered bacon fat.

As a result, Veracruzan cuisine can be many things to many people, if not all things to all people. If you favor a "Mediterranean diet" approach to cooking, with olive oil as the one basic fat, you will find many suitable dishes in this book. I confess that for me, this is one of the most attractive features of the cuisine. (But please note that Veracruzan cooks are not sticklers for extra-virgin olive oil — let your palate be your guide in deciding what grade to use.) I think, however, that it would be misleading not to point out that Veracruzan cooks deeply value butter for its delicacy and lard for the satisfying way it rounds out or complements other flavors.

LARD: If you have never tasted good lard, give it a try before disdaining it. I am beginning to read excited tributes to lard in gourmet publications that used to treat it like toxic waste. All, however, stress that the flavorless commercial packaged lard sold in our supermarkets is not the real thing. It contains preservatives and is partly hydrogenated to a consistency that makes it useful for a few baking purposes but somewhat unpleasant in terms of "mouth feel." The best lard you can buy usually comes from Hungarian, German, or Latin butchers. The best lard of all will probably be that you make yourself.

Home-rendered lard is not at all difficult to make. This task is part of the ordinary kitchen routine in Mexico. You can work with any desired amount — because I use it generously almost every day, I routinely make a sizable batch. There is a great bonus: you will also end up with a trove of the pork cracklings (*chicharrones*) that all Mexicans adore from childhood on.

To Render Lard

BUY *unsalted* pork fat from a good pork butcher. (I don't usually bother looking for the expensive leaf lard that comes from above the kidneys; the plain has always given me excellent results.) I generally buy about 3 pounds. If you are new to lard making, you may want to experiment with smaller amounts (maybe ¹/₂ pound or ³/₄ pound) to get the hang of the process. With a large sharp heavy knife, cut it up into cubes no larger than ¹/₂ inch. (For this — the worst part of the process — I usually half-freeze the fat to make it easier to work with.) Place it in a Dutch oven or heavy pot over low heat, stirring frequently to make sure the pieces are not clumping together or sticking to the bottom. On my stove, in a large Dutch oven with a diameter of 12 inches, it takes about 30 minutes for 3 pounds of cubed pork fat to render most of the fat without getting dark or scorched. You may get a different timing on your first attempt; it's something you have to get a feel for by practice. The pieces should be separated but not marooned in space, they should get partly crisp without totally shriveling up, and the rendered fat should be clear and pale. When it reaches this stage, remove the pot from the heat and let it cool slightly for a few minutes (the rendered fat is hotter than it looks). Carefully pour off the melted lard through a mesh strainer into a heatproof container (a 3-to-4-cup container if you started with 3 pounds of fat), trying to stop pouring before any of the grainy residue goes through. What you should have is unclouded, unbrowned rendered fat that will cool into pure, clear lard. Set the container aside. When it has cooled to room temperature, refrigerate, well sealed. It is what is generally meant in any of my recipes calling for home-rendered lard.

MEANWHILE, return the pot — with the residue and partly finished pork fat cubes — to the stove over low heat. Now you must monitor the pot constantly, because things can change very fast. You are watching for the stage when the frying morsels have rendered up the rest of their fat *without starting to burn* and when the remaining rendered lard is at most a delicate light brown. A moment's inattention, and the whole thing will be scorched and bitter. Let cool slightly and drain as before, but using a smaller (1-to-2-cup) container for the fat, which will be slightly darker and stronger-flavored than the first batch. The pork bits should now be crisp, delicious cracklings.

USE this second rendering of lard whenever you want very distinctive lard flavor, and eat the cracklings to your heart's content. Or, for one of the great Veracruzan treats, crush the cracklings and any residue to a coarse paste and recombine them with the second rendering of lard.

Cheeses

MANCHEGO CHEESE: This is the overwhelming favorite for melted toppings in Veracruz. It will not necessarily be the real thing, from La Mancha in Spain, since a domestic imitation from cows' rather than sheep's milk is widely available in the state.

QUESO BLANCO (OR QUESO JAROCHO): When Veracruzan cooks want a bland cheese to melt into a sauce or filling, they use *queso blanco* (white cheese), locally known as *queso jarocho* (Veracruzan cheese), a slightly more pliant uncured white cheese that is grated or cubed before being added. You can substitute domestic Muenster or a mild white cheddar cheese.

QUESO FRESCO: The most important Mexican-type cheese in Veracruz is *queso fresco* (fresh cheese), an unaged, slightly salty white cheese that crumbles nicely between the fingers to make a lovely uncooked topping. *Queso fresco* never melts but keeps its crumbly consistency. I used to go through terrible contortions trying to find substitutes. Now *queso fresco* is available here in any town where there's a Latin grocery and can even be mail-ordered. If you are absolutely desperate, replace it with a young ricotta salata.

When aged, *queso fresco* is called **queso cotija**, or **queso añejo**, and can be used in exactly the same ways, except that its sharper, more intense flavor gives it a more condiment-like quality. My preferred substitute is an aged ricotta salata. Another crumbly cheese is **requesón**, made like ricotta with some of the whey saved from making other cheeses. But, unlike ricotta, it is drained and pressed to a firm consistency. The closest substitute here is hoop cheese, which was popularized by some fad diet a few years ago. A very firm, well-drained farmer cheese will do.

Canned Milk and Mexican *Crema*

Veracruz is one of Mexico's foremost dairy states. Traveling along on almost any road, you pass the occasional pasture of grazing cows, often the hump-shouldered East Indian zebus that are thought to do best in a torrid climate. The care and feeding of the animals is very backward by the standards of the United States, where computerized

rations and untiring efforts to increase the volume of milk per cow are the norm. As a result, fresh milk tastes richer and better in Veracruz. But much of it is not drunk fresh. This is one of the best cheese-making areas of Mexico and also produces a lot of butter and commercial as well as artisanal ice cream. Cream is used fresh for some purposes, but when you see the word *crema* in a local recipe, you can usually assume that it means the delicious Mexican and Central American–style cultured cream.

CANNED CONDENSED OR EVAPORATED MILK: These are by far the most popular forms of milk in Mexico. Do not wince and start thinking of more elegant products that you can substitute. The use of condensed and evaporated milk is a part of Latin American (not just Mexican) culture that deserves to be understood, not sneered at. For close to a hundred and fifty years, they have been valued not only because they keep safely in tropical heat but because people like the taste. Condensed milk is a prized sweetening agent; evaporated milk is valued for its concentrated flavor and richness. There are dishes where Mexicans actually use both at once. Many parts of Central America enjoy a sort of trifle called *tres leches*, with evaporated, condensed, and fresh milk mixed! I get impatient listening to well-meaning purists talk as if it were all just bad taste or a corporate plot. Follow the recipe when you see canned milk in an ingredients list, and I believe you will come to the conclusion that cooks in Mexico know what they are doing.

CREMA: This is not the same thing as our sour cream. *Crema* is more pourable and has a nutty, slightly salty quality that makes sour cream seem too buttery and bland by comparison. In about the last eight or ten years, I've been delighted to find approximations of the real thing being made in this country for a Mexican, Salvadoran, and Honduran clientele. The quality varies; some are heavily dosed with emulsifiers and preservatives. Look in Latin markets for little plastic bottles labeled *Crema Salvadoreña*, *Crema Tipo Centroamericana*, and *Crema Criolla*. Comparison-shop to find the one you prefer. *Crema* is fabulous with — among other things — any kind of fried plantains.

Chocolate

When the Spanish came to Veracruz, cacao for chocolate was widely grown in the area. It remained fairly important in colonial times but has now been abandoned as a commercial crop. What a pity — cacao trees still grow wild in parts of Veracruz, and some people (like the family of Luisa Reyna Mortera Aguirre in Otatitlán) continue to gather the fruit and ferment the beans for a household source of chocolate.

One of the main pre-Hispanic uses of chocolate was as an element in intricately flavored sauces. This persists in modern Mexico, along with several chocolate-based beverages. When you see chocolate called for in a recipe, always use the grainy, spiced Mexican chocolate (Ibarra or La Abuelita brands) sold here in most Latin groceries. The effect is completely different from American and European sweetened or unsweetened chocolate.

Sugars

If there is any region of Veracruz where sugarcane doesn't grow, I haven't seen it. Driving on the highways, you pass mile after mile of the tall green reeds, sometimes crowned with the ethereal silvery tassels that are the flower clusters.

All along the Gulf coast of Mexico (indeed, in all sugar-growing parts of the Caribbean and Latin America), this sight used to be varied by the small-scale artisanal sugar mills that dotted the countryside. These simple facilities, or *trapiches*, ground the harvested cane and boiled the juice in a series of evaporating pans. Few *trapiches* are left now, but their tiny output is highly prized by Veracruzan connoisseurs who know sugars as substances full of fascinating nuances, not standardized sweeteners. At every stage of boiling, there is a different balance of pure sucrose and the many cane-juice residues. At the end of the process, the unclarified molten sugar is poured into molds where it hardens into brown loaf sugar. The syrupy residue (molasses, the fraction of cane juice that won't crystallize) is equally valued. It is not identical to our commercial molasses, because it is not as completely separated from the sucrose. This delicious cane syrup, known as *miel de caña* or just *caña*, is the wonderful accompaniment to many a Veracruzan pastry.

The molded brown sugar and *caña* from *trapiches* are a revelation

to people who have tasted only mass-produced sugar and molasses. The sugar maker's taste and skill emerge in the blend of sweetness and winy depth. Sadly, *trapiches* are disappearing, and artisanal sugar making is becoming a curiosity rather than a part of daily life in the old African slave territories.

Today most people use brown loaf sugar and molasses made in large factories. But even the factory products have a lot of flavor. They are definitely to be preferred to the brown sugar of this country, which is really nothing but mass-produced white sugar mixed with mass-produced molasses. It is acceptable in some recipes where the nuances of taste are not terribly important, but do not try substituting it when true brown loaf sugar is the main ingredient.

PILONCILLO (MEXICAN BROWN LOAF SUGAR): This is one of the culinary treasures of the old slave lands, widely sold in Latin neighborhood groceries in the United States. Ask for *piloncillo* (made in narrow conical shapes) or *panela* (thick flat rounds). Depending on the store, it may come from any of half a dozen Latin American countries that had parallel sugar-raising and slave-owning pasts. There is no one standard size and, in fact, no standard grade of refinement. Some are darker and more interesting, some lighter in both color and taste. See Brown Loaf Sugar Syrup (page 342) for suggestions on handling.

WHITE SUGAR: Refined white sugar is indeed used in modern Veracruzan cooking, especially for confectionery. Yet even today you will notice that the whitest sugar of Veracruz has a tiny hint of tan, indicating that a vestige of molasses remains. It is also just fractionally moister and stickier than ours. This is a distinctive preference inherited from the past.

IF YOU REALLY WANT TO COOK LIKE ME

*I*T'S LIKE MEETING AN ACCUSER. Someone marches up to me at my restaurant or after a book signing and announces with an injured air: "You know, there's something wrong with this recipe. I did everything it said to, and it didn't taste *anything* like yours!"

I always try to do a little tactful detective work on the possible reasons for the disappointment, but in my head I already know what happened: She used Minute Rice for the rice. He used clam juice out of a jar for the fish stock. She used some stale dried herb mix for the chopped fresh herbs. And they *DON'T KNOW WHAT THEY DID!*

The following hints are for people who honestly want their food to taste like mine and are willing to take a good look at their kitchen habits. I can't guarantee that every recipe in this book will turn out like an absolute clone of the same dish as it might be made in my own kitchen or at my restaurants — there are a lot of tiny variables that no recipe on earth can do justice to. But I would like to point out some factors that make all the difference between singing the melody as written and whistling it off-key.

$\mathcal{R}$EMEMBERING these precepts will make your cooking better no matter what type of cuisine you are interested in. Well, it's true that some of them especially concern Mexican cooking, but the attitude behind them can be applied to all kinds of good cooking.

A dish can only be as good as the ingredients that go into it. The ingredients won't be good unless you learn what "good" is and insist on it. So it is imperative to find a first-class butcher, fishmonger, and produce purveyor. Spend as much time as you can in their shops asking questions, until they know you mean business about quality. With that, you'll already have half the battle won when you come home from shopping and unpack your purchases.

Any cook trying to get her or his bearings in a particular cuisine should be able to recognize some crucial ingredients and stock them in the pantry, refrigerator, or freezer. If you look at my recipes you will see that it is wise to have on hand:

Good tomatoes

White onions

Limes

Several kinds of dried chiles (see page 47)

Fresh jalapeños and/or serranos (see page 46)

Plain white rice (not instant or converted)

Fresh (or frozen) corn masa and masa harina (see page 51)

Dried black beans

Olive oil

Good butter

Good lard, preferably home-rendered (see page 66)

Queso fresco and *queso blanco* (see page 67)

True cinnamon (*canela*; see page 44)

Cumin seeds

Homemade bread crumbs from good French or Italian bread; or, lacking that, fresh soda crackers (Saltines) to crush for crumbs

Homemade stock (chicken, pork, and fish; see pages 142, 144, and
 145)

Piloncillo or *panela* (Latin American brown loaf sugar; see pages
 69–70)

Any serious cook should understand the difference between an ingredient that's called for and a substitute or stopgap. It's not that
Mexican cooks never use substitutes. But they certainly *know* when
they are using one!

FOR THE RECORD

- Fresh herbs are not dried herbs. Even when their flavor may happen to be acceptable, dried herbs will never contribute body to a
  puree-based sauce, as herbs are meant to in many of these
  recipes.

- Homemade chicken stock or pork stock is not water, and it isn't a
  bouillon cube or powdered base. (Mexican cooks do use these —
  but as a flavoring ingredient, not to replace stock. In a pinch,
  canned low-sodium chicken broth will do — but do not take this
  as a blanket endorsement.)

- Fish stock (made at home or purchased from your fishmonger)
  is not bottled clam juice.

- Fresh fish, poultry, or meat is not equivalent to the same thing
  frozen and thawed. (Unfortunately, none of us has any choice
  with some kinds of seafood, like shrimp and conch — virtually
  everything in the stores here has been frozen.)

- Limes are not lemons, and freshly squeezed lime juice is not bottled lime juice.

- Plain white rice is not instant rice, converted rice, or a presea-
  soned "pilaf" mix.

- Butter is not margarine, and lard is not vegetable shortening.
  Olive oil is not some nameless vegetable oil or treated "light"
  olive oil.

- True cinnamon (*canela*) is not the stuff labeled cinnamon in our
  stores, which is really a relative named cassia with a totally un-
  Mexican flavor.

➣ It is equally true that one cooking method is not another. You will never achieve the right results with tomatoes, chiles, garlic, and onions unless you realize that griddle-roasting is not oven-baking or broiler-roasting. The only method that brings out the natural sugars of these ingredients is dry-roasting the vegetable on a griddle or heavy-bottomed skillet (see page 58).

➣ It is usually a bad idea to radically change the amount given for any ingredient in a recipe. (This often happens when well-meaning people are trying to cut down on fat.) Using more or less of one ingredient can throw off the whole "orchestration."

➣ By the same token, leaving out any one stage of a recipe — for example, chopping fresh ingredients as directed, frying something in fat before cooking it in liquid, or working a processed mixture through a mesh sieve — guarantees that you will never get the desired result.

➣ Spices are best bought very fresh, in small quantities. When a recipe calls for ground spices, it is infinitely better to grind them yourself. First toast them for a minute or two in a small skillet over medium or medium-high heat, then grind them using an electric coffee or spice mill or a sturdy mortar and pestle.

THE EXTRA SOMETHING

BEYOND THE FACT that I use good ingredients with great care, I have to say that quite often my food tastes as it does because "I did it MY way." This is not to put down cooks here or in Mexico who would do it another way. But my passion is certain kinds of distinct, rounded, many-dimensional flavors. As a restaurateur, I am constantly searching for ways to enrich and define the flavors I'm working with. And, like any cook, I also have my pet ingredients that are just part of my palette. Here are the most important examples of what I do to make a dish "mine":

➣ In my kitchen, olive oil is always extra-virgin. I use a premium fruity oil for salads, one with less pronounced flavor for sautéing and frying.

➣ When I use a vegetable oil (for example, for deep-frying), it's always corn or safflower oil.

- In recipes calling for sherry, I use a *fino*.

- For most rice dishes, I like to use a medium-grain variety (preferably imported Valencia).

- I have a constant struggle to get the pork here to taste like pork instead of cardboard. I usually buy it bone-in (shoulder butt is the best cut), bone it myself, and simmer the bones in the pot along with the meat.

- As another aid in the search for flavor, I'll regularly add a frying step to recipes that might not have originally had one. Herb or spice mixtures and pureed sauces always have more depth if fried in a little fat before being combined with the other ingredients.

- Supermarket chicken is another product that needs all the help it can get. If I can't buy a nice, tasty free-range chicken, I almost always try to give a mass-produced one a little boost by briefly cooking it until golden in a small amount of fat before adding it to a sauce or soup.

- I am very extravagant with homemade stock. Being a restaurateur, I always have a plentiful supply on hand and can use it unstintingly where other people might use water. I know that this generosity with stock will not be practical for every home cook. But I think anyone will get immeasurably better results by using chicken stock to cook rice or pasta pilaf-style, soften dried chiles, poach chicken breasts, and make most soups. The same goes for using fish stock to poach the seafood that will go into salads, fillings, seafood and rice dishes, and almost any dish that calls for a seafood mélange. The more often you can make up a good batch of stock and have it in your freezer, the richer and fuller a dish will be.

- The same is true of home-rendered lard. I hate to run out of it, because it is vitally important in so many different kinds of dishes. I like to be able to count on the flavor of lard the way some people count on salt and pepper. Get in the habit of making up a modest-sized batch at frequent intervals, and you won't have to groan and rack your brain for bad substitutes when you see it in my recipes.

*T*HERE'S A CERTAIN IRONY in the fact that appetizers have always numbered among my most popular dishes. Even now, I can't help smiling at the idea, because appetizers as such barely exist in Mexico. But although we have no equivalent of the "starters" part of the typical menu of the United States, we do have a glorious array of little dishes, nibbles, and irresistible street foods that we fit into windows of opportunity at almost every hour between breakfast, the mid-day main meal, and the modest, rather late supper.

Sometimes, in fact, it seems that our way of life in Mexico is nothing but a blur of these small meals! Hearty breakfast dishes double as supper dishes, and some supper dishes are just as apt to appear in the morning. Many of our beloved snacks are the corn

dishes that Mexicans fondly call *antojitos*, or "little whims," a subject so vast that it could easily have been a book in itself. (The Veracruzan corn kitchen deserves its own chapter; see page III.) We have as well a whole other repertoire of tidbits called *botanas*, which we munch with drinks, much as the Spanish eat *tapas*, but this drinks-and-conversation time is a leisurely interval in its own right, not a prelude to a meal.

It's no wonder that diners in this country immediately seized upon these small meals and snacks and appropriated them as appetizers when Mexican food entered the culinary mainstream here. This is how I usually serve them to guests. The recipes in this chapter have been pulled from many original contexts and concentrate largely — though not exclusively — on the popular seafood *cocteles* (cocktails), hashes, and salads of Veracruz. (You'll find that some of them make fine main dishes for a light lunch or supper.) A strong Spanish accent is evident in many of these dishes, making itself felt in the frequent use of ingredients like olive oil, thyme, and the caper-olive-almond complex. The plantain dishes, however, belong squarely to the state's Afro-Caribbean heritage.

Coctel de Aguacate

AVOCADO COCKTAIL

*T*HIS SIMPLE BUT LUXURIOUS PREPARATION TURNS UP AS
an appetizer in Veracruz, piled into individual goblets. I also like to
serve it as a side dish. Take care to choose ripe, flavorful avocados and
tomatoes — inferior ingredients will really let down the dish. Be sure
to chop everything immediately before use.

If you like, substitute 1–2 habanero chiles for the jalapeños or
serranos. Their fruity, aromatic quality is especially nice with avocado.

1	large ripe tomato, peeled and seeded
2	jalapeño or serrano chiles, stemmed and seeded
1	small white onion
12–15	cilantro sprigs
	Juice of 1 lime
2	tablespoons olive oil
2	large firm but ripe Mexican-type avocados (such as Hass or Fuerte)

CHOP the tomato, chiles, onion, and cilantro very fine. In a
medium bowl, whisk together the lime juice and oil. Add the
chopped ingredients and mix thoroughly.

PEEL and pit the avocados. Cut them into $1/2$-inch dice, fold into
the other ingredients, and serve at once.

Ensalada de Camarones

SHRIMP SALAD

Makes 6–8 servings

Veracruzans prize seafood salads made with either medleys of different kinds or one particular variety. The version I give here, a good appetizer or first course, is based on my own happy experiences with many Veracruzan *ensaladas de mariscos.*

In dishes garnished with raw onion, like this, I really value the freshness of Mexican onions, which are used much sooner after pulling than our common storage onions. Often they are like the middling-sized pearly white onions with green tops still attached that you'll find in some ethnic groceries as "bulb onions" or "spring onions" (but don't confuse them with scallions). Red onions make a good substitute, especially the kind that are new-looking and shiny, without papery skins.

> 6 cups Basic Fish Stock (page 145) or water
> 1 small white onion, unpeeled
> 2 garlic cloves, unpeeled
> 3 bay leaves
> 10–12 black peppercorns
> 1½ teaspoons salt, or to taste
> 1 pound medium shrimp (sold as 16–20 count), in the shell
> Juice of 1 lime
> 3 tablespoons olive oil
> Freshly ground black pepper
> 1 fresh bulb onion (see above) or 1 medium-small red onion, sliced into thin half-moons
> 3 jalapeño chiles (seeded if desired to mitigate the heat—I don't bother) and finely julienned
> 1 ripe Mexican-type avocado (such as Hass or Fuerte), peeled, pitted, and finely diced
> 10 cilantro sprigs, stripped of leaves

PLACE the fish stock or water, onion, garlic, bay leaves, peppercorns, and 1 teaspoon of the salt in a medium saucepan. Bring to a boil over high heat and cook, uncovered, for 10 minutes to infuse the flavors. Add the shrimp and cook, uncovered, for about 2 minutes, or until the shrimp turn pink. Quickly cool by emptying into a colander set under cold running water. Drain thoroughly. Peel the shrimp and cut lengthwise into halves.

IN a small bowl, combine the lime juice and oil with a generous grinding of black pepper and about $1/2$ teaspoon more salt. Place the shrimp in a large bowl with the onion, chiles, avocado, and cilantro. Pour the lime-juice dressing over the salad and toss to distribute evenly. Taste for seasoning and add a little more salt and pepper if desired. Serve at once.

VARIATIONS

The same recipe works well with virtually any kind of seafood, though each has to be cooked according to its own optimal timing. For *Ensalada de Calamares* (Squid Salad), start with $1-1^{1}/2$ pounds squid (cleaned weight). Peel off the outer membrane and cut the meat into $1/2$-inch rings. Cook as directed for shrimp, or just until tender. Continue as directed.

Ensalada de Mariscos "Rafapar"

SEAFOOD SALAD IN AVOCADO HALVES

THIS DISH IS THE CREATION AND NAMESAKE OF RAFAEL Pardiño, at Restaurant Riviera Pardiños in Boca del Río. It is always served there in avocado halves. But if you want to combine the avocado flesh with the rest of the salad, there are two possibilities. Scoop out the flesh, chop it, and mix it with the rest of the salad ingredients, then fill the avocado shells with the mixture, or put it in a serving bowl or on individual plates (presented this way, the salad could serve up to 9 or 10). In the latter case, serve with soda crackers or fried tortilla chips. (Yes, soda crackers are "authentic"!)

Riviera Pardiños prepares the salad with roughly equal parts of octopus, conch, shrimp, and crabmeat. Vary the choices according to what's best and freshest in your local fish store. When I can't find Caribbean conch, I sometimes substitute whelk, usually called scungilli in mid-Atlantic markets. Another option is to leave out the conch or whelk altogether and use 4 ounces cleaned squid or bay scallops (add together with the shrimp to cook).

Note that with octopus you must allow for some loss of weight after cleaning and even more after cooking. A $1\frac{1}{2}$-to-2-pound octopus yields 1–$1\frac{1}{2}$ pounds of meat after it is cleaned, which will shrink to about 4 ounces after cooking.

Makes 8 large servings if served in avocado halves (more if served in a bowl)

1 pound octopus (cleaned weight; see above)
4 ounces Caribbean conch steak or scungilli (North Atlantic whelk)
1 small white onion, unpeeled
2 garlic cloves, unpeeled
10 black peppercorns
3 bay leaves
1 large fresh thyme sprig or $\frac{1}{2}$ teaspoon crumbled dried thyme
2 teaspoons salt, or to taste
8 large or medium shrimp (sold as 12–16 count or 16–20 count), in the shell
2 medium-sized ripe globe tomatoes or 2 large ripe plum tomatoes, peeled and seeded
1 fresh bulb onion (see the headnote on page 78) or 1 medium-small red onion

1 jalapeño chile

10–12 cilantro sprigs

4 ounces lump crabmeat, picked over to remove any bits of shell or cartilage

¼ cup olive oil

Juice of 2 limes

¼ cup mayonnaise, or to taste (optional)

4 ripe Mexican-type avocados (such as Hass or Fuerte)

PLACE the octopus and conch or scungilli in a medium saucepan or small pot with the unpeeled onion and garlic, peppercorns, bay leaves, thyme, and 1 teaspoons of the salt. Add enough water to cover by about 2 inches and bring to a boil over high heat. Reduce the heat to maintain a low rolling boil; skim off any froth that rises to the surface. Cook, partly covered, for 45 minutes. Remove from the heat and let cool in the stock.

LIFT out the octopus and cut it into small (about ⅓-inch) chunks; set aside. If using scungilli, pare off the black skin with a small knife. Cut the conch or scungilli into the same size chunks. Set aside.

STRAIN the cooking stock, return to the pot, and bring to a boil over high heat. Add the shrimp and cook just until they start to turn pink, 2–3 minutes. Quickly lift out with a skimmer or strainer before they can overcook. Peel, chop coarsely, and set aside. Strain the stock and save for another purpose, if desired.

CHOP the tomatoes, onion, jalapeño, and cilantro quite finely; place in a large bowl. Add the crabmeat, octopus, conch or scungilli, and shrimp. Combine the oil, lime juice, and mayonnaise, if using, and the remaining ½ teaspoon salt in a small bowl. Pour over the salad ingredients and toss to mix thoroughly.

CUT the avocados in half, remove the pits, and fill with the seafood salad. Serve at once.

Coctel de Caracol o Callos con Aguacate

CONCH OR SCALLOP COCKTAIL
WITH AVOCADO

Makes 4–6 servings

*B*OCA DEL RÍO, THAT HAVEN OF EXCELLENT SEAFOOD cooking, sprawls around a little confluence of river mouths including an estuary simply called El Estero. On the bank of the estuary, Isidro Uscanga, a Veracruzan descended from colonial Afro-Cuban ancestors, has a restaurant proudly titled after himself, El Negro del Estero. This is my attempt to re-create one of his various seafood cocktails, justly known as the freshest and best in the area.

Caracol (snail) is what Gulf coast Mexicans call the large Caribbean conch. Do not try to substitute the smaller, dark-skinned North Atlantic whelk commonly sold as "conch" in this country. My usual substitute for *caracol* is fresh scallops.

1	pound (out of the shell) Caribbean conch steak or scallops
1	fresh bulb onion (see page 78) or ½ medium red onion
1	ripe Mexican-type avocado (such as Hass or Fuerte)
2	habanero chiles (see page 45), stemmed, seeded, and deveined
10–12	cilantro sprigs, chopped
1	teaspoon salt, or to taste
	Freshly ground black pepper
	Juice of 3 limes

WITH a razor-sharp thin-bladed knife, cut the conch steak or scallops into tissue-thin slices. Arrange on a wide flat serving platter. Slice the onion very thin. Peel and pit the avocado; slice very thin. Cut the chiles into thin rings and scatter the onion, avocado, and chiles over the conch or scallops. Garnish with the cilantro. Season with the salt and a few grindings of black pepper.

POUR the lime juice over the conch or scallops and vegetables; let stand for about 10 minutes (no longer) to "cook" the conch. Serve at room temperature.

Minilla

HASHED FISH WITH FRESH HERBS AND OLIVES

Makes 6–8 servings

MINILLA IS A LOCAL VERACRUZAN TERM FOR WHAT OTHER Mexicans might call *salpicón de pescado*. For a dozen or more years I've been serving a somewhat related red snapper *salpicón* (a name for shredded mixtures or mishmashes) at my original restaurant. But now I've fallen equally in love with the subtler, less "sweet"-spiced *minilla* of Veracruz. This version is based on one that I encountered at Las Brisas del Mar in Boca del Río. I love the different things Tomasita Meléndez has going on here with the flavorings, especially the wonderful accent of mint and the rounded mellowness of the garlic-butter mixture. *Minilla* makes a great topping for tostadas or filling for empanadas or tacos. You can also use it in a main-dish context, as a filling for cold stuffed poblano chiles.

In Veracruz, people often make *minilla* with leftovers. Feel free to do likewise if you happen to have about 4 cups of cooked fish on hand. In that case, omit all steps and ingredients before heating the oils and sautéing the onion. But don't try it if the fish is already the least bit overcooked or if it's a strong-flavored oily type like salmon or bluefish. The kinds to use for this recipe are firm white-fleshed roundfish like sea bass, striped bass, Pacific rockfish, red snapper, or tilefish.

4 cups water

4 garlic cloves, unpeeled

1 small white onion, unpeeled

6 bay leaves

1 teaspoon salt, or to taste

2 pounds fish fillets (see above), skin left on, any pinbones removed with tweezers

2 tablespoons olive oil

2 tablespoons vegetable oil

1 large white onion, finely chopped

1 large or 2 medium-sized ripe tomatoes (about 8 ounces), finely chopped

1 cup fresh Italian parsley leaves, chopped

1 cup fresh mint leaves, chopped

2 large thyme sprigs, chopped
½ cup pimiento-stuffed green olives, finely chopped
½ cup pickled jalapeño chiles, seeded and finely chopped
2 teaspoons Garlic Butter Enrichment (page 300)

PUT the water, garlic, unpeeled onion, 2 of the bay leaves, and the salt in a medium saucepan and bring to a boil over high heat. Reduce the heat to low, add the fish, and cook very gently, uncovered, just until the flesh turns opaque, 5–7 minutes. Lift the fish from the cooking stock (which you can strain and save for another purpose) and set aside until cool enough to handle.

REMOVE the skin and any remaining bones from the fish; separate the flesh into shreds.

IN a large skillet, heat the oils over medium-high heat until rippling. Add the chopped onion and cook, stirring occasionally, until translucent, about 3 minutes. Add the tomatoes, parsley, mint, thyme, and remaining 4 bay leaves. Reduce the heat to medium and cook, stirring frequently, until most of the moisture has evaporated.

STIR in the fish, olives, jalapeños, and garlic butter. Cook for another 5 minutes to marry the flavors and remove the bay leaf before serving.

Salpicón de Mariscos

HASHED SEAFOOD MÉLANGE

*T*HIS IS ANOTHER OF THOSE BASIC COASTAL VERACRUZAN seafood recipes that lend themselves to different interpretations. This recipe, based on an excellent *salpicón* that I had at Restorán Acuario in Boca del Río, has a briny note of pickled seasonings. It is a versatile mixture that can serve as a taco or empanada filling, a tostada topping, or a great stuffing for a whole fish. Combinations like this are often used to fill coconut halves and served with a little manchego cheese melted under the broiler.

At Acuario, the cooking liquid is good fish stock. You can use water, but you'll lose some of the full richness. The choice of seafood can be fairly fluid. I had it with crabmeat, shrimp, and fillets of a white-fleshed roundfish called *robalo* (best matched here by something like sea bass, red snapper, or Pacific rockfish). But there's no reason not to substitute small oysters, bay scallops, or anything else that looks good. Just remember that you want about 2½ pounds of usable fish and shellfish meat in all—and that everything must be extremely fresh.

Makes 6–8 servings

2 cups Basic Fish Stock (page 145) or water

8 ounces shrimp in the shell (any size)

1 pound fillets or deboned steaks of firm nonoily fish (see above)

2 tablespoons olive oil

4 bay leaves

5 fresh thyme sprigs or 1 teaspoon crumbled dried thyme

2 tablespoons butter

1 large white onion, finely chopped

3 garlic cloves, minced

2 large ripe tomatoes (about 1 pound total), peeled, seeded, and finely chopped

¼ cup fresh Italian parsley leaves, chopped

1 pound lump crabmeat, picked over to remove any bits of shell or cartilage

1 cup pimiento-stuffed green olives, finely chopped

3 tablespoons capers, rinsed and finely chopped

3 pickled jalapeño chiles, seeded and finely chopped

Salt (optional)

IN a medium saucepan, bring the fish stock or water to a boil over medium-high heat. Add the shrimp and cook just until it turns pink, about 3 minutes. At once lift out with a skimmer or slotted spoon, draining well. Set aside in a bowl and let cool.

REDUCE the heat to medium-low and add the fish. Cook just until opaque, about 5 minutes; remove from the stock and set aside in the same way.

WHEN it is cool enough to handle, peel the shrimp and chop fine. Remove any skin or bones from the fish and pull into shreds. (Strain the stock and save for another purpose.)

IN a large sauté pan, heat the oil over medium-high heat until rippling. Add the bay leaves and thyme and cook for 2–3 minutes, just until they impart their fragrance to the oil. Remove with a skimmer or slotted spoon and discard (don't worry about any bits of thyme that remain).

ADD the butter to the oil and heat until it is fragrant and foaming. At once add the onion and garlic and cook, stirring frequently, until the onion is translucent, about 3 minutes. Add the tomatoes and parsley and cook for another 3–5 minutes, stirring to evaporate some of the moisture.

ADD the crabmeat and the chopped shrimp and shredded fish. Stir in the olives, capers, and pickled jalapeños, distributing all ingredients evenly. Cook, stirring occasionally, until heated through, about 5 minutes. Taste for seasoning; add a pinch or two of salt if desired. Serve hot or warm.

Taquitos de Mariscos

FRIED ROLLED TORTILLAS WITH SEAFOOD FILLING

I HAD THESE MARVELOUS CRISP LITTLE CYLINDERS FOR breakfast at Las Brisas de Papaloapan, a restaurant overlooking the massive Papaloapan River in the gentle, brightly painted colonial town of Tlacotalpan. They're what diners in restaurants here usually call flautas. The conventional wisdom is that such fried tortilla-wrap specialties are best when served piping hot. But the ones at Las Brisas arrived at room temperature, by either intention or circumstance, and I thought they were just right.

Tlacotalpan has a varying seasonal selection of both freshwater and saltwater fish, shrimp, crabs, and other species, so the ingredients in the seafood filling aren't a fixed formula. I suggest that you use 2 cups of any preferred filling, such as Hashed Seafood Mélange (page 86), Hashed Fish with Fresh Herbs and Olives (page 84), or Shrimp Filling (page 173). You could also limit yourself to just one or two kinds (shrimp only, crab only, shrimp and crab combined). The only real essentials are that the seafood ingredients be given a good flavor kick by way of onion, tomatoes, and other seasonings, as in the individual filling recipes, and that they be chopped quite fine to fit neatly in the tortilla wrapping.

Makes 16 tacos;
4 servings

FOR THE TACOS

16 commercial thin corn tortillas

2 cups any preferred seafood filling (see above), finely chopped

Vegetable oil for frying

FOR THE GARNISH

2 cups Mexican *crema* (see page 67) or crème fraîche

2 cups finely shredded iceberg lettuce

FOR THE TACOS

SOFTEN the tortillas, preferably by placing them, in batches of 4 at a time, in a small plastic bag and microwaving them on full power for 30–40 seconds (depending on the wattage of your model). A steamer basket or other improvised steaming arrangement also works fairly well: wrap all the tortillas in a tea towel and steam for 2 minutes, then keep warm wrapped in the towels.

WORKING quickly, while the tortillas are still pliable, place about 2 tablespoons of the filling in the center of each tortilla, roll into a tight cylinder, and secure with toothpicks. As you work, place the filled tortillas in a larger plastic bag before they can dry out, which would make them crack in frying.

WHEN they are all filled, pour oil into a medium deep skillet or heavy saucepan to a depth of about $1^{1}/_{2}$ inches. Heat over medium-high heat to 375°F. Deep-fry the tortillas, 4 at a time, until golden, about 5 minutes per batch. Lift out onto paper towels and let drain briefly.

ARRANGE the *taquitos* on a platter and top with the *crema* (which can be thinned with up to $^{1}/_{2}$ cup of milk if it is very thick) or crème fraîche. Scatter the shredded lettuce over the platter and serve at once.

Salpicón de Jaiba con Alcaparras

HASHED CRAB WITH CAPERS

*T*HIS MAKES A GREAT TOPPING FOR TOSTADAS. BUT ITS light, piquant personality makes it even better with fresh corn tortillas, the way I first tasted it from Elena Gutiérrez of Santiago's Club in Tamiahua. It is also a wonderful filling for empanadas. Or enjoy it on its own with just a sprinkle of fresh lime juice.

Makes 2–2$^1/_2$ cups
(4 plated servings
by itself)

2 tablespoons lard, preferably home-rendered (see page 66), or olive oil

1 medium-sized white onion, finely chopped

4 ripe plum tomatoes (about 1 pound), finely chopped, or 4 medium globe tomatoes, seeded and finely chopped

2 bay leaves

2 pickled jalapeños, seeded and finely chopped

1 tablespoon large capers, drained

2 tablespoons butter

1 pound lump crabmeat, picked over to remove any bits of shell or cartilage

Lime wedges for garnish

IN a medium skillet, heat the lard or oil over medium-high heat until rippling. Add the onion and cook until translucent, about 3 minutes. Add the tomatoes and bay leaves. Cook, stirring occasionally, until the mixture is somewhat concentrated, 3–4 minutes. Add the pickled jalapeños and capers and cook, stirring occasionally, until most of the juices have evaporated, about 3 minutes.

MEANWHILE, in another medium skillet, melt the butter over medium heat. When it is fragrant, add the crabmeat and cook, stirring, to heat through, about 2 minutes.

GENTLY stir the crabmeat into the tomato-caper mixture. Cook, stirring, for another minute, remove the bay leaf, and serve with lime wedges.

"Pardiñolas"

THIS IS ONE OF THE SIGNATURE *BOTANAS* (TIDBITS TO nibble with drinks) of Restaurant Riviera Pardiños in Boca del Río. The crabs used there look very similar to our Florida stone crabs, with the best meat in the claws. Each diner dips the partly shelled claws in a chipotle-spiked mayonnaise and gnaws away in contentment. Most fish stores in this country sell stone crab claws already cooked, either fresh or frozen.

Makes 4 servings

2 cups fine bread crumbs
8–10 garlic cloves
1/2 cup freshly squeezed lime juice
1/2 cup light beer (lager, not "lite")
1 teaspoon salt, or to taste
Freshly ground black pepper
2 teaspoons powdered chicken stock base or 1 chicken bouillon cube
12 large stone crab claws (see above)
2 large eggs
Vegetable oil for frying
Chipotle Mayonnaise (page 307)

TOAST the bread crumbs by spreading on a baking sheet and placing in a preheated 350°F oven for 7–8 minutes.

MINCE the garlic and place in a mixing bowl with the lime juice, beer, salt, a few grindings of black pepper, and the stock base or bouillon cube. (The cube will dissolve better if it is first crushed with a little water.)

CRACK the crab claws in several places using a heavy nutcracker (or whack with the flat of a heavy knife or cleaver blade). Remove all the shell except for the movable hinged pincer tip, which should be left intact to use as a "handle." Add the shelled claws to the garlic-lime marinade and let sit for 30 minutes.

SPREAD the bread crumbs on a plate or shallow dish. Have ready another plate to hold the prepared claws. In a small mixing bowl, lightly beat the eggs.

REMOVE the crab claws from the marinade. One at a time, dip them in the eggs, letting the excess drip off, then roll in the bread crumbs to coat evenly, shaking off the excess. Place the breaded claws on the second plate and refrigerate, covered, for at least 30 minutes or up to 3 hours to help firm the coating.

POUR oil into a deep, heavy skillet to a depth of about 1 inch. Heat over medium-high heat to 375°F. Working in 2 or 3 batches, deep-fry the crab claws until golden, about 3 minutes. Serve at once, with the chipotle mayonnaise. (Tip: I have seen eager guests extracting the final nuggets of meat by breaking off the pincer shell and using it as a miniature excavating tool.)

Tostadas de Jaiba

TOSTADAS WITH HASHED CRAB

I HAD THE WORLD'S MOST DELICIOUS CRAB TOSTADAS IN Tlacotalpan, made with spanking fresh crabmeat from the peerless *jaibas* (relatives of our Chesapeake blue crabs) fished from the Papaloapan River system. Here I usually make the dish with jumbo lump crabmeat.

The mixture is very good as a simple crab salad, but I still think it beats all competitors as a topping for tostadas. Now, I know that some people will take the path of least resistance with tostadas and use commercial corn tortilla chips. I suggest that you put in just a little more effort and make your own miniature tostadas by cutting 3-inch rounds from commercial thin corn tortillas with a cookie cutter. Fry the tortilla rounds until crisp and golden (a handful at a time) in vegetable oil heated to 375°F and drain on paper towels.

Makes 2–2¹/₂ cups crab salad (6 servings)

¹/₂ cup mayonnaise
1 tablespoon olive oil
1 pound lump crabmeat, picked over to remove any bits of shell or cartilage
1 large ripe tomato or 2 medium (about 8 ounces), peeled, seeded, and finely chopped
1 small white onion, finely chopped
3 thyme sprigs, chopped
2 tablespoons finely chopped cilantro
1 ripe but firm Mexican-type avocado (such as Hass or Fuerte), peeled, pitted, and finely diced
Salt and freshly ground black pepper
12 3-inch tostadas, either commercial or freshly made (see above)
Green She-Man Sauce (page 312)

IN a medium bowl, beat together the mayonnaise and oil. Add the crabmeat and mix well. Stir in the tomatoes, onion, and herbs. Fold in the diced avocado. Add salt and pepper to taste (they will lose some of their effect on chilling, so don't be shy). Let sit, covered, in the refrigerator for at least 1 hour to marry the flavors.

SERVE with the tostadas, topping each with about ¹/₄ cup of the crab mixture. Pass the sauce on the side.

Camarones al Ajillo

GARLICKY STIR-FRIED SHRIMP

Makes 4 servings

THIS IS A UBIQUITOUS DISH IN VERACRUZ AND CUBA, AS well as Spain (where it is called *gambas al ajillo*). I have eaten and loved many versions, but I think my all-time favorite is the one served at Las Brisas del Mar in Boca del Río. Most cooks just throw the garlic and chile into a pan to fry, then add the shrimp. This produces a good dish but doesn't equal the distinct flavors that Tomasita Meléndez achieves by marinating and stir-frying the shrimp before combining them with the separately cooked garlic and chile. I also love the richness of the spoonful of luxurious garlic-butter paste that Tomasita adds. Another interesting touch is the use of small dried chiles (árbol or dried serrano) instead of the commoner large guajillos. The heat and chile flavor seem to diffuse better with the small chiles. You can vary the amount to taste, but since they are used whole, they shouldn't make the dish too incendiary.

In Veracruz, people eat the shrimp with corn tortillas. Cubans sop up the oil with bread.

1	large head garlic, separated into cloves and peeled
1	teaspoon coarse salt, or to taste
	Juice of 2 limes
	Freshly ground black pepper
1	pound shrimp (any size; I generally use small), peeled and deveined
3	tablespoons olive oil
3	tablespoons vegetable oil
20	árbol or dried serrano chiles (see page 45)
1	tablespoon Garlic Butter Enrichment (page 300; optional)
	Lime wedges for garnish

WITH a heavy pestle, crush 2 of the garlic cloves to a paste with the salt in a medium bowl. Stir in the lime juice and a good grinding of black pepper. Add the shrimp and toss well to combine. Let stand for 5 minutes; drain and set aside.

USING a mortar and pestle or the flat of a heavy knife blade, crush the remaining garlic cloves just enough to bruise the surface while leaving the cloves nearly intact. Add 1 tablespoon each of the olive and vegetable oil to a small skillet and heat over medium heat until rippling. Add the bruised garlic and cook, stirring occasionally, for about 2 minutes, or until golden. Add the chiles and cook, stirring constantly, for another minute, being careful not to scorch the chiles. Set the pan aside.

IN a medium skillet, heat the remaining 4 tablespoons olive and vegetable oil over medium-high heat until rippling. Stir in the garlic butter, if using. Add the drained shrimp and cook, stirring constantly, for 2 minutes, or until they change color. Add the garlic-chile mixture and cook, stirring constantly, just to heat through, about 1 more minute. Serve at once with lime wedges.

Mariquitas

DEEP-FRIED GREEN PLANTAIN CHIPS

*T*HESE IRRESISTIBLE GOLDEN CHIPS ARE A FAVORITE snack in all Afro-Caribbean communities. *Mariquitas* play a role in Cuba and the remnants of the slave colonies very close to that of potato chips in the United States and are munched with great joy at home, on the street, or at the movies. It is crucial that the plantains be sliced wafer-thin, as thin as potatoes for chips. Unless you have terrific knife skills, the best tool is a French mandoline or one of those plastic mandoline-type gizmos that periodically turn up under different brand names. Please note that the plantains must be green. The black ones don't have the right starchiness.

Makes 4 servings,
at an optimistic guess
(they go fast!)

2 large green plantains
  Vegetable oil or peanut oil for frying
  Salt
  Lime juice (optional)
  Garlic powder (optional)
  She-Man Sauce (page 310)

PEEL the plantains as directed on page 60. Preferably using a mandoline, cut either crosswise or (more traditional among Cubans) lengthwise into the thinnest possible slices. (If slicing lengthwise, it may help to cut them in half crosswise first.) Some people drop the slices into a basin of cold water as they are cut and soak them for 40–60 minutes to prevent them from discoloring. If you do this, you must drain them all and blot *completely* dry with paper towels to eliminate any trace of moisture that might ruin the frying.

POUR oil into a large heavy skillet to a depth of at least 1 inch and heat over medium-high heat to 375°F. A handful at a time, add the chips and fry until golden, about 2 minutes. Watch the temperature and adjust the heat as necessary to keep it constant. As the chips are done, lift them out with a slotted spoon onto paper towels to drain. Eat hot and crisp, sprinkled with salt and the lime juice, if desired, or serve with She-Man Sauce. Or take the unconventional advice of my son Aarón, who learned to season *mariquitas* with a dash of garlic powder while working for the gifted Latin restaurateur Douglas Rodríguez.

Plátanos Rellenos

STUFFED PLANTAINS

*T*HESE LITTLE FILLED FRITTERS OF MASHED PLANTAIN ARE one of the classic Veracruzan appetizers, made with all kinds of fillings from *picadillo* (the ubiquitous Mexican chopped meat mixture) to grated cheese. My favorite is the following version from Raquel Torres, featuring pureed black beans perfumed with avocado leaf. Be sure to use only plain, fatless boiled beans that are just slightly undercooked. For some reason, refried beans cause the filled fritters to burst when they hit the hot oil.

Plantains vary a lot in cooking time, depending on the degree of ripeness, which can be hard to gauge when you buy them. For this recipe, you want them fairly ripe, mottled yellow and black. To tell when they are done, start testing with a knife tip after about 25 minutes of cooking and continue to cook until you feel no resistance. Stubborn ones can take as long as an hour.

Makes 20–24 fritters
(8 servings)

3 ripe plantains (yellow liberally spotted with black)
1 cup Cooked Black Beans (page 283), a little underdone, drained
1 teaspoon salt, or to taste
2 teaspoons powdered dried avocado leaf (see page 41)
Vegetable oil for shaping and frying the plantains

Any preferred salsa or Mexican *crema* (see page 67; optional)

CUT the unpeeled plantains in half crosswise. You may be able to gauge their ripeness from looking at them: riper ones will have almost no visible core, while greener ones will display a central core nearly ¼ inch thick. Place the plantains in a medium saucepan and add water to cover by about 1 inch. Bring to a boil over high heat; reduce the heat to maintain a low rolling boil and cook until they are soft enough to mash, starting to test with a knife tip as described above after about 25 minutes. Drain and let cool.

WHILE the plantains cook, place the beans in a small mixing bowl with the salt and powdered avocado leaf. Using a potato masher or heavy pestle, mash to a fine puree. Set aside.

PEEL the plantains, place in a large mixing bowl, and mash very thoroughly with a (clean) potato masher or pestle. (Alternatively, you can puree them in a food processor, but take care to stop before they become overprocessed and gluey, which makes them hard to work with.)

LIGHTLY oil a cookie sheet. Rub a light film of oil over your palms and shape the mashed plantains into 20–24 balls about the size of golf balls. Remoistening your hands with oil as necessary, place the balls one at a time on a lightly oiled plate or work surface and flatten with your fingertips into a round 2¹⁄₂–3 inches across. Place about 2 teaspoons of the mashed-bean mixture in the center of each round; fold up the sides and press together to make a stubby cigar shape with well-sealed edges. Place the filled "cigars" seam side up on the cookie sheet as they are shaped and cover with a moist tea towel. (They can be made up to 2 hours in advance of cooking, though I recommend refrigerating if they have to sit longer than 15–20 minutes.)

WHEN you are ready to cook the fritters, place a medium deep, heavy skillet over medium-high heat and add oil to a depth of at least 1 ¹⁄₂–2 inches. Heat to 375°F. Fry the filled rolls 3 or 4 at a time, turning to cook evenly on all sides, for about 3 minutes, or until golden. As they are done, lift out with a skimmer or slotted spatula and let drain briefly on paper towels. Serve hot, with salsa or *crema*, if desired.

Chiles Capones Rellenos de Picadillo de Puerco

STUFFED "NEUTERED" CHIPOTLE CHILES

Makes 6–8 servings

THE FAMOUS CHIPOTLE CHILES OF VERACRUZ ARE CALLED *chiles capones*, or "capon chiles," when prepared for stuffing by removing their seeds and veins. The name comes from the fact that this "neuters" their heat. They can still be pretty hot, but the sting is softened.

Restorán Doña Josefina, in the picturesque town of Naolinco, makes one of my favorite *chiles capones* dishes, an appetizer featuring the endlessly useful Mexican chopped meat mixture known as *picadillo*. A classic *picadillo* consists of shredded or minced cooked pork (or chicken) sautéed with seasonings like raisins, capers, and thyme. There are any number of delightful variations used as fillings for tacos, empanadas, and stuffed chiles.

I like to serve these as a first course, but I find that they also make an inspired addition (unfried) to Almond Soup (page 164).

20–24	large dried (*not* canned) chipotle chiles, preferably morita-type (see page 48)
1¹/₂	cups Pork Picadillo (page 104)
¹/₂	cup plus 2 tablespoons all-purpose flour
3	large eggs, separated
	Vegetable oil for frying
	Thin Tomato Sauce (page 317), warmed

WEARING protective gloves, cut a shallow 1-inch slit lengthwise down each chile and carefully remove the seeds and veins, trying not to tear the skin. Place in a bowl, cover with boiling water, and let sit for 30 minutes. Drain thoroughly and blot away every trace of moisture with paper towels.

FILL each of the chiles with a little of the *picadillo*, just enough so that the cut edges will still close over the filling. Put them in a shallow dish or on a plate and dredge with ¹/₂ cup of the flour, turning to coat each chile lightly and shaking to remove any excess.

IN a mixing bowl, beat the egg whites to stiff peaks. Beat in the egg yolks one at a time. The mixture should be very light and glossy. Sprinkle the remaining 2 tablespoons flour over the beaten eggs and fold in carefully.

POUR oil into a heavy medium saucepan or deep skillet to a depth of about 1 inch; heat to 375°F over medium-high heat. Working in batches of 2 or 3 at a time, dip the stuffed chiles in the egg mixture and fry until puffed and golden, about 1 minute on each side. As they are done, lift out with a slotted spoon and let drain on paper towels. Serve at once, with the tomato sauce.

Picadillo de Puerco

PORK PICADILLO

*I*F YOU ARE COOKING THE MEAT FOR THE *PICADILLO* FROM scratch, start with about ½ pound boneless pork.

Makes about 2½ cups

3 tablespoons vegetable oil
1 small white onion, finely chopped
1 garlic clove, minced
1½ cups Shredded Cooked Pork (page 144)
1 medium-sized ripe tomato, peeled, seeded, and finely chopped
½ ripe plantain, peeled (see page 60) and finely diced
2 tablespoons dark raisins, chopped
1 tablespoon capers, chopped
½ teaspoon crumbled dried thyme
½ teaspoon crumbled dried oregano
Salt and freshly ground black pepper (optional)

HEAT the oil in a large skillet over medium-high heat. When it ripples, add the onion and garlic and cook until the onion is translucent, about 3 minutes. Reduce the heat to medium, add the shredded meat, and stir to distribute evenly. Stir in the tomato, plantain, raisins, capers, and dried herbs. Cook for about 10 minutes, or until the flavors are well blended. Taste the mixture for seasoning and add a little salt and pepper, if desired. Let cool to room temperature before using as a filling for chiles.

VARIATION
For *Picadillo de Pollo* (Chicken Picadillo), substitute Shredded Cooked Chicken (page 142) for the pork.

Chiles Xalapeños Rellenos en Vinagreta

STUFFED JALAPEÑO CHILES
IN VINAIGRETTE

Veracruzan cooks love stuffed jalapeños in many guises: fresh and green, smoke-dried, even lightly marinated, as in this unusual appetizer or snack. I came across several different versions, all including the preliminary cooking with sugar (said to take out some of the heat) and instant coffee. This recipe is based on one that I had from Gregoria Arreola, the cook at Restorán El Tabachín in Córdoba.

If you are starting with uncooked chicken breast, use about 8 ounces boneless, skinless chicken and cook following the directions for Shredded Cooked Chicken on page 142.

Makes 6–8 servings

24–30	large jalapeño chiles with stems
6	cups water
1/4	cup sugar
2	tablespoons instant coffee
1/2	cup cider vinegar
1	head garlic, separated into cloves and peeled
1/2	cup olive oil
1	medium-sized white onion, finely chopped
1	large ripe tomato, peeled, seeded, and finely chopped
1/4	cup fresh Italian parsley leaves, chopped
1/4	cup slivered blanched almonds, toasted (see page 64) and finely chopped
1/4	cup pimiento-stuffed green olives, chopped or thinly sliced
2	tablespoons capers, chopped
1/2	teaspoon crumbled dried thyme
1/2	teaspoon crumbled dried Mexican oregano (see page 43)
1 1/2	cups finely shredded cooked chicken breast
1	teaspoon salt, or to taste
	Freshly ground black pepper
5	large carrots, peeled and sliced
2	large white onions, sliced into very thin half-moons
5	bay leaves
10	allspice berries

KEEPING the stems intact, cut a shallow slit down almost the whole length of each chile and very carefully remove the seeds and veins. (You may want to wear protective gloves for this task.)

IN a large nonreactive saucepan, combine the water with the sugar, instant coffee, and $1/4$ cup of the vinegar and bring to a boil over high heat. Add the chiles, reduce the heat to medium-low, and cook for 5 minutes. Drain and discard the cooking liquid. Cover the chiles with cool water and let stand for 1 hour to remove some of their heat. Change the water and let stand for another hour. (If you like, you can repeat the process one or two more times to cancel out any trace of heat, but I find two soakings sufficient.)

MINCE 2 of the garlic cloves. In a large deep skillet or sauté pan, heat $1/4$ cup of the oil over medium-high heat until fragrant. Add the minced garlic and chopped onion and cook, stirring frequently, until the onion is translucent, about 3 minutes. Add the tomato, parsley, almonds, olives, capers, and dried herbs. Reduce the heat to medium and cook, stirring frequently, until most of the moisture has evaporated, about 15 minutes.

STIR in the chicken and cook for 5 minutes longer to heat through. Taste for seasoning; add up to 1 teaspoon salt, if desired, and a good grinding of black pepper. Remove from the heat and let cool to room temperature.

CAREFULLY fill each chile with about 2 tablespoons of the chicken mixture (the amount will vary with their size). Arrange, slit side up, in a shallow serving dish or deep platter.

PLACE the remaining $1/4$ cup oil in a medium nonreactive saucepan over medium heat. Add the carrots, sliced onions, and remaining garlic cloves, along with the bay leaves and allspice. Cook, stirring, until the onions are translucent, about 3 minutes. Add the remaining $1/4$ cup vinegar and bring to a boil. Remove from the heat and let cool to room temperature.

POUR the vinegar mixture over the chiles. Let stand for several hours, occasionally spooning the marinade over the chiles. The chiles will keep in the refrigerator, tightly covered, for up to 2 days, but be sure to bring to room temperature before serving. Place the chiles on a tray and pass as an appetizer, or plate individually and serve.

Pambazos

FLOUR-DUSTED SANDWICH BUNS
WITH FILLINGS

*I*F VERACRUZ HAD AN OFFICIAL SANDWICH, IT WOULD BE *pambazos,* also affectionately called *pambacitos.* They are lovely little yeast buns that you split and fill with something irresistible, like beans and chorizo. At a glance, a *pambazo* looks a little like a Sloppy Joe, but the resemblance ends there. *Pambazos* are among the best yeast rolls I've ever eaten, a tender and delicate contrast to the rich flavors of the fillings. They are a favorite dish at *cenadurías* (places that serve simple supper dishes) in Xalapa and Orizaba, but they are loved in other parts of the state as well. You can also buy the rolls at bakeries and take them home to serve with your own fillings.

Miguel Ángel Montano, who owns an excellent small bakery in Xalapa and makes his own delivery rounds on foot, gave me this recipe.

A helpful tool for this recipe is the right sort of rolling pin—short, thin, and light. A 6-inch length cut from a plain wooden broomstick would do perfectly; if you're not given to sawing up broomsticks, a really sturdy cardboard tube from a roll of plastic wrap or fax paper is about the right weight and diameter.

The rolls should be used very fresh.

Makes 16 (4-inch) buns

FOR THE ROLLS

1/3 ounce compressed fresh yeast (about half of a 0.6-ounce cake), or 2 teaspoons dry yeast

1 1/3 cups warm water

1 tablespoon sugar

About 4 cups unbleached all-purpose flour (1 pound), plus about 1 cup more for kneading and dusting

1 teaspoon salt

1 tablespoon vegetable shortening, at room temperature

4 ounces Spanish-style chorizo, chopped, or Chile-Spiced Pork Sausage (page 246), removed from casings and crumbled (about 1 cup), cooked

4 ounces *queso fresco* (see page 67), well drained, crumbled

1/2 small white onion, thinly sliced

1 medium-sized ripe tomato, sliced

3 pickled jalapeño chiles, seeded and sliced

IN a small bowl, dissolve the yeast in the warm water. Add the sugar and stir to dissolve well. Stir in about $1/2$ cup of the flour and let sit at room temperature for about 15 minutes, or until foamy.

MOUND $3^1/2$ cups of the flour on a pastry board or countertop and make a well in the center, building up the walls carefully. Add the salt and shortening to the dissolved yeast and pour the mixture into the well. Quickly start scooping the flour into the liquid ingredients, mixing with your fingertips and trying not to let the liquid overflow the walls before it can be absorbed. As the dough comes together (it will be very sticky), start kneading it vigorously with both hands. Knead for about 15 minutes, adding a few more tablespoons of flour if necessary, until the dough is very silky and elastic but no longer sticky.

SHAPE the dough into a neat ball, place in a large greased bowl, and turn to coat. Cover with a damp towel and set in a warm, draft-free spot (such as a turned-off gas oven) to rise until doubled in volume, $1^1/2$–2 hours. (Please note that the rising time may vary greatly; check at intervals after about 50 minutes.)

VERY lightly grease two baking sheets. Punch down the dough and turn it out onto a work surface. With a knife or bench scraper, cut it first into halves, then into quarters, eighths, and so forth, to yield 16 equal pieces. Quickly and gently roll each into a ball. With bunched fingertips, twist up a nipple-sized knot (like a Hershey's Kiss) on top of each. Lightly dust each with flour. With a small thin rolling "pin" (see the headnote), roll out each ball to a disk about 3 inches across. Dust all over with flour. Place the disks side by side, not quite touching, on the greased baking sheets. Let rise, loosely covered with a cloth, until about doubled in size, 1–$1^1/2$ hours (depending on the temperature of the kitchen).

PREHEAT the oven to 400°F.

BAKE for 20 minutes, or until the surface of the rolls, but *not* the flour, is lightly browned. (If the flour browns, it will have a harsh taste.) Let cool.

TO SERVE, split the rolls horizontally in half and fill with the sausage, cheese, onion, tomato, and chiles.

VERACRUZ WAS THE FIRST PLACE on earth where a European tasted Mexican corn. What Cortés and his companions tasted on the shores of Veracruz had the distinctive, haunting flavor that every Mexican loves from birth — *nixtamal*, corn treated with natural alkalis that make it into a new and magical substance.

The Spanish took to Mexican maize cooking very quickly. Two kinds of preparation attracted their interest from the first. One was the griddle-baked Mexican daily "bread," which they called tortillas (little round cakes). Another was the people's favorite celebration food, richly moist corn mixtures steamed inside leaf wrappings. Trying to pronounce the name in the language of the Aztecs, the newcomers came up with the now familiar word *tamales*.

THE

VERACRUZAN

CORN

KITCHEN

Eventually the plain griddle-baked tortilla became every Veracruzan's — and every Mexican's — idea of the indispensable everyday bread. (Don't expect to see flour tortillas here; they belong to the north.) But plain tortillas were only the beginning. The famous culinary intermingling of European and Indian ways rapidly took off when the Spanish introduced pigs and the idea of cooking things in lard. It gave rise to an incredible number of variations on the original corn tortilla. I have never seen anything to equal the Veracruzan creations in this category — what Mexicans call *antojitos*, or "little whims," which serve as street food, supper food, breakfast food, all-round comfort food. The word "tortilla" is inadequate to convey their scope.

People in Veracruz started doing things like mixing the corn masa (dough) with lard and/or pork cracklings to make *tortillas con momocho*, or pleating the surface of large tortillas into little ridges to catch and hold a good layer of lard with cracklings (*pellizcadas*). Or they formed corn cakes into little rimmed containers like tart shells, fried them in lard and served them topped with sauces and garnishes (*picadas* and *garnachas*). They also invented all kinds of filled variations. In yet another wrinkle on the fried tortilla idea, they shaped the dough into little cakes enclosing a pocket of bean filling, then fried the whole thing (*tapaditas*). Someone discovered that mixing some wheat flour with the masa made it light enough to puff up like a balloon when it hit a pan of hot fat, and the *gorditas infladas* of Veracruz were born. Someone had the further bright idea of splitting *gorditas* and putting a filling—usually beans—into the pocket. People also learned to mix the dough with mashed beans before frying it, to produce *gorditas de frijol*.

There are places — especially the Huastec communities of the north — where people still eat plain tortillas in something close to the pre-Hispanic fashion, dipped in a simple chile sauce and folded in half. (These were the original enchiladas.) The north also preserves the state's largest repertoire of tamales, including both savory and sweet kinds that I have never seen elsewhere. This region is famed for the most spectacular tamale in all of Mexico, the *sacahuil*, or *zacahuil*, a mammoth creation that can be six feet long and contains a seriously heavy-duty masa-and-meat filling wrapped in banana leaves. After ten or twelve hours in a large wood-fired outdoor oven, the mighty dish is unwrapped to release clouds of intense steam in which the several meats have cooked all that time while becoming exquisitely tender.

*T*HE CORN KITCHEN of Veracruz is probably the area where the African presence is least noticeable. Most of the masa dishes that people eat today are blended from indigenous and Spanish elements. But there are some delicious exceptions—for example, tortillas made with mashed plantain in the dough. The state's most famous Afromestizo corn dish is the sumptuous *tamal de cazuela*, which resembles a polenta or savory pudding with a chile-laced meat sauce and is a close cousin of the Cuban *tamal en cazuela*. It has become one of my favorite party dishes.

Masa de Masa *Harina*

MASA FROM DEHYDRATED MIX

*M*ASA RECONSTITUTED FROM PACKAGED MIXES IS
acceptable for most uses, though it will never be as good as true masa
made at home or bought from a Mexican *tortillería*. As I explain on
page 51, people commonly if incorrectly lump together all brands
under the name of "masa harina," which was invented by the Quaker
Oats Company. When Mexican home cooks use the instantized product, they generally reconstitute it with water. I often use chicken stock
instead, to give the resulting masa-equivalent a little more life, but
this is up to individual preference.

The process is simple: Place the masa harina in a bowl, add lukewarm water or stock, and work with a wooden spoon or your hands to
form a stiff dough for tortillas, a slightly more yielding one for
tamales. I have indicated the specific proportions of liquid to masa
harina in each recipe. As a rough rule of thumb, use 2 cups (about 1
pound) masa harina to $1^1/_8$–$1^1/_4$ cups warm water or Basic Chicken
Stock (page 142) to obtain the equivalent of $2^1/_2$–3 cups (1 pound)
fresh masa. For tamales, allow 1 cup more liquid; the weight will be
slightly more.

Tortillas de Maíz

BASIC CORN TORTILLAS

WHEN MEXICANS SAY "TORTILLA," YOU CAN USUALLY BET that they are not thinking of the blah versions of flour tortillas so popular in the United States—not much different from all those other flabby all-purpose "wraps." In Veracruz and nearly everywhere in Mexico, the bread of life is corn tortillas. The very best ones are made using fresh masa ground from the finest Mexican corn and will always have a slight edge over tortillas made from our corn. However, we can still make excellent tortillas here.

Please try this at least once with fresh masa. Even though tortillas from masa harina are all right for everyday purposes, you will taste a striking difference with real masa. The following recipe is a standard pan-Mexican formula for basic corn tortillas—but Veracruz is also known for some fascinating tortilla variations. Once you've mastered the basic procedure, be sure to try the plantain-masa tortillas (page 116) or the ones with crushed pork cracklings (page 117).

Read through the recipe and have everything ready for pressing out the tortillas before you begin. I urge you to acquire a simple aluminized cast-iron tortilla press from one of the sources listed on page 365, or from just about any Mexican neighborhood grocery. Wooden presses are even better (especially if you want to make outsize tortillas) but are less easy to find outside of Mexico. There is one alternative method that works well: shaping the tortillas by pressing out each ball of dough using a small round heavy object with a perfectly flat bottom, such as a very small cast-iron skillet. Prepare an antistick liner as directed in the recipe below, place the dough between the two plastic flaps, and press down on the dough, keeping the bottom of the skillet absolutely parallel with the countertop—if it is ever so slightly tilted, the tortillas will be of uneven thickness.

Makes 10–12
(5-to-6-inch) tortillas

1½ pounds (about 3 cups) masa, fresh or reconstituted by mixing 2 cups masa harina with about 1 cup plus 2 tablespoons warm water (see page 51)

2–3 teaspoons vegetable oil, or as needed, for the griddle

LIGHTLY work the masa with your fingers to test the consistency; it should be like a slightly stiff but pliable cookie dough. Work in 2–4 tablespoons water if necessary.

MAKE an antistick liner for your tortilla press by cutting open the two sides of a 1-quart zip-closing plastic freezer bag (or other heavy-duty plastic bag of the same size) to form a long rectangle about 12 x 6 inches. Open the press and place the plastic strip in it, with the fold next to the hinge.

DAMPEN your hands with cool water and shake off the excess. Shape the masa into 10–12 balls the size of Ping-Pong balls, occasionally remoistening your hands and covering the masa balls with a damp cloth as they are prepared.

HEAT a griddle or medium cast-iron skillet over high heat until a drop of water sizzles on contact. Moisten a bunched-up paper towel with a dab of vegetable oil and quickly rub it over the griddle. Press a ball of masa into a tortilla by placing it on the bottom of the tortilla press (on the plastic), closing the hinged top, and pressing on the handle. You want a round of dough 5–6 inches in diameter and about $1/16$ inch thick. Open the press and gently detach the plastic from the tortilla, remoistening your hands if necessary to keep it from sticking to your fingers. Place the tortilla on the hot griddle and cook for 1–2 minutes, until lightly flecked with brown on the underside. Flip it with a spatula and let the other side cook for about $1^{1}/2$ minutes longer. It may puff slightly: if not, quickly and firmly press down on the surface with a bunched-up tea towel or a weight like a heavy can. (If you're using a skillet rather than a griddle, watch out for the hot sides.) Flip it again, press the other side, and then quickly lift out onto a plate. Wrap the hot tortilla snugly in a cloth napkin or tea towel.

REPEAT with the remaining balls of dough, working with one or two at a time and stacking them on top of one another inside the cloth wrapping as they are done. Keep checking the temperature of the griddle or pan and adjust the heat as necessary to maintain a uniform heat.

CORN tortillas are best when eaten hot and fresh — though leftover ones have as many secondary uses as stale bread.

Tortillas de Masa y Plátano Verde

CORN MASA–GREEN PLANTAIN TORTILLAS

SLIGHTLY SWEETER AND STARCHIER THAN ORTHODOX tortillas, this popular variation extends and enriches the original corn masa with the starchy plantains that came to the whole Caribbean region during the slave era. You can use them as you would any fresh corn tortilla, but I find that they tend to stick to the griddle more — no problem if you grease the griddle a little more often and more generously than usual. My first introduction to these delicious tortillas came from the anthropologist-cook Raquel Torres.

Makes about 15 (5-to-6-inch) tortillas

1	small or ½ large green plantain
1	pound masa, fresh or reconstituted by mixing 2 cups masa harina with about 1 cup plus 2 tablespoons warm water (see page 51)
1	teaspoon salt, or to taste
2–3	tablespoons all-purpose flour
3–4	tablespoons vegetable oil, or as needed, for oiling the griddle

PEEL the plantain, following the directions on page 60. Using the medium-fine side of a box grater, grate it into a large mixing bowl. Add the masa and salt and work with your hands to combine thoroughly. It should form a somewhat stiff but pliable dough, a little heavier than a usual corn tortilla dough but not too pasty to handle. If it is difficult to work with, add a little flour, about 1 tablespoon at a time, and knead it in thoroughly until the consistency is smoother.

SHAPE the mixture into about 15 golf-ball-sized balls. Following the directions on page 115, press them out into 5-to-6-inch rounds about 1/16 inch thick and griddle-bake.

Tortillas con Momocho

TORTILLAS WITH PORK CRACKLING SPREAD

Makes 10–12
thick tortillas

*M*OMOCHO, OR *MOSMOCHO*, THE DELICIOUS VERACRUZAN mixture of crackling bits and the grainy layer that sinks to the bottom of homemade lard, is a great addition to plain corn tortillas. When I sing the praises of good Mexican lard and urge people to get into the habit of making up a little batch from time to time, I'm thinking not only of its excellent cooking qualities but also of bonuses like this. When you have lard and cracklings on hand, be sure to see how they can transform a simple tortilla. Serve them with a meal as you would plain tortillas or enjoy as a snack.

1 pound masa, fresh or reconstituted by mixing 2 cups masa harina with about 1 cup plus 2 tablespoons warm water (see page 51)
1 teaspoon salt, or to taste
³/4 cup fresh pork cracklings (see page 66)
¹/2 cup home-rendered lard (see page 66)

PLACE the masa in a large mixing bowl. Place the salt, cracklings, and lard in a bowl or large mortar and crush together with a wooden pusher or a pestle. Add to the masa and work with your hands to distribute the ingredients evenly.

SHAPE the mixture into 10–12 golf-ball-sized balls. Following the directions on page 115, press out each into a round about 4 inches across and ¹/4 inch thick and griddle-bake, using medium heat and allowing 1¹/2–2 minutes per side. The tortillas should be just golden, not browned.

Pellizcadas

LARGE "PINCHED" TORTILLAS

PELLIZCADAS ARE ONE OF MANY CHANGES THAT Veracruzan cooks ring on the theme of a fresh corn tortilla formed into an unusual shape and spread or filled with something flavorful. They are large tortillas, sometimes up to 8 inches across on their home ground of the Tuxtlas region, with a curious textured surface that is produced by pinching up tiny folds of the exposed side while the tortilla is still hot and pliant from the griddle. (The effect reminds me of wave crests in paintings of the sea.) The little pleats catch and hold whatever is spread over the *pellizcada*, classically lard mixed with pork cracklings. If you can't see your way to a home-rendering session, you can produce a tasty result with bacon drippings, preferably on the grainy side. Serve as you would ordinary tortillas.

Makes 8
(6-inch) *pellizcadas*

1 pound masa, fresh or reconstituted by mixing 2 cups masa harina with about 1 cup plus 2 tablespoons warm water (see page 51)
$1/2$–$3/4$ cup home-rendered lard mixed with 2–3 tablespoons finely crushed pork cracklings (see page 66)
2 teaspoons coarse salt, or to taste
1–$1/2$ cups Los Tuxtlas–Style Chile-Lime Sauce (page 305)

SHAPE the masa into 8 golf-ball-sized balls. Following the directions on page 115, press out each into a fairly thick (about $1/8$ inch) 6-inch round.

LIGHTLY grease a griddle or large cast-iron skillet and heat over medium-high heat until a drop of water sizzles on contact. Place a tortilla on the hot griddle and griddle-bake for $1/2$–2 minutes. Turn and cook on the other side for about 1 minute longer, just until it puffs slightly. Quickly remove to a work surface. Be prepared to work fast, before the tortilla can cool. With your fingertips, swiftly pinch up little pleats (about $1/2$ inch long and $1/2$ inch high) all over the upper surface. (Some people also pinch out a slightly raised rim, but this isn't necessary.)

SPREAD the still warm *pellizcada* with a few tablespoons of the lard-crackling mixture. Sprinkle a little salt over it. Set aside. Continue baking, pinching, and spreading the tortillas one at a time. Serve at once, with a bowl of the sauce.

Enchiladas de Pepián Verde Huasteco

ENCHILADAS WITH HUASTECA-STYLE GREEN PEPIÁN

*I*N VERACRUZ'S NORTHEASTERN HUASTECA REGION, THE term "enchiladas" usually refers, not to the rolled and filled versions you have probably encountered elsewhere, but to a minimalist dish consisting of tortillas dipped in a chile sauce and folded in half sans filling. Virginia Villalón, chef-owner of Doña Virginia restaurant in Pánuco, serves several versions for breakfast. I am especially fond of this pumpkin-seed sauce example.

Makes 16 enchiladas

1 pound masa, fresh or reconstituted by mixing 2 cups masa harina with about 1 cup plus 2 tablespoons warm water (see page 51)
3 cups Huasteca-Style Green Pepián (page 322)
2 hard-cooked eggs, minced (optional)

FOLLOWING the directions on page 115, form the masa into 16 small balls, press out into thin 4-inch tortillas, and griddle-bake. Have the sauce barely simmering over low heat.

AS the tortillas come off the griddle, dip each in the sauce and fold in half. Arrange on a serving platter or individual plates and serve at once, topped with the hard-cooked egg, if desired.

Picadas

CRIMPED MASA TARTLETS

PICADA, LITERALLY, "PINKED" OR "PRICKED," REFERS TO the way you're supposed to crimp up the edges of a small tortilla so as to form a shallow tartlet shell for spreading with a few simple toppings and serving as either a breakfast or a supper snack. You may have encountered similar masa preparations, in different shapes and sizes, under names like *sopes* or *chalupas*. *Picadas* usually come to the table in Veracruz in colorful pairings of red and green: one shell spread with *salsa roja* or chipotle sauce, its mate with some kind of *salsa verde*. The other toppings (usually crumbled or grated cheese and Mexican *crema*, sometimes also a little chopped onion) are arranged over the sauce. (See the photograph on page 122.) Some people add shredded meat as well, but I think it distracts from the simple flavor of the sauce. The size can vary. I've seen them as large as 5 inches in diameter, which is manageable at a dinner table but too messy for a passed appetizer, which is how I like to serve them. Three inches is the most useful size.

I am giving directions for briefly frying the *picada* shells in hot lard, the authentic Veracruzan technique. But when I serve them, I often simplify things by reheating the shells on a griddle and brushing lightly with melted lard. This saves a lot of calories and not a little mess! Reduce the amount of lard to 2–3 tablespoons if you choose this option.

Makes 20–22 *picadas*

FOR THE *PICADAS*

1 teaspoon salt, or to taste

1 pound masa, fresh or reconstituted by mixing 2 cups masa harina with about 1 cup plus 2 tablespoons warm water (see page 51)

1/2 cup lard, preferably home-rendered (see page 66)

FOR THE TOPPINGS

1 cup Red Sauce from Orizaba (page 313), Tomato Sauce with Chipotle Chiles (page 319), or any red salsa

1 cup Green Sauce with Avocado (page 308) or any green salsa

8 ounces *queso fresco*, crumbled, or *queso añejo* (see page 67), grated (about 2 cups)

1/2 cup Mexican *crema* (see page 67) or crème fraîche

1 small white onion, finely chopped (optional)

FOR THE *PICADAS*

WITH your hands, work the salt into the masa. Shape it into 20–22 walnut-sized balls. Following the directions for tortillas on page 115, press them into rounds about 3 inches across and 1/8 inch thick. Set them side by side (not stacked) on baking sheets as they are shaped, covering them with a damp cloth.

LIGHTLY grease a griddle or large cast-iron skillet and heat over medium-high heat until a drop of water sizzles on contact. Have ready a basket lined with tea towels. Now you must work quickly, because the masa will be supple enough to shape for only a few seconds after baking. Place 2 of the prepared masa rounds on the hot griddle and cook for about 1½ minutes, until the edges shrink away slightly from the pan and lose their raw look. Turn and cook the other side for another 1–1½ minutes. Transfer to a plate or work surface and, while they are still hot, quickly pinch up the edges of each into a slightly raised rim. Place them in the basket and cover snugly with the towels. Continue with the remaining masa rounds, 2 at a time.

LINE a baking sheet with paper towels. In a small skillet or saucepan, heat the lard over medium heat until hot but not quite rippling. Using kitchen tongs, slide each *picada* into the hot fat and let it cook for 10–20 seconds. Before it starts to brown, lift out, letting it drain well, and set on the prepared baking sheet.

WHEN all the *picadas* are done, spread half of them with a little of the red sauce, the remainder with the green sauce. Scatter some of the grated cheese over the sauce, top with a swirl of *crema* or crème fraîche and some chopped onion, if desired, and serve.

Encacahuatadas

ROLLED FILLED TORTILLAS IN PEANUT SAUCE

Makes 12 enchiladas

*J*UST AS *ENCHILADAS* REFERS TO TORTILLAS THAT HAVE been "en-chile'd" — that is, coated in a chile sauce—*encacahuatadas* means tortillas that have been "en-peanutted" in the same way. My recipe is based on one from Raquel Torres and a related version in *Cocina Veracruzana de Abolengo*, a most useful collection whose title is the Veracruzan equivalent of Mayflower Descendants' Cuisine. Serve as an appetizer.

The general idea of the dish is very simple, but it takes a certain amount of assembling. You must have the stock and the meat filling prepared before you start making the rich sauce. The tortillas must also be ready for the assembly line at the right moment—thin, flexible tortillas like the ones that would be used in Veracruz for this overall family of dishes. (If you are not skilled at handling fresh tortillas, by all means use thin commercial ones.) Some good homemade lard also has to be on hand for softening the tortillas before they are dipped in the sauce. And then there is the sauce itself, which some cooks unfamiliar with Mexican sauces will be surprised to find requires both a blender *and* a food processor. The processor is more adept at grinding seeds and nuts. The short, straight blades of the blender bite into reconstituted dried chiles much more efficiently. So you'd do yourself no favor by trying to combine all the processing in one machine.

3 ancho chiles, stemmed and seeded
4–5 cups Basic Pork Stock (page 144)
8 ounces (about 2 cups) sesame seeds
8 ounces (about 2½ cups) roasted peanuts
1 3-ounce tablet Mexican chocolate (see page 69)
5 tablespoons lard, preferably home-rendered (see page 66), or vegetable oil
About 2½ cups Pork Picadillo (page 104), heated
12 thin 5-inch corn tortillas, store-bought or homemade (page 114)

PLACE the chiles in a small saucepan and add 2 cups of the stock. Bring to a boil over medium-high heat and cook until softened, about 10 minutes. Let the chiles and cooking liquid cool slightly, then pour into a blender and process until smooth. Leave the mixture in the blender.

PLACE the sesame seeds in a medium heavy skillet over medium heat and toast, stirring constantly and shaking the pan, until light golden, 3–5 minutes. Before they can darken, quickly scoop into a food processor and process to a smooth puree. (It can take a while for the blades to connect with the tiny seeds, so be patient.) Add the peanuts and process to a paste. Scrape the mixture into the blender with the chile mixture. Start processing again, trying to gauge how well the blender is coping with the seeds and nuts.

WITH the motor running, gradually add another 2 cups of the stock to form a rich but easily pourable sauce. If the mixture thickens more than you expect, slowly add up to 1 cup more of stock (or water) to thin it as necessary.

LINE a baking sheet with paper towels. Using the coarse side of a box grater, grate the chocolate into a bowl. In a heavy medium saucepan, heat 2 tablespoons of the lard or oil over medium-high heat until rippling. Add the pureed mixture, watching out for splatters, and stir in the grated chocolate. Reduce the heat to maintain a simmer and cook, stirring frequently, for about 5 minutes, or until the chocolate is well amalgamated. Remove from the heat.

AT once heat the remaining 3 tablespoons lard or oil in a medium skillet over medium-high heat until rippling. Using tongs, quickly slide each tortilla through the hot fat to coat lightly and set on the prepared baking sheet. Dip one tortilla at a time into the hot peanut sauce, set on a plate, place about 2 tablespoons of the *picadillo* in the center, and roll up into a cylinder. Arrange the filled tortillas seam side down on individual serving plates, spoon the remaining sauce over them, and serve at once.

Garnachas de Masa Cocida con Camote

MASA–SWEET POTATO SHELLS
WITH FILLINGS

Makes 15–16 *garnachas*

THERE ARE MANY VARIATIONS ON THE MEXICAN theme of a fried masa base with an array of toppings. One of the classic instances in Veracruz is *garnachas*. I found a fascinating interpretation at the Hotel Doña Lala in Tlacotalpan. Rosa María Castro Chisanto, the head cook, is known for her version of *garnachas* consisting of shallow oval shells topped with a rich, complex filling that contains refried beans, cubed potatoes, some cooked meat (crumbled chorizo or other sausage, or shredded or minced chicken or pork), grated or crumbled cheese, Mexican *crema*, and any preferred piquant salsa.

Two things set them apart from ordinary corn masa preparations: first, the masa is boiled in water before shaping, and second, it is combined with cooked and mashed sweet potato. The resulting dough has a wonderful elusive sweetness, but it can be a bit tricky to work with. The boiled masa tends to harden and resist shaping almost as soon as it comes from the hot water, so you must work *very* quickly to mash it with the sweet potato. After frying, you will be rewarded with a nicely crunchy but sturdy vehicle for the lively assortment of toppings.

FOR THE GARNACHAS

- 1 medium sweet potato, boiled until tender and peeled while still warm
- 1 pound masa, fresh or reconstituted by mixing 2 cups masa harina with about 1 cup plus 2 tablespoons warm water (see page 51)
- 2 teaspoons salt, or to taste

  Vegetable oil for frying

FOR THE TOPPINGS

- 1/2–3/4 cup Refried Beans with Butter (page 285)
- 1 medium potato, boiled, peeled and cut into very fine (less than 1/4-inch) dice (1/2–3/4 cup diced)
- 1/2–3/4 cup crumbled Chile-Spiced Pork Sausage (page 246; removed from casings) or Spanish-style chorizo or 1/2–3/4 cup Shredded Cooked Chicken (page 142) or Pork Picadillo (page 104)

4 ounces *queso fresco*, crumbled, or *queso añejo* (see page 67), grated (about 1 cup)

3/4 cup salsa, such as Los Tuxtlas–Style Chile-Lime Sauce (page 305), Green She-Man Sauce (page 312), or Chipotle Chile Paste (page 306), diluted with a little water to taste

1/2 cup Mexican *crema* (see page 67; optional)

FOR THE *GARNACHAS*

LINE two baking sheets with parchment or waxed paper. Mash the sweet potato in a large shallow mixing bowl; set aside. Divide the masa into 4 equal pieces and shape them into round cakes like large hamburger patties.

CHOOSE a skillet or wide shallow saucepan large enough to hold the masa cakes without touching and add water to a depth of 2–2¹/₂ inches. Add the salt and bring to a boil. Add the masa cakes, making sure that they don't touch, and cook, covered, at a good boil over medium-high heat for 15 minutes. Drain thoroughly, add to the mashed sweet potato, and *at once* start mashing the masa into the sweet potato with a potato masher or heavy wooden pusher, working the mixture until the ingredients are roughly combined. Transfer it to a food processor and process for about 2 minutes, until the texture is smooth but not gluey.

QUICKLY start shaping the dough into 15–16 balls just a little smaller than Ping-Pong balls. Place them on a work surface and, with your fingertips, shape each into an oval about 3¹/₂ x 2 inches, with a raised rim about ¹/₄ inch high. As they are done, place on the prepared baking sheets and keep covered with a damp tea towel. They can stand for up to 4 hours, until you are ready to assemble them.

POUR oil into a large deep skillet to a depth of about 1¹/₂ inches; heat to 375°F. Add the masa shells 3 or 4 at a time and fry just until golden, about 1 minute per side (they get hard and tough if you leave them longer). Lift out onto paper towels as they are done.

FOR THE TOPPINGS

FOR the best flavor, have the beans, potato, and meat hot (you can warm them briefly in small saucepans or a microwave). Spread each *garnacha* with about 1 tablespoon of the refried beans. Scatter with a little of the potato, sausage, chicken or pork, and grated cheese. Top with a small dollop of the salsa and the *crema*, if using; serve at once.

Tapaditas de Frijol

SMALL FRIED MASA CAKES WITH BEAN FILLING

*T*HESE SAVORY LITTLE MORSELS — MASA ADROITLY SHAPED around a pocket of bean filling—are one subspecies of the *gorditas* that you find all over the state. (See the photograph on page 126.) Shaping *tapaditas* without having them spring a leak can be difficult. Every cook has a different stratagem. I've mastered a method that gives good results, though it's not exactly the technique of the cook who gave me this excellent recipe, Carmen Martínez Barrales, at Casa Bonilla in the north central hill town of Coatepec.

Should you have access to the small, fragrant Veracruzan comapa chiles, use 12–15 of them instead of the chiltepín chiles. Do not be tempted to substitute leftover refried beans for the plain semi-cooked ones I specify. Beans precooked in fat will make the masa cakes burst open when they go into hot oil.

Makes 12–15 *tapaditas*

½–1 teaspoon dried chiltepín chiles (see page 48)

1 garlic clove

2 teaspoons salt, or to taste

4 dried avocado leaves or 1 tablespoon ground avocado leaf (see page 41)

1 cup Semicooked Black Beans (page 284), very well drained

1 pound masa, fresh or reconstituted by mixing 2 cups masa harina with about 1 cup plus 2 tablespoons warm water (see page 51)

½ cup all-purpose flour

Vegetable oil for frying

Red Sauce from Orizaba (page 313), Green Sauce with Avocado (page 308), or Green She-Man Sauce (page 312)

IN a small skillet, gently toast the chiles over the lowest possible heat until darkened and brittle but not burned, about 10 minutes. Immediately remove from the heat.

USING a Mexican *molcajete* or other large mortar and pestle, pound the garlic to a paste with 1 teaspoon of the salt and then the toasted chiles. Add the whole or ground avocado leaves and the beans; mash to a paste. If the beans are very chalky and dry, you can add about ¼ cup water to help in mashing, but the mixture should not be wet—the ingredients should only just come together. (I some-times do this in a food processor, but remember that it's easy to over-process—it must not get gluey.)

LINE a baking sheet with parchment or waxed paper. With your hands, work together the masa and flour with the remaining 1 tea-spoon salt in a mixing bowl. When the dough is smooth and uni-form, shape it into 12–15 golf-ball-sized balls. With your thumb and forefinger, hollow out each to make a little cup with a lip about $^1/_4$ inch thick. Carefully place 1–1$^1/_2$ teaspoons of the bean mixture into each cup and close the dough cleanly over it. Mold each *tapadita* into a convex disk like a fat magnifying lens or a miniature flying saucer. As they are finished, place them on the prepared baking sheet and cover with a damp cloth. They can be held for up to 2 hours.

WHEN you are ready to cook the *tapaditas*, pour oil into a medium skillet to a depth of 1 inch and heat to 375°F over medium-high heat. Add the filled masa cakes 2 or 3 at a time and fry until golden and puffed, turning once and allowing 1–1$^1/_2$ minutes per side. Lift out onto a baking sheet lined with paper towels to drain. Serve at once with the chosen sauce.

Bolitas de Masa

THE FUNNY INDENTED SHAPE OF THESE DUMPLINGS helps them cook faster when added to a soup or stew. They are a frequent and welcome addition to dishes such as Chicken Chileatole (page 156) and Spicy Shrimp Stew (page 151); follow the cooking directions in the individual recipes. I would not try to substitute a fat other than lard. It holds them together compactly while making them fluffy, without a hint of greasiness.

The recipe can easily be multiplied for a larger yield, but *bolitas* don't keep very well. I usually make only what I need for the moment. However, they can be frozen for up to 2 weeks. Drop them into the boiling stew or soup while still frozen and add a couple of minutes to the cooking time.

Makes 12–15 dumplings

1 tablespoon lard, preferably home-rendered (see page 66)

½ teaspoon salt

1 cup masa, fresh or reconstituted by mixing ¾ cup masa harina with about ⅔ cup warm water (see page 51)

LINE a baking sheet with parchment or waxed paper.

IN a small mixing bowl, stir the lard and salt into the masa to make a smooth dough. Shape the mixture into balls the size of a large marble, slightly flattening each one and using your index finger to press a small indentation into each dumpling. Use at once, or let stand on the prepared baking sheet covered with a damp tea towel for up to an hour.

VARIATION

Some cooks like to add a bit of a chopped fresh herb such as epazote (see page 41), cilantro, or *hoja santa* (see page 42) to the dumplings, either mixing the herb into the dough or firmly pushing a small bit into the indentation in each.

Gorditas *Infladas*

FRIED PUFFED TORTILLAS

*V*ERACRUZ'S ANSWER TO THE INDIAN *PURI* IS THE *GORDITA* *inflada* (literally, "puffed-up little fat one"). In talking about them most people leave out the *inflada*, which can be confusing, since the name *gordita* by itself refers to a motley family of different tortilla-like masa cakes. They are eaten in some form or other in many parts of Mexico, but everyone knows that Veracruz state is headquarters for the most varied and delicious *gorditas*.

Some *gordita* variations, such as *tapaditas* (page 129), have a filling, but *gorditas infladas* are not meant to be filled.

You may think that getting a *gordita inflada* to inflate takes aeons of practice. Not so. If the oil is at the right temperature and you have a large spoon handy to keep flicking the hot fat over the upper surface, they'll puff as if by magic. The following dough is for basic *gorditas infladas* as commonly made around the port city and the Sotavento region. It uses a combination of masa, wheat flour, and mashed plantain that produces a pliable, subtly flavored, and easily puffed dough. The cooks of the region often shape their *gorditas* by hand into rounded ovals, which does take a little extra skill; I've opted for round ones made with a tortilla press.

Please note that the recipe calls for a chunk of plantain at the last stage of ripeness, black and thoroughly softened. If you have to use one that is still a little hard and starchy, soften it as follows: Increase the amount of milk to $1/2$ cup and simmer the sliced plantain in the milk in a small saucepan for about 15 minutes. Let cool and proceed as directed below.

Makes about 12 *gorditas*

$1/4$ large ripe plantain, peeled (see page 60) and cut into $1/4$-inch slices

$1/4$ cup milk

1 pound masa, fresh or reconstituted by mixing 2 cups masa harina with about 1 cup plus 2 tablespoons warm water (see page 51)

$1/4$–$1/2$ cup all-purpose flour, or more as necessary

$1/2$–$3/4$ teaspoon salt, or to taste

Vegetable oil for frying

THE *V*ERACRUZAN *C*ORN *K*ITCHEN

PUREE the plantain with the milk in a blender. In a medium mixing bowl, combine the mixture with the masa, $1/4$ cup of the flour, and $1/2$ teaspoon of the salt. With your hands, mix the ingredients into a dough, working in more flour $1/2$ tablespoon at a time just until it has a smooth, somewhat pliable but firm consistency. Taste for salt and work in a little more if desired.

SHAPE the dough into about 12 balls the size of Ping-Pong balls and keep them covered with a damp cloth as you work. Following the directions on page 115, press out each ball of dough into a 5-inch round, and place on baking sheets lined with parchment or waxed paper.

POUR oil into a deep-fryer or deep, heavy skillet to a depth of $1-1^1/2$ inches and heat over medium-high heat to 375°F, or until a morsel of dough sizzles on contact. Have ready a large cooking spoon and a skimmer or slotted spatula. Line a large baking sheet with paper towels. Slip the *gorditas* into the oil one at a time. They will sink to the bottom at first, then come to the top. As the *gordita* rises to the surface, start flicking spoonfuls of the oil over it to make it puff evenly. Fry, without turning, for 20–25 seconds; it should be no darker than lightly golden. Turn and fry for 10–15 seconds more. At once lift out with the skimmer, letting as much oil as possible drain back into the pot and set on the prepared baking sheet. Watch the temperature carefully as you work, and adjust the heat as necessary to maintain the oil at 375°F.

IT'S impossible to predict just how long it will take a *gordita inflada* to deflate. But they will be at their tenderest and most irresistible if eaten hot, hot, hot, as they come out of the pan.

VARIATIONS

For *Gorditas Dulces* (Sweet Gorditas), add $2/3$ cup very finely grated *piloncillo* (Mexican brown loaf sugar; see page 70) to the plantain mixture along with the masa, flour, and salt. (You can substitute $2/3$ cup packed brown sugar, but the *piloncillo* has a more complex and delicate flavor.) For *Gorditas de Anís* (Anise-Flavored Gorditas), add 1 tablespoon lightly bruised aniseed along with the *piloncillo*. The fragrance is exquisite.

Gorditas de Frijol

FRIED PUFFED TORTILLAS
WITH BLACK BEANS

*T*HIS VERSION OF *GORDITAS INFLADAS*, FROM TOMASITA
Meléndez at Brisas del Mar in Boca del Río, has beans mixed into the
dough. The flavor is close to that of the *gorditas* on page 133, but a little earthier, and the color is dusky from the black beans. If you can
make up a batch of each kind at the same time, they make a delightful picture together on a plate.

Makes about 12 *gorditas*

1 cup Semicooked Black Beans (page
      284), very well drained
1/4 large ripe plantain, peeled (see page 60)
      and cut into 1/4-inch slices
1/4 cup milk
1 pound masa, fresh or reconstituted by mixing 2 cups masa
      harina with about 1 cup plus 2 tablespoons warm water (see
      page 51)
1/4–1/2 cup all-purpose flour, or more as necessary
1/2–3/4 teaspoon salt
      Vegetable oil for frying

PLACE the beans in a food processor and process to a coarse
puree. Add the plantain and milk; process until smooth but not
gluey.

IN a medium mixing bowl, combine the bean mixture with the
masa, 1/4 cup of the flour, and 1/2 teaspoon of the salt. With your
hands, mix the ingredients into a dough, working in more flour 1/2
tablespoon at a time just until it has a smooth, somewhat pliable but
firm consistency. Taste for salt and work in a little more if desired.

SHAPE into about 12 Ping-Pong-sized balls, press out, and fry
following the instructions on page 134. Serve hot.

Empanadas de Champiñones

MUSHROOM EMPANADAS

THIS RECIPE WAS GIVEN TO ME BY CARMEN RIVERA DÍAZ in Papantla, but I have had very similar versions of the dish elsewhere. It is popular in all the high-rainfall areas where mushrooms flourish. It is quite good made with *champiñones* (cultivated white mushrooms), even better with the many varieties of wild mushrooms that are gathered locally. Feel free to substitute any preferred kind of mushroom.

This is one dough that I generally make with masa harina rather than fresh masa, because it's easier to incorporate with the wheat flour.

Makes 12–14 empanadas

FOR THE FILLING

- 1 pound cultivated white mushrooms
- 2 tablespoons vegetable oil
- 1 small white onion, finely chopped
- 2 garlic cloves, finely chopped
- 1 large poblano chile, roasted, peeled, and seeded following the directions on page 58, finely chopped
- 4 large epazote sprigs, leaves only, finely chopped, or 1 tablespoon crumbled dried epazote (see page 41) or 6–8 cilantro sprigs
- 1½ teaspoons salt, or to taste
- Freshly ground black pepper
- 4 ounces *queso blanco* (see page 67), finely diced

FOR THE DOUGH

- 2 cups masa harina (see page 51)
- ½ cup all-purpose flour
- 2 tablespoons lard, preferably home-rendered (see page 66)
- 1 teaspoon salt, or to taste
- Approximately 1 cup warm water

- Vegetable oil for frying
- Ranch-Style Red Sauce (page 318), She-Man Sauce (page 310), or any light, simple salsa

WIPE the mushrooms clean with a damp cloth. Trim the stems even with the base of the caps (reserve the stems for another purpose). With a large heavy knife, chop the mushroom caps very fine.

IN a large skillet, heat the oil over medium-high heat until rippling. Add the onion and garlic and cook, stirring occasionally, until the onion is translucent, about 3 minutes. Add the chile and epazote or cilantro; cook, stirring occasionally, for another 2 minutes. Stir in the mushrooms, salt, and a generous grinding of pepper. Cook, stirring occasionally, until the mushroom juices have evaporated, 10–12 minutes. Remove from the heat and let cool to room temperature, then stir in the diced cheese. Set aside while you make the dough.

FOR THE DOUGH

PLACE the masa harina, flour, lard, and salt in a large bowl and add the warm water (it may take slightly more). With a wooden spoon or your hands, mix the ingredients to form a smooth, pliable dough.

LINE a baking sheet with parchment or waxed paper. Shape the dough into 12–14 balls the size of Ping-Pong balls. Following the directions for tortillas on page 115, press them into 4-inch rounds. Place 2 tablespoons of the mushroom filling in the center of each round, fold into a turnover shape, and press the edges together to seal well. As they are done, place on the prepared baking sheet and cover with a damp cloth until you are ready to cook. They can sit, covered, for 2–4 hours.

POUR vegetable oil into a medium deep skillet to a depth of about 1 inch and heat to 375°F over medium-high heat. Fry the empanadas 3–4 at a time, allowing about 1 minute per side. Lift out onto paper towels as they are done. Serve hot with the chosen sauce.

VARIATIONS

This is one of the best empanada recipes I know when made with mushrooms, but don't stop there! Almost any shredded or hashed meat, poultry, or seafood mixture — for example, Pork Picadillo (page 104), Chicken Picadillo (page 104), or Hashed Seafood Mélange (page 86) — will make an excellent filling.

Tamal de Cazuela

"POT TAMAL" WITHOUT A WRAPPING

Makes 8–10 servings

CUBANS HAVE THEIR BELOVED *TAMAL EN CAZUELA*, A cross between a savory stovetop corn pudding and a polenta, with aromatic seasonings (tomato, onion, green pepper) and chunks of braised pork. Veracruzans have this near relative that must go back to kindred roots in African slave kitchens.

The Veracruzan *tamal de cazuela* has almost the same ingredients as the Cuban one. It is made sometimes as a stovetop dish, sometimes as a baked casserole. Sometimes the meat — usually either pork or chicken — is cooked separately in its sauce and served as a topping for the corn mixture. I like to think of the dish as the original tamale pie.

The recipe here is a composite version based on several that I've eaten and enjoyed in different parts of the state. I especially like the anise-like fragrance of the *hoja santa*, the only strong accent in a rather gently seasoned dish. Don't be puzzled by the range in the suggested amount of pork or chicken stock; I like to soak the chiles and reconstitute the masa harina in stock rather than water, but I know some cooks will prefer all or part water, despite the loss of flavor. I often fill this tamal with Chile-Braised Spareribs from the Huasteca (page 238) instead of the Shredded Cooked Pork.

2	ounces ancho chiles (about 6 large chiles), stemmed and seeded
8–9	cups Basic Pork Stock, Chicken Stock (page 144 or 142), or water
2	garlic cloves, coarsely chopped
1¹/₂	cups lard, preferably home-rendered (see page 66)
2	jalapeño chiles
3	medium-sized ripe tomatoes (about 1 pound)
6	cups Shredded Cooked Pork (page 144)
2	pounds fresh masa or 4 cups masa harina (see page 51)
2–3	teaspoons salt, or to taste
6	large or 12 small fresh *hoja santa* leaves or 12 dried leaves (see page 42)

RINSE and griddle-dry the ancho chiles following the directions on page 50. Meanwhile, bring 2 cups of the stock or water to a boil.

Place the chiles in a deep bowl, cover with boiling stock or water, and let sit for 20 minutes. Drain the chiles and puree in a blender with the garlic and enough additional stock or water to help the action of the blades (¹/₄–¹/₂ cup).

IN a medium saucepan, heat 2 tablespoons of the lard over medium heat until rippling. Add the chile mixture (set the blender container aside), reduce the heat to low, and cook, covered, for 5 minutes, stirring frequently. Remove from the heat and set the pan aside.

PLACE the jalapeño chiles and tomatoes in a small saucepan, cover with boiling water, and cook over medium heat for 10 minutes. Drain and let sit until cool enough to handle.

PEEL the jalapeños and tomatoes. Puree in the blender and add to the chile mixture in the pan. Cover and cook, stirring occasionally, over medium-high heat until the fat starts to separate, about 15 minutes. Remove from the heat, stir in the shredded pork, and set aside.

PLACE the masa in a large mixing bowl and combine as smoothly as possible with 6 cups of the stock or water (warm or at room temperature), working the mixture with your hands to break up the masa. With a wooden spoon or pusher, force the mixture through a medium-mesh strainer into a large heavy saucepan.

MELT the remaining lard and stir into the masa mixture, along with the salt. Cook over low heat, stirring constantly to prevent sticking or lumping, for 10–12 minutes. The mixture should have a smooth sheen and be thick enough to start coming away from the pan, and you should see a hint of a thin crust starting to form on the bottom. Remove from the heat and let sit until just cool enough to handle. (If allowed to cool completely, it will thicken into a jelled mass that's hard to spread.)

PREHEAT the oven to 350°F.

ARRANGE half of the *hoja santa* on the bottom of a 13-x-9-inch Pyrex baking dish or other shallow 4-quart baking dish. Spread half of the warm masa over the *hoja santa*. Pour the meat mixture over this and top with the remaining masa and *hoja santa*. (The tamal can be assembled ahead of time and refrigerated for up to 1 day before baking; let stand at room temperature for 15–20 minutes before it goes in the oven.)

COVER the dish with aluminum foil and bake for 20 minutes. Remove the foil and bake until the top is lightly browned, about another 5 minutes. Scoop out portions onto individual plates and serve.

*I*N MY EXPERIENCE OF MEXICAN CUISINE, I've never seen any place that rivals the wide-ranging Veracruzan repertory of soups. Pre-Hispanic Mexico had a wealth of soupy dishes that resembled sauces or stews and were eaten as important meals in their own right. Many of these soup-stews were based on fish or seafood. Many involved vegetables and/or corn masa—sometimes as a thickener, sometimes in the form of indented dumplings hardly larger than gnocchi. Some were fiery with chiles or fragrant with herbs. Veracruz never lost this extraordinary heritage. To the Spanish, the idea of soup-stews would not have been entirely strange, and the Spanish influence may have been one reason that they persisted in Veracruz.

They are not limited to any one part of the state, although a par-

ticular name will sometimes have an association with a particular region. *Chileatole, chilpachole, tesmole,* and *huatape* are some of the most important names, but the soup-stew family can't be reduced to a few simple labels. You will find examples not only here but throughout the fish, poultry, and meat chapters. When planning a menu, think of these soup-stews as main dishes.

But other types of soups have thrived here as well. There are soups that anyone in the state would call *moles,* because they involve ingredients ground or crushed to a paste. Then there are the many varieties based on European-style stocks and broths—not only the chicken and pork stocks used throughout Mexico but fish and shellfish stocks as well. Veracruzans are emphatic about the importance of good seafood stocks.

On top of all this, they adore *cremas,* or cream soups, which are a usual first course in restaurants serving a daily *comida corrida* (blue plate lunch special). These are delicate European-style pureed soups based on some chosen vegetable. Most are creamy in the sense of smooth and silky rather than cream-enriched, and they can be as varied as the season's vegetables. They are among the easiest Veracruzan dishes to prepare and also among the most elegant in their pure simplicity.

Caldo de Pollo/Pollo Cocido

BASIC CHICKEN STOCK/ SHREDDED COOKED CHICKEN

Makes 8–9 cups stock, 3 cups shredded cooked chicken

Why do Mexican recipes so often involve home-made chicken or pork stock? Believe me, it's not because people go in for elaborate, time-consuming *fonds de cuisine*. The true reason is that the preferred everyday cooking method for chicken or pork — the two basic meats — is boiling. (All right, "poaching," if that sounds better.) This means that cooks are often able to dip out a few ladlefuls from a pot with a chicken-in-progress and apply it to some other purpose, like thinning a *mole*.

I use stock more liberally than most people in Mexico because I'm always seeking to compensate for the dullness of much of the produce here. Good stock isn't exactly a substitute for wonderful tomatoes, onions with the edge of freshness still on them, or really luscious beans. But it can add depth and dimension when the basic ingredients are a little insipid.

My vegetarian readers will notice many recipes in which chicken stock is the only nonvegetarian ingredient; I've indicated where they can substitute water and still have a flavorful dish. Note that the timing is for a usual supermarket chicken. If you are lucky enough to come by a free-range chicken, it will take somewhat longer to cook but give the stock much more flavor. This recipe can easily be doubled (the degreased stock freezes well). If cooked chicken meat isn't part of your plans, you can substitute 4 to 5 pounds chicken backs, wings, and necks for the whole chicken, though the flavor won't be quite as good.

1	3¹/₂-to-4-pound chicken, whole or quartered
1	medium onion, unpeeled
3	garlic cloves, unpeeled
1	carrot, unpeeled, well scrubbed
2	bay leaves
1	teaspoon black peppercorns, bruised
1	teaspoon salt, or to taste
10–12	cups cold water

PLACE all the ingredients in a small stockpot or large deep saucepan. Add enough water to cover the chicken and bring to a boil over high heat. Reduce the heat to maintain a low rolling boil; skim off the froth that rises to the surface. Cook, partly covered, until the meat is just tender, 30–35 minutes.

LIFT out the chicken, letting it drain well, and set aside to cool. Strain the stock through a fine-mesh sieve and set aside to cool; discard the solids.

WHEN the chicken is cool enough to handle, remove and discard the skin. Carefully pull the meat from the bones, discarding any fat or gristle. Pull the meat into fine shreds. It will keep in the refrigerator, tightly covered, for 3–4 days.

WHEN the stock has cooled to room temperature, refrigerate for at least 1 hour, or until the fat can easily be skimmed off. It will keep, tightly covered, for 4–5 days in the refrigerator or up to 6 months in the freezer.

VARIATION

For *Caldo de Pollo Sazonado* (Seasoned Chicken Stock), prepare the stock through the stage of removing the fat. In a medium saucepan, slowly bring the stock to a boil over medium-low heat. Meanwhile, heat 2 tablespoons lard or vegetable oil in a medium skillet over medium-high heat. Add 1 cup chopped white onion and 1 minced garlic clove and cook, stirring occasionally, until the onion is translucent, about 3 minutes. Add 1 large ripe tomato, chopped, and cook for 3 minutes longer.

ADD the sautéed mixture to the hot stock, reduce the heat to low, and cook, uncovered, for 10 minutes to marry the flavors. Strain through a fine-mesh sieve, discarding the solids.

Caldo de Puerco/Carne de Puerco Cocida

BASIC PORK STOCK/
SHREDDED COOKED PORK

*T*HIS SIMPLE STOCK CAN BE USED FOR SOME OF THE SAME purposes as Basic Chicken Stock, but the flavor is more distinctive and does not blend into other dishes as flexibly. The recipe can easily be doubled and any surplus stock frozen.

If you have no need for the cooked pork butt, you can use pork bones instead. I suggest a combination of pork neck bones and meaty spareribs, in about a 2:1 ratio. For a stock with more body, add 1 or 2 fresh pork hocks as well.

Makes 8–9 cups stock,
3–4 cups shredded
cooked pork

3 pounds bone-in pork shoulder butt,
 trimmed of all but a thin layer of fat
1 head garlic, unpeeled, cut in half crosswise
1 teaspoon black peppercorns, bruised
4 bay leaves
1 teaspoon salt, or to taste
10–12 cups cold water

PLACE all the ingredients in a small stockpot or large deep saucepan. Add enough water to cover the meat well and bring to a boil over high heat. Reduce the heat to maintain a low rolling boil; skim off any froth that rises to the surface. Cook, partly covered, until the meat is tender, 2–2¹/₂ hours.

LIFT out the pork, letting it drain well, and set aside to cool. Strain the stock through a fine-mesh sieve and set aside to cool; discard the solids.

WHEN the meat is cool enough to handle, remove and discard any visible fat. Pull the meat from the bones and tear it into long shreds. It will keep, tightly covered, in the refrigerator for 3–4 days.

WHEN the stock has cooled to room temperature, refrigerate for at least an hour, or until the solidified fat can easily be removed. It will keep, tightly covered, for 4–5 days in the refrigerator or up to 6 months in the freezer.

Caldo Sencillo de Pescado

BASIC FISH STOCK

Makes 7–8 cups

I DO NOT COME FROM SEAFOOD COUNTRY. ALTHOUGH dishes based on homemade chicken stock and pork stock have always been integral to my idea of good Mexican cooking, somehow the same hasn't held true of fish stock. But in the seafood paradise of Veracruz, I soon realized that seafood stocks were crucial in many dishes. They're the quickest to make of any stock and can be as flexible as you like—at the bare minimum, a bunch of fresh fish trimmings and an onion and a little water. Use the following formula as a rough rather than strict guide. If you leave out a carrot or a seasoning or throw all the ingredients together in the pot instead of sautéing them, you'll still have a respectable stock. A dash of white wine or lime juice is all to the good. So are a few shrimp or crab shells. The only two absolutes are that the fish must be totally fresh, with the gills and all traces of blood scrupulously removed, and that you must choose varieties with lean white flesh, such as red snapper, sea bass, cod, whiting, flounder, Pacific rockfish, halibut—*never* strong-flavored fish like salmon or mackerel. Fish heads are especially prized for adding body and flavor.

2–3 pounds cleaned fish frames and/or heads, with any available scraps and trimmings

1–2 tablespoons olive oil, vegetable oil, or butter

2 medium-sized white onions, coarsely chopped

2 garlic cloves, coarsely chopped

1–2 medium carrots, scrubbed and coarsely chopped

1 large or 2–3 medium-sized ripe tomatoes, coarsely chopped

6–8 black peppercorns, lightly bruised

1 teaspoon salt, or to taste

3–4 parsley sprigs

3–4 cilantro sprigs

3–4 fresh thyme sprigs or 1/2 teaspoon crumbled dried thyme (optional)

1–2 bay leaves

8 cups water

BREAK or chop the fish frames into pieces that will fit comfortably into the pot used for the stock. Large fish heads will cook better and faster if whacked in half by the fishmonger (desirable but not necessary). Set aside.

IN a small stockpot or large saucepan, heat the oil or butter over medium-high heat until fragrant. Add the fish bones and cook, stirring and tossing constantly, until any visible flesh is opaque, 3–4 minutes. Add the onions, garlic, and carrots, stirring and tossing to distribute the ingredients, then cook for 5–8 minutes, or until the onion is translucent and the carrots somewhat softened.

STIR in the tomatoes, peppercorns, salt, and herbs. Add the water and bring to a boil. Reduce the heat to medium-low and cook, covered, for 20–25 minutes, or until the vegetables are thoroughly cooked. (Longer cooking doesn't improve a fish stock.) Strain through a fine-mesh sieve; discard the solids. Let cool. Store the stock in the refrigerator, tightly covered, for up to 3 days or in the freezer for up to 3 months.

Caldo de Pescado

FISH SOUP

Makes 4 servings
as a first course

*I*N VERACRUZ, THIS SOUP WOULD BE MADE WITH *ROBALO* —snook, a versatile white-fleshed fish that unfortunately doesn't show up often north of Florida. The best substitute here is a 2-to-3-pound red snapper, sea bass, Pacific rockfish, or any mild, firm-fleshed fish in the same size range. Or you could use steaks from a larger fish like halibut.

Caldo de robalo is a specialty at the Restorán Doña Daría in Zempoala. There they use a whole fish and cook it in just water. The resulting broth is delicious, but when I make this at home, I like to use steaks and make the broth with fish stock.

3 large ripe tomatoes, coarsely chopped

1 garlic clove, coarsely chopped

2 tablespoons vegetable oil

1 medium-sized white onion, sliced into thin half-moons

1 2-to-3-pound fish (see above), cleaned and scaled, or four 6-to-8-ounce fish steaks

2 pickled jalapeño chiles, stemmed, seeded, and cut into thin slices

2 large fresh *hoja santa* leaves, cut into thin strips, or 4 dried leaves, crumbled (see page 42)

8 cups water or Basic Fish Stock (page 145)

1½ teaspoons salt, or to taste

PUREE the tomatoes and garlic in a blender or food processor.

IN a stockpot or other pot large enough to hold the fish, heat the oil over high heat until rippling. Add the sliced onion and cook, stirring occasionally, for 3 minutes, or until fragrant and translucent. Stir in the tomato mixture, reduce the heat to medium, and cook for 10 minutes, or until somewhat thickened, stirring occasionally.

ADD the whole fish or steaks, the pickled jalapeños, *hoja santa*, water or stock, and salt. Bring to a boil over high heat; adjust the heat to maintain a low rolling boil. Cook until the fish is just firm, about 10 minutes.

DIVIDE the fish among individual serving bowls, pour the broth over it, and serve at once.

Caldo Verde de Pescado con Tomatillos

FISH SOUP WITH GREEN HERBS AND TOMATILLOS

*I*N THIS ROBUST SOUP, THE SHARPNESS OF THE LIME JUICE and tomatillos is a wonderful counterpoint to the trio of herbs. The original at Brisas del Mar used the head of a big *robalo* to make the all-essential stock. This adds a lot of gelatin and flavor. Use a fish head if you can get one, but never from an oily variety like salmon or bluefish. You could substitute fresh tarragon for the *hoja santa*.

Makes 4 servings
as a main course

Juice of 2 limes
1¹/₂ teaspoons salt, or to taste
2 garlic cloves, minced
4 6-ounce fish steaks
8 medium tomatillos (about 12 ounces), husks removed, rinsed, and cut into quarters
2 jalapeño chiles, stemmed and coarsely chopped
10 large cilantro sprigs
3 large fresh epazote sprigs, leaves only, or 1 tablespoon crumbled dried epazote (see page 41)
6 fresh *hoja santa* leaves or 8 dried leaves, crumbled (see page 42)
About 1 cup water
2 tablespoons butter
8 cups Basic Fish Stock (page 145)

COMBINE the lime juice, salt, and garlic in a large bowl. Add the fish steaks, turning them to coat well with the mixture. Let sit while you prepare the ingredients for the stock enrichment.

PLACE the tomatillos, chiles, cilantro, epazote, and 5 of the fresh *hoja santa* leaves (6 if dried) in a blender and add just enough water to facilitate blending. Process to a smooth paste.

IN a large saucepan or Dutch oven, heat the butter over medium heat until bubbling. Add the tomatillo puree and cook for 3 minutes, stirring occasionally. Add the stock and bring to a boil over high heat; adjust the heat to maintain a low rolling boil and cook, uncovered, for about 5 minutes.

ADD the fish and cook for 7–10 minutes, or until just opaque (the Mexican preference would be until the fish is almost falling apart).

WHILE the fish is cooking, puree the remaining *hoja santa* in the blender with a little water or some of the cooking liquid. Just before serving, add to the pot and cook for another minute or two. Place the fish steaks in individual serving bowls and pour the soup over them.

Chilpachole de Camarón

SPICY SHRIMP STEW

*M*Y RESEARCH TRIPS TO VERACRUZ HAVE BEEN MADE immeasurably more productive by Victor Agustín Benítez, who must be one of the world's most knowledgeable guides. Victor is a man of great sensibilities—which extend to his cooking. This recipe is my version of *his* version of a Veracruz soup-stew that is made with either ocean shrimp or the excellent crabs of the region. Some versions, like this, are enriched with little dumplings (*bolitas*) of masa floating in the broth. In others, the soup is simply thickened with some masa or crushed corn tortillas. Cilantro (about 8 sprigs) may be used in place of the epazote, if you must, but the effect won't be the same.

Makes 4–6 servings as a first course, 2–3 servings as a main course

1 recipe Corn Masa Dumplings (page 131)
2 large ripe tomatoes, peeled
1/2 small white onion, coarsely chopped
2 garlic cloves, coarsely chopped
2 tablespoons olive oil
8 cups water
2 teaspoons salt, or to taste
1 1/2 pounds extra-large shrimp (sold as 14–16 count) in the shell, preferably with heads on
1–2 tablespoons Chipotle Chile Paste (page 306)
2 large fresh epazote sprigs, leaves only, or 1 tablespoon crumbled dried epazote (see page 41)
Lime wedges for garnish

SET the dumplings aside, covered with a damp towel, while you prepare the stew.

PUREE the tomatoes, onion, and garlic in a blender.

IN a stockpot or a large saucepan, heat the olive oil over medium-high heat until fragrant. Add the tomato mixture and cook, uncovered, stirring frequently, for about 15 minutes, or until slightly reduced and concentrated.

WHILE the mixture cooks, bring the water, salted to taste, to a boil in a large saucepan. Add the shrimp and cook over high heat just until they change color, 2–3 minutes. Quickly lift out with a slotted spoon and set aside in a bowl. (You can shell the cooked shrimp if you want, but this wouldn't be done in Veracruz.)

STRAIN the hot cooking liquid into the tomato mixture; add the chipotle paste and cook, uncovered, for 15 minutes. Add the epazote and the dumplings; reduce the heat slightly and cook until they float to the surface, about 3 minutes. Add the shrimp and cook for 1–2 minutes longer, or just until heated through.

SERVE with lime wedges.

Chileatole Verde

GREEN CHILEATOLE

*T*HIS VEGETABLE SOUP FROM MARÍA DEL CARMEN Virués de Izaguirre, one of the best cooks in Xico, is thickened with a medley of pureed greens and aromatics with sesame seeds. Doña Carmen uses all kinds of greens or vegetables, depending on what's in the market. I suggest that you do likewise. I've sometimes used tarragon for the *hoja santa* and replaced the chayotes or zucchini with other vegetables. Try corn kernels, green beans, peas — any firm-textured vegetable that looks inviting. Young fava beans are a standard addition (you can substitute fresh or frozen young lima beans). If using fava beans, shell them and blanch them in boiling water for 1 minute, then plunge the drained beans into an ice-water bath. The skins will slip off easily.

The soup is fatless (except for the natural oil in the sesame) and meatless if you use water rather than stock. I tend to prefer the latter. Doña Carmen sometimes cooks pork, beef, or chicken for the same meal and uses a little of the cooking stock to puree the sesame seeds and greens.

Makes 4–6 servings
as a main course

2	ounces ($1/2$ cup) sesame seeds, lightly toasted (see page 64)
2	fresh *hoja santa* leaves (see page 42), or 1 small bunch tarragon
40	cilantro sprigs (1 large bunch)
20	Italian parsley sprigs ($1/2$ bunch)
6	fresh epazote sprigs, leaves only, or 3 tablespoons crumbled dried epazote (see page 41)
1	bunch spinach, trimmed, rinsed in several changes of water, and shaken dry
3–4	jalapeño chiles, stemmed, seeded, and cut into quarters
2	large tomatillos, husks removed, rinsed, and quartered
$1/2$	small white onion, coarsely chopped
2	garlic cloves, coarsely chopped
4	cups water, Basic Chicken Stock (page 142), or any preferred stock (see above)
$1^{1}/2$–2	teaspoons salt

3 chayotes, peeled and pitted (see page 55), cut lengthwise into eighths

1 cup (about 8 ounces) young fava beans or fresh or frozen lima beans, skins removed (see headnote, page 153)

3 medium zucchini, cut into 2-inch lengths

PLACE the sesame seeds in the blender with a little water and process until they are pasty. Working in batches as necessary, add the *hoja santa* or tarragon, cilantro, parsley, epazote, spinach, tomatillos, chiles, onion, and garlic and process to a smooth puree, using about 2 cups in all of the water or stock to facilitate blending. Pour each batch as it is done into a stockpot or medium-large Dutch oven. Rinse out the blender with the remaining 2 cups water or stock and add the contents to the pot.

BRING to a boil over high heat. Add the salt, a little at a time, tasting until it is to your liking. Add the chayotes, beans, and zucchini and cook, uncovered, for 10 minutes. Serve immediately.

Chileatole de Pollo

CHICKEN CHILEATOLE

CHILEATOLE IS ONE OF THOSE UNTRANSLATABLE Mexican terms like enchilada or tamal. In the central Gulf coast states, including Veracruz, *chileatoles* are usually soup-stews made with a masa thickening and either fresh or dried chiles. Probably the most delicious ones I've tasted have come from the mountain-foothill towns of inland Veracruz. Often they're made with assorted fresh vegetables; sometimes little masa dumplings (*bolitas*) are added in place of a masa thickening.

This is a version I tasted at the home of Raquel Torres, an anthropologist and the owner of the popular *cenaduría* (a restaurant specializing in homey supper dishes) La Churrería del Recuerdo, in Xalapa.

Makes 4 servings
as a main course

1 recipe Corn Masa Dumplings (page 131)
2 large ripe tomatoes
2 ancho chiles
1/2 small white onion, coarsely chopped
2 garlic cloves, coarsely chopped
3 tablespoons lard, preferably home-rendered (see page 66), or vegetable oil
1 3 1/2-to-4-pound chicken, cut into 8 pieces
1 1/2–2 teaspoons salt
1/2 teaspoon black peppercorns
About 8 cups water
2 large ears corn (preferably not a super-sweet variety), kernels stripped from cobs (2–2 1/2 cups), or one 10-ounce package frozen shoepeg corn
2 large chayotes, peeled and pitted (see page 55), cut lengthwise into quarters
3 large epazote sprigs or 1–2 tablespoons dried epazote (see page 41) or 8–10 cilantro sprigs

SET the dumplings aside, covered with a damp towel, while you prepare the remaining ingredients.

PLACE the tomatoes in a small saucepan with hot water to cover, bring to a low rolling boil, and cook for 8–10 minutes. Lift out and set aside to cool. Add the chiles to the pan and cook for 5 minutes; lift out and set aside.

WHEN the tomatoes are cool enough to handle, puree them in a blender with the onion, garlic, and chiles. With a wooden spoon or pusher, force the mixture through a medium-mesh sieve into a bowl.

IN a medium saucepan, heat the lard or oil over medium heat until rippling. Add the tomato mixture and cook for 15–20 minutes, stirring occasionally.

MEANWHILE, place the chicken in a stockpot or large saucepan with the salt, peppercorns, and 8 cups water, or enough to cover by 2 inches. Bring to a boil over high heat; quickly reduce the heat to maintain a low rolling boil and skim off any froth that rises to the top. Cook, partly covered, for about 15 minutes.

POUR the tomato-chile mixture into the pot with the chicken. Add the corn kernels, chayotes, and epazote or cilantro and cook, uncovered, for 10 minutes.

ADD the dumplings and cook for 3–4 minutes, or until they float to the surface. Serve hot.

Caldo de Pollo con Fideos

SANTA MARÍA'S CHICKEN SOUP WITH NOODLES

I LOVED THE BROTHY SOUP WITH PILAF-STYLE NOODLES (you brown them in hot oil before cooking them in the broth) that I grew up with in northern Mexico. So I was delighted to find a closely related dish from the Huasteca region of northeastern Veracruz. Santa María de Guadalupe Armenta Guzmán—"Lupita" among friends, Santa María on formal occasions—tells me that this soup is a special ceremonial dish often served at wakes or prayer vigils among local ranch families. Lupita suggests serving the soup with small freshly made tortillas and, if desired, Refried Beans with Butter (page 285). It's also sometimes made with rice instead of pasta. The ancho chiles give the soup great depth of flavor, but it also has the freshness of mint. Look for the nested thin noodles sold as *fideos* in Latin American neighborhoods or *fedelini* in Italian ones. Vermicelli also works well in this dish.

Makes 6–8 servings as a first course

- 1 3½-to-4-pound chicken, cut into quarters
- 2 small white onions, 1 unpeeled
- 6 garlic cloves, 2 unpeeled
- 1½–2 teaspoons salt
- 10 black peppercorns
- 15 mint sprigs (1 small bunch)
- 7–8 cups water
- 3 ancho chiles, stemmed and seeded
- ¼ cup vegetable oil
- 1 10-ounce package *fideos* (nested thin noodles; see above), or about 8 ounces vermicelli
- Freshly ground black pepper (optional)

PLACE the chicken in a stockpot or Dutch oven with the unpeeled onion, the 2 unpeeled garlic cloves, 1 teaspoon salt, the peppercorns, and 3 sprigs of the mint. Add enough water to cover by 2 inches and bring to a boil over high heat. At once reduce the heat to maintain a low rolling boil; skim off any froth that rises to the top. Cook, partly covered, until the chicken is tender, 20–25 minutes. Remove the pot from the heat and let the chicken cool in the stock.

LIFT out the chicken pieces. Discard the skin, remove the meat from the bones, and cut it into bite-sized pieces. Strain the stock into a bowl, discarding the solids. Rinse out and dry the pot.

PLACE the chiles in a small bowl and cover with 2 cups of the hot stock. Let sit for 20 minutes. Transfer the chiles and soaking liquid to a blender and puree with the remaining onion and 4 garlic cloves.

ADD the oil to the clean stockpot and heat over medium-high heat until rippling. Add the nests of *fideos* and brown lightly on both sides; if using vermicelli, stir-fry until lightly browned. Lift out with a slotted spoon and drain on paper towels.

POUR off all but a thin film of the oil from the pot. Add the pureed chile mixture, reduce the heat to low, and cook for 10 minutes, stirring frequently. Add the chicken, fried noodles, and the remaining stock. Bring to a boil and taste for salt, adding a little if it seems flat. Cook over low heat until the noodles are al dente, 5–7 minutes.

MEANWHILE, chop the remaining mint. Add most of the mint to the soup; serve immediately, with a sprinkling of the remaining mint and, if desired, a few grindings of black pepper.

Crema de Palmitos

PUREED HEARTS OF PALM SOUP

Makes 6 servings
as a first course

MOST RESTAURANTS IN VERACRUZ INCLUDE A SMOOTH pureed soup based on a vegetable (fresh corn, summer squash, leafy greens, or whatever) as part of the lunch special. Soups of this type — called *cremas* whether or not they actually contain cream — are incredibly simple (assuming you have a blender) and can be lovely vehicles for pure, direct vegetable flavor.

Crema de palmitos, a typical example, is made in Veracruz with the fresh hearts of young palm trunks. In the United States, we have to use *palmitos* put up in jars or cans, imported from (usually) Brazil or Costa Rica. Luckily, hearts of palm are one of the best canned products I know. This soup is delicious with or without cream. Taste it at the end of cooking, and if you crave a little extra suavity, stir in up to ¼ cup heavy cream.

3 bunches scallions (18–20 large scallions), trimmed, white and pale green parts separated

2 garlic cloves

2 tablespoons olive oil

1 28-ounce or two 14-ounce cans or jars hearts of palm, drained and coarsely chopped

6 cups chicken stock, preferably homemade (page 142)

FINELY chop the scallion whites and the garlic. You should have about 1 cup.

IN a large saucepan or Dutch oven, heat the oil over medium-high heat until rippling. Add the scallion whites and garlic and cook until wilted, about 3 minutes. Reduce the heat to medium, add the hearts of palm, and cook for about 8 minutes to mellow the flavors. Meanwhile, finely chop the scallion greens and set aside.

LET the garlic mixture cool slightly, then puree in a blender, using a little of the chicken stock if necessary to help the action of the blades. Return to the pan, stir in the rest of the stock, and bring to a boil. (The soup can be prepared and held for several hours at room temperature, or refrigerated overnight; return to a boil before serving.)

SERVE garnished with the scallion greens.

Sopa de Setas

MUSHROOM SOUP

Makes 6 servings
as a first course

LUNCH SPOTS IN MEXICO USUALLY HAVE A DIFFERENT fixed-price *comida corrida* every day. The phrase means "meal in courses" and refers to a menu that usually starts with a soup and also includes a pilaf-style rice or pasta, a stewed meat or chicken dish, dessert, and a beverage. The *comida corrida* at La Fuente, the restaurant of the Hotel Pluviosilla in Orizaba, has a devoted fan club and no wonder — the food is delicious and the entire meal costs 22 pesos (about $2.20). The first course is often a mushroom soup made with the season's pick of the wild mushrooms that grow everywhere in the cool, misty hills of the region. I tasted it with the kind locally called *setas*, which look like oyster mushrooms. In my New York kitchen, I've arrived at a version based on equal parts of shiitake and oyster mushrooms.

You can experiment with different combinations. Unless your mushrooms are absolutely riddled with grit and sand, wipe them clean with barely dampened paper towels rather than washing them — nothing is more discouraging than cooking waterlogged mushrooms. Epazote is the natural seasoning complement to mushrooms, but you can make do with cilantro in a pinch.

3 pasilla or mulato chiles (see page 50), stemmed and seeded

4 cups chicken stock, preferably homemade (page 142), heated

6 ounces streaky slab bacon, cut into fine dice (1/3–1/2 inch)

1 medium-sized white onion, finely chopped

3 garlic cloves, minced

1 pound mixed mushrooms (see above), cleaned and coarsely chopped

2 large fresh epazote sprigs or 1 tablespoon crumbled dried epazote (see page 41)

1/2 teaspoon salt, or to taste

RINSE and griddle-dry the chiles following the directions on page 50. Place in a medium bowl, cover with some of the hot chicken stock, and let stand for 20 minutes.

TRANSFER the chiles and the soaking liquid to a blender.

Process until smooth. With a wooden spoon or pusher, force the puree through a medium-mesh sieve into a bowl; set aside.

IN a medium skillet, fry the bacon over medium-high heat, stirring occasionally, until crisp and golden, 5–7 minutes. Scoop out the bacon with a slotted spoon and let drain on paper towels. Pour about 2 tablespoons of the bacon fat into a medium pot and discard the rest. Heat over medium-high heat until fragrant. Add the onion and garlic; cook, stirring occasionally, until the onion is translucent and light golden, about 5 minutes. Stir in the mushrooms and cook for 2–3 minutes to bring out and lightly concentrate their juices. Add the bacon and the chile puree, along with the remaining chicken stock and the epazote. Cook, uncovered, over medium-low heat for 20 minutes, or until the flavors are richly melded. It should be brothy, not thick. Add salt to taste and serve hot.

Caldo de Almendra

ALMOND SOUP

Makes 4–6 servings
as a first course

᠁

*H*ERE IS ONE OF THE MANY SOPHISTICATED AND DELICATE recipes that I was taught by María del Carmen Virués de Izaguirre, a proud cook of Xico whose family name has been practically synonymous with the town for more than a hundred and fifty years. I can never thank her enough for introducing me to Xico's rich culinary tradition.

If using ground almonds as a binder makes you think of old Moorish-Iberian influences, you're right. That's one original source of the popular Veracruzan soups thickened with nuts and (often) crushed stale bread. The Spanish almond tradition is very strong in Veracruz, but people might also use pine nuts or pecans for a soup like this. It makes a very rich first-course soup.

1	3¹/₂-to-4-pound chicken, cut into 8 serving pieces
1	medium-sized white onion, unpeeled
4	garlic cloves, unpeeled
2	teaspoons salt, or to taste
7–8	cups water
¹/₄	cup home-rendered lard (see page 66), or vegetable oil
¹/₂	cup (about 3 ounces) unblanched whole almonds
1	small French roll (3–4 ounces), cut into 4 slices, or 4 small slices good French or Italian bread
2	dried (*not* canned) chipotle chiles, preferably morita-type (see page 48)
2	large epazote sprigs (see page 41), leaves only, or 6 cilantro sprigs

PLACE the chicken, onion, garlic, and salt in a small pot or large deep saucepan and add enough water to cover by 2 inches. Bring to a boil over high heat, then reduce the heat to maintain a low rolling boil, skimming off any froth that rises to the top. Cook, partly covered, until the chicken is tender, 25–30 minutes. Lift the chicken pieces into a bowl. Strain the stock, discarding the onion and garlic; you should have 6–7 cups. Set aside. Wash and dry the stockpot.

IN a medium heavy skillet, heat the lard or oil over medium-high heat until rippling. Add the almonds, reduce the heat to medium, and fry, stirring constantly, for 8–10 minutes, or until browned but not scorched. Lift out with a slotted spoon and drain on paper towels. In the same skillet, fry the bread slices until golden, about 1 minute on each side. Lift out, drain in the same way, and let cool slightly. Set the skillet aside.

IN a food processor, grind the fried almonds and bread to a paste.

STRAIN the fat from the skillet into the clean stockpot and heat over medium heat. When the fat ripples, add the chiles and fry for 1 minute. Lift out and set aside. Add the almond-bread mixture and cook, stirring constantly, for about 5 minutes, or until golden brown. Stir in the reserved stock. Add the chiles, chicken pieces, and epazote or cilantro. Bring to a boil over high heat, adjust the heat to maintain a low rolling boil, and cook, uncovered, for 10 minutes, or until the chicken is heated through. Remove the chiles and serve immediately.

VARIATION

I sometimes like to float a stuffed chipotle chile in the soup. Follow the recipe for Stuffed "Neutered" Chipotle Chiles (page 102) up to stuffing the chiles, but omit the dredging with flour, batter coating, and frying. The sweet *picadillo* of the filling melds wonderfully with the pureed almonds, and the smokiness of the chipotles adds a haunting note.

$\mathcal{T}$HE LOVE OF SEAFOOD is one of Veracruz's important links with Spain.

The Spanish invaders were astonished by the wealth of fish and shellfish that they found in the province. Close offshore, there were ocean fish with sweet, tender flesh, such as snook, various Atlantic-Caribbean snappers, and *mojarra*, a group of fish somewhat resembling ocean perch or bass, as well as little anchovy-like fish. The coastal shallows, lagoons, and mangrove swamps contained other riches, including many kinds of crabs, shrimp, clams, and oysters. Deep-sea creatures like bonito, octopus, and squid could be fished in fantastic plenty almost within sight of the coast.

Then there were the rivers, creeks, and lakes. Because so much

FISH

AND

SEAFOOD

of Veracruz is waterland, it contains creatures well adapted to many different aquatic habitats. The conquerors found that many of the best ocean fish also flourished far inland in tidal rivers like the Papaloapan, effortlessly adjusting to different saltwater/freshwater balances and competing for food with neighbors like catfish. Some of the saltwater species spawned upstream and the fry could be fished up from riverbeds when still almost microscopic, while others that swam in to spawn could be taken for the sake of the roe. Different kinds of river shrimp, land crabs, and crayfish proved to be incredibly abundant during various seasons. Freshwater cichlids (relations of tilapia) filled Lake Catemaco, along with a succulent water snail called *tegogolo*. (Should you ever find yourself in the Catemaco area, every local restaurant serves *tegogolos* in a simple salsa as well as irresistible little crisp-fried fish called *topotes*, somewhere between the size of whitebait and small smelts.)

Before Cortés, the local people cooked their seafood in chile-based sauces or used it in a variety of chile-spiked soup-stews. To this day, similar dishes — with a few European touches — are passionately loved all over Veracruz state. The Indians had also perfected the technique of cooking fish in leaf wrappers, such as the aromatic *hoja santa*. For their part, the Spanish introduced all kinds of frying and sautéing to the New World. Among their gifts was the idea of a garlic-oil (or lard) combination applied to fish, sometimes with citrus juice as well. This concept was adopted by Africans and others in all the sugar colonies of the Hispanic Caribbean, from Cuba to Veracruz.

Salt cod from the North Atlantic became an important food in the African slave territories, because in many places it was almost the only thing approaching a meat ration that was regularly handed out to the plantation slaves.

Today you could live in Veracruz on nothing but fish or shellfish and still taste something different every day of the year. Perhaps the most unusual and characteristic dishes are the ones using seasoned seafood medleys—assorted shellfish, fish, and/or mollusks, shredded or cut up quite fine and put to many culinary uses. In Veracruz, almost any seafood mélange would include the clean-tasting, nutty oysters of the great Tamiahua lagoon far in the north. They have to be among the world's finest oysters—but also among the smallest, seldom much bigger than the first joint of a thumb. The only thing that comes close would be the prized Olympia oysters of the Pacific Northwest, which are rare and nearly unaffordable. So oysters (along with *tegogolos* and *topotes*) are among the specialties that I have regretfully omitted from my coverage of Veracruzan seafood cookery.

$\mathcal{A}$LL OF THE FOLLOWING RECIPES are Veracruzan classics in their own different ways, but I must single out two as probably the most famous seafood dishes of the entire state. Both have a pronounced Spanish character. *Torta de mariscos* takes the Spanish concept of the flat omelet (*tortilla*) and fills it chock-full of magnificent seafood. *Arroz a la tumbada* recalls the rice dishes of Spain's Levantine coast. It is a rich mélange of fish and seafood—the more kinds, the merrier—stirred into a rice dish that suggests both paella and risotto.

Torta de Mariscos

SEAFOOD FRITTATA

Makes 8 servings

*T*HIS WOULD HAVE TO BE CLOSE TO THE TOP OF ANY LIST of classic, peerless, sensational Veracruzan dishes. You find different versions everywhere, but it belongs mostly to the central-southern coast and waterways of Sotavento. The Veracruzan *torta de mariscos* consists of seafood and eggs combined and cooked in a skillet. There are three-inch versions, and others the size of large pies. There are some with a little seafood suspended in a lot of egg, and some that are nearly all seafood just barely bound together with an egg or two. The kind I like best is somewhere between a thick, tender pancake and a fluffy, moist flat omelet cooked until golden on all sides. It is best if the egg whites are beaten separately and then combined with the yolks, but I've had good versions where they weren't. It makes a brunch, lunch, or dinner dish with (or without) Ranch-Style Red Sauce (page 318) or Tomato Sauce with Chipotle Chiles (page 319).

Possibly the best *torta de mariscos* I ever tasted was at La Viuda restaurant in the fishing town of Alvarado. The quality of the fresh seafood was exquisite, and it was used so generously that the omelet was practically falling apart with shrimp, crabmeat, and tiny baby squid. The recipe is not an exact rendition of that lovely *torta*, but I've adopted a few of its special touches, like the combination of fresh herbs and the delicate binding of fine crumbs.

At La Viuda, the crumbs were *pan rallado*—"grated bread," fine bread crumbs rasped from a stale loaf using a grater. Because the crumbs packaged in supermarket containers are guaranteed to ruin anything they come in contact with, I suggest that you use finely crushed soda cracker crumbs—unless you are prepared to take good homemade bread crumbs seriously.

Like many Veracruzan seafood dishes, this one depends on a versatile mishmash of seafood cut up quite fine. Cooks automatically prepare a *relleno* (filling) or *salpicón* (hash) from the best ingredients on hand or the ones they feel like sampling at the moment. They might add tiny sweet oysters, hashed fish, or cooked diced conch or octopus. Play with the mixture as you like, but remember that it shouldn't be watery and that you want a total of 2–2½ pounds. You can start with cooked seafood instead of cooking it specifically for the *torta* as I do, but it must be very fresh and not at all overcooked.

Plan ahead for flipping the *torta* to brown on the second side. I use a 10-inch Calphalon omelet pan. It's easy to slide the omelet out onto a plate when the first side is done, then slide it back into the pan on the other side. You can use any brand of nonstick or well-seasoned skillet of this size, but it should have rounded, not straight, sides.

3	small white onions, 1 unpeeled
2	garlic cloves, unpeeled
5	bay leaves
1^{1}/$_{2}$–2	teaspoons salt, or to taste
8	cups water
1	pound shrimp (any size), in the shell
^{1}/$_{2}$	pound cleaned squid, cut into ^{1}/$_{4}$-inch dice (about 1 cup)
1	pound lump crabmeat, picked over to remove bits of shell or cartilage
2	large or 4–5 medium-sized ripe tomatoes (about 1 pound), peeled and seeded
2	jalapeño chiles, stemmed and seeded
15	Italian parsley sprigs (^{1}/$_{2}$ small bunch), leaves only
15	cilantro sprigs (^{1}/$_{2}$ bunch), leaves only
15	mint sprigs (^{1}/$_{2}$ small bunch), leaves only
6–8	oregano sprigs, leaves only
^{1}/$_{3}$–^{1}/$_{2}$	cup finely crushed soda cracker crumbs (such as Saltines) or best-quality fine dry bread crumbs from good French or Italian bread (no substitutes)
5	large eggs, separated
4	tablespoons olive oil

PLACE the unpeeled onion, garlic, bay leaves, 1 teaspoon of the salt, and water in a large saucepan. Bring to a boil over high heat; reduce the heat to maintain a low rolling boil and cook for 5 minutes. Add the shrimp and cook for 2–3 minutes (depending on their size), skimming off any froth that rises to the top. Quickly lift out the shrimp with a mesh skimmer or slotted spoon, letting them drain well, place in a bowl, and set aside to cool. Remove the onion and garlic from the stock and discard. Add the squid and cook for 1 minute. Drain in a colander, reserving the stock for another purpose (it would make a delicious fish soup).

PEEL and devein the shrimp. Coarsely chop and place in a large mixing bowl, along with the squid and crabmeat. Finely chop the remaining 2 onions, the tomatoes, jalapeños, and fresh herbs. Add to the bowl of seafood and toss to distribute the ingredients evenly. Sprinkle the cracker or bread crumbs and $1/2$–1 teaspoon salt over the mixture and toss very thoroughly.

IN a medium mixing bowl, beat the egg whites until they form glossy, not-quite-stiff peaks. Add the egg yolks, one at a time, beating well after each addition. With a rubber spatula, gently fold the eggs into the seafood mixture.

IN a medium (about 10-inch) heavy omelet pan or skillet (see above), heat the oil over medium-high heat until fragrant but not quite rippling. Reduce the heat to low. Pour or spoon the seafood mixture into the pan, smoothing it firmly with a spatula to spread it evenly without any air pockets on the bottom. Cook, uncovered, for 8 minutes, or until it is just set in the center. Flip the *torta* by sliding it out onto a pan lid or plate (see above) and slipping it back into the pan. (If necessary, loosen it first with a spatula, but I've never had a problem.) Cook for another 3 minutes, or until golden on the underside.

TRANSFER to a platter or large plate and serve hot, cut into wedges.

Niño Envuelto

"SWADDLED BABY" SEAFOOD OMELET

Makes 1 serving

I HAD NO IDEA WHAT TO EXPECT WHEN WE PICKED THIS dish from a menu at La Viuda restaurant in Alvarado. What they brought us was a folded omelet enclosing the restaurant's beautiful version of a seafood *relleno* (filling).

The dish has become a much-demanded favorite at my home in New York, but I've made one major readjustment. The original was a tender, moist 3- or 4-egg omelet meant to serve several people. I prefer to make it in individual servings, with 1/2–1 cup of any chosen filling wrapped in a very thin 1-egg omelet, with a good sprinkling of fresh chives.

1 large egg

1/2 teaspoon salt, or to taste

2 tablespoons minced fresh chives

1/2–1 tablespoon butter or vegetable oil

1/2 cup (for a first-course serving) or 1 cup (for a main-course serving) hot or warm Shrimp Filling (facing page)

Thin Tomato Sauce (page 317), Ranch-Style Red Sauce (page 318), or Tomato Sauce with Chipotle Chiles (page 319)

BEAT the egg in a small bowl with the salt and chives. (Alternatively, reserve the chives to sprinkle over the omelet in the pan.)

IN a 7-inch omelet pan (either nonstick or well-seasoned), heat the butter or oil over medium-high heat until very hot but not scorching. Add the egg, tilting the pan to let it flow over the bottom in a thin, even layer, like a crepe. Cook for 45 seconds to 1 minute, until set but barely browned on the bottom. Flip and cook the other side in the same way. Add the prepared seafood, quickly fold the sides of the omelet over the filling and slide it onto a plate.

SERVE with a well-flavored tomato sauce. I prefer to spread a little of the sauce over the plate and slide the omelet onto it, but you can top it with the sauce if you like.

Relleno de Camarón

SHRIMP FILLING

$\mathcal{A}$ RECIPE LIKE THIS IS REALLY AN INVITATION TO PLAY around. The choice of herbs and the amount of olives and pickled jalapeños, tomatoes, and seasonings are all up to your judgment. Are you planning to serve something else with a lot of olives, like Duck with the Curé's Sauce (page 221)? Then you may want to reduce or eliminate the olives from the *relleno*. Do you feel unenthusiastic about the lime-and-Worcestershire marinade? Leave it out. Would you prefer to use all olive oil instead of part vegetable oil? Go right ahead. Would you like to tone down the parsley, or combine it — maybe even replace it — with fresh mint and oregano? Great idea. Do bay scallops look good in your fish market? Substitute them for all or part of the shrimp. What we're talking about here is a basic method or approach, not a fixed recipe. This can be served hot as a first course or in omelets, or cold as a seafood salad or in tacos and empanadas.

Makes 3–4 cups

Juice of 2 limes
2 garlic cloves, minced
1 tablespoon Worcestershire sauce
1 teaspoon salt, or to taste
1 pound shrimp (any size), peeled and deveined
2 tablespoons olive oil
2 tablespoons vegetable oil
1 large white onion, finely chopped
5 large ripe tomatoes (about 2½ pounds), seeded and finely chopped
2 teaspoons Garlic Butter Enrichment (page 300)
1 cup finely chopped fresh Italian parsley
2 large thyme sprigs, leaves only
4 bay leaves
½ cup pimiento-stuffed green olives, finely chopped, plus 1–2 tablespoons of their brine
½ cup pickled jalapeño chiles, seeded and finely chopped, plus 1–2 tablespoons of their pickling juice

IN a medium mixing bowl, combine the lime juice, garlic, Worcestershire sauce, and 1 teaspoon salt. Add the shrimp, toss thoroughly, and let stand for 5 minutes. Drain, discarding the marinade. Chop the shrimp into bits no larger than 1/4 inch. Set aside.

IN a large skillet, heat the olive and vegetable oils over high heat. Add the onion and cook, stirring, for 1–2 minutes. Add the tomatoes, garlic butter, parsley, thyme, and bay leaves. Reduce the heat to medium and cook, stirring occasionally, for 15 minutes, or until the flavors are somewhat concentrated.

ADD the shrimp, olives, olive brine, jalapeños, and the pickling juice. Cook, stirring frequently, for 5 minutes, or until most of the liquid has evaporated. Taste for salt and add another pinch if desired. Remove the bay leaves. Serve hot as a first course or as an omelet filling; otherwise, let cool to room temperature before using. This will keep overnight, tightly covered, in the refrigerator, but I prefer to use it at once.

Arroz a la Tumbada

"THROW-IT-TOGETHER" RICE AND SEAFOOD

Makes 6–8 servings

THIS IS ONE OF THE FIRST VERACRUZAN DISHES I TASTED, a true classic that is made everywhere in the state. However, not every version is worth going across the street for. The real thing—said to have originated in the fishing village of Alvarado—is what you might get by crossing paella with risotto with a wonderful seafood soup. I suspect that the name may have originally referred to chucking in any tasty odds and ends of fish or shellfish from the day's catch. But you certainly do not just throw this together, though I tasted many disappointing examples where somebody had done exactly that with some already cooked rice, cooked (or overcooked) seafood, and fish stock. The first true *arroz a la tumbada* I encountered was at El Varadero, María Luisa Andrade's waterside restaurant in Boca del Río. What a difference! The rice had absorbed the good tomato and onion flavors before soaking up gradual additions of excellent fish stock and being finished at the last minute with the fresh seafood.

As with all great rice dishes, you need to pay attention to the kind of rice. I have experimented with different varieties, and the one I like best is a medium-grain rice imported from Valencia, Spain. I find that it absorbs the flavors perfectly. The medium-grain or "Valencia-type" rice sometimes sold in supermarkets in the United States is acceptable but not quite so firm-textured; if you have to use it, shave a few minutes off the cooking times during the last few additions of stock. The same goes for long-grain rice. People do use it in Veracruz, but it will not absorb as much of the liquid and tends to have an unappealing texture if cooked for longer than about 15 minutes.

The selection of seafood given here is typically Veracruzan but not carved in stone. Feel free to omit or substitute anything you like, as long as it is all sparkling fresh and the total amount is 2½–3 pounds. However, I do think that you'll miss a lot of the effect if you don't use at least four kinds. Some good possibilities besides the ones mentioned include small shucked clams, mussels, scallops, or oysters. Any of these should be added with the third installment of fish stock.

<table>
<tr><td>2</td><td>cups medium-grain rice, preferably imported Spanish Valencia</td></tr>
<tr><td>1/4</td><td>cup olive oil</td></tr>
<tr><td>2</td><td>medium-sized white onions, sliced into thin half-moons</td></tr>
<tr><td>2</td><td>garlic cloves, minced</td></tr>
<tr><td>4</td><td>large, ripe plum tomatoes (about 1 pound), coarsely chopped</td></tr>
<tr><td>2</td><td>tablespoons butter</td></tr>
<tr><td>5–6</td><td>cups Basic Fish Stock (page 145)</td></tr>
<tr><td>6</td><td>large fresh epazote sprigs, leaves only, coarsely chopped, or 2 tablespoons crumbled dried epazote (see page 41)</td></tr>
<tr><td>2</td><td>serrano or jalapeño chiles, griddle-roasted and peeled following the directions on page 58, seeded, and chopped</td></tr>
<tr><td>8</td><td>ounces medium shrimp (sold as 16–20 count), peeled and deveined</td></tr>
<tr><td>1</td><td>small skinless fillet from firm white-fleshed fish, such as red snapper, grouper, or Pacific rockfish, cut into 1/2-inch dice</td></tr>
<tr><td>10–12</td><td>ounces cleaned squid, cut into 1/4-inch rings (to yield about 1 cup)</td></tr>
<tr><td>8</td><td>ounces cooked octopus, prepared according to the directions on page 82 (start with 1 1/2–1 3/4 pounds cleaned raw octopus), cut into 1/4-inch dice (to yield about 1 cup)</td></tr>
<tr><td>8</td><td>ounces conch meat, cooked following the directions on page 82 and coarsely chopped (about 1 cup; optional)</td></tr>
<tr><td>8</td><td>ounces lump crabmeat, picked over to remove any bits of shell or cartilage</td></tr>
</table>

PLACE the rice in a strainer and rinse very thoroughly under cold running water until the water runs clear. Set aside to drain.

HEAT 2 tablespoons of the oil until rippling in a medium skillet set over medium-high heat. Add half the onion and garlic; cook, stirring occasionally, until the onion is translucent, about 3 minutes. Stir in the chopped tomatoes and cook, stirring occasionally, for about 5 minutes. Remove from the heat and let cool.

POUR the tomato mixture into a blender and process for about 2 minutes, to make a smooth puree. With a wooden spoon or pusher, force the mixture through a medium-mesh sieve into a bowl; set aside.

IN a large pot or Dutch oven, combine the butter and the remaining 2 tablespoons olive oil and heat over medium-high heat.

When the mixture foams, stir in the drained rice, with the remaining onion and garlic. Cook, stirring constantly, until the rice is well coated with the fat and the onion is translucent, about 3 minutes. Add the pureed tomato mixture and cook, stirring constantly, for 3 minutes longer.

HEAT the fish stock until not quite boiling. Stir the epazote and chiles into the rice mixture and add $1^1/_2$ cups of the stock. Cook, stirring frequently, for about 5 minutes (for firm-textured rice, which I prefer) or 8 minutes (for a softer consistency, preferred in Veracruz). The liquid will be only partly, not completely, absorbed. Add another $1^1/_2$ cups of stock and continue cooking in the same manner for another 5 to 8 minutes. The rice grains will have swelled somewhat but still be slightly chalky at the center, and some of the liquid will remain unabsorbed.

ADD the shrimp, fish, squid, octopus, and conch, if using. Stir in another 1 cup of the fish stock, bring back to a boil, and cook, stirring frequently, for 5 minutes longer. Add the crabmeat and enough of the remaining stock to lend the dish a loose, semi-soupy consistency. Cook for another 1–2 minutes to heat the crab through. Serve immediately in soup plates.

Pescado en Chile Limón

FISH WITH FRESH LIME AND CHILE DRESSING

CHILE LIMÓN, THE INSPIRED CHILE-AND-LIME COMBINATION served everywhere around Lake Catemaco, may be the best thing that ever happened to fish—especially the local *mojarra*, a fish with remarkably sweet and delicate flesh. Probably the most popular approach is panfrying, traditionally over a wood fire, which imparts a tantalizing smokiness to the fish. But people also love the sauce with grilled or broiled fish. If you prefer either of those methods, you may want to omit the butter for a slightly leaner dish.

Makes 4 servings

Fresh Lime and Chile Dressing for Fish (page 315)

1 3-pound fish, such as red snapper, grouper, sea bass, or Pacific rockfish, scaled and cleaned

1–1½ teaspoons coarse salt

½ cup olive oil

2 teaspoons butter, cut into several pieces

MAKE the chile-lime sauce and keep it warm.

RINSE the fish, inside and out, under cold running water, being sure to remove all traces of blood and gills. Blot thoroughly dry, inside and out. Lightly sprinkle the cavity and skin with the salt.

IN a large skillet, heat the oil over medium-high heat until rippling. Add the fish and cook, turning several times with two spatulas or a fish turner, until light golden and nearly firm to the touch, about 10 minutes.

HOLDING the fish in place with a spatula, carefully drain off most of the fat from the pan. Pour the chile-lime sauce over the fish and cook for another 5 minutes. Remove from the heat, add the butter, and swirl the pan so it melts into the sauce. Serve at once, with the sauce spooned over.

Pámpano en Acuyo

POMPANO WRAPPED IN *HOJA SANTA*

Makes 4 servings

 *P*OMPANO IS ONE OF THE GREAT FISH OF VERACRUZ.
Specimens of three to four pounds are not uncommon, and the beautiful silvery creatures glistening on ice are one of the most enchant-
ing sights in fish markets everywhere in the state. Perhaps the best-
loved way of cooking it is in parchment or aluminum foil packets
lined with *hoja santa* (popularly called *acuyo* in many districts). This
is not a case in which dried *hoja santa* can be substituted for the fresh
green leaf in all its aromatic glory. If you cannot find fresh *hoja santa*
leaves, don't try the dish.

 If pompano doesn't happen to be in your local fish market or
doesn't look ultra-fresh, the dish also works well with sea bass, red
snapper, or Pacific rockfish. Serve with Pilaf-Style White Rice (page
291) or Steamed Potatoes (page 279).

 1 3-pound pompano, scaled and cleaned
 4 tablespoons (½ stick) butter
 1 teaspoon salt, or to taste
    Freshly ground black pepper
 9 medium or 7 large fresh *hoja santa* leaves (see page 42)
 1 large white onion, sliced into thin half-moons
 6 garlic cloves, coarsely chopped
 3 jalapeño chiles (or more to taste), stemmed and sliced into
    rounds
 1 cup Basic Chicken or Fish Stock (page 142 or 145)

 PREHEAT the oven to 350°F.

 RINSE the fish, inside and out, under cold running water to remove any traces of gills or blood. Blot thoroughly dry, inside and out.
Rub the butter liberally inside the cavity and over the skin; season
well inside and out with the salt and pepper. Cut or tear 1 of the *hoja
santa* leaves into several pieces. Place the larger part inside the cavity
of the fish and stuff the remainder into the mouth.

 CUT two 16-inch lengths of heavy-duty aluminum foil (18-inch
width) and place one on a baking sheet. Arrange half the remaining
hoja santa leaves in a line down the center and scatter with half the

onion, garlic, and chiles. Place the fish over this bed and scatter with the remaining onion, garlic, and chiles. Cover with the remaining *hoja santa*.

FOLD up a 1/2-inch border along all four edges of the foil to make a shallow "box," being sure to pinch the corners so no liquid can escape. Pour the stock over the fish. Place the second sheet of foil over the whole arrangement and pleat all the edges together to seal very securely. Bake for about 35 minutes, until the flesh is just tender enough to flake.

REMOVE the baking sheet from the oven and carefully transfer the foil packet to a serving platter deep enough to hold the juices. (If you've used strong foil, you should be able to pick it up by the ends or slide it by tugging from one end.) To serve, pierce the foil with a knife and carefully pull it back on all sides to expose the fish. Be sure each person gets some of the *hoja santa* and the delicious pan juices.

Huachinango a la Veracruzana

RED SNAPPER VERACRUZ STYLE

Makes 4–5 servings

*T*HIS IS, BY ALL ODDS, VERACRUZ'S MOST CELEBRATED contribution to world cuisine. The *salsa a la veracruzana* is too wonderful to be used only with red snapper, but there's no denying that the combination is inspired. The olives, capers, and pickled chiles are the perfect foil for the delicate flesh of the fish.

Luckily, red snapper happens to be one of the best and most readily available fish in many parts of the United States. But if it doesn't look good in your market on any given day, feel free to turn the dish into Sea Bass, Rockfish, or Any Good Fish Veracruz Style. A Veracruzan cook would never hesitate to make such a substitution.

Serve with hot Pilaf-Style White Rice (page 291).

> Double recipe Veracruz-Style Sauce (page 320)
> 1 3-pound red snapper, scaled and cleaned
> Salt and freshly ground black pepper
> 2–3 bay leaves (optional)
> 3–4 thyme sprigs (optional)
> 1 small white onion, thinly sliced (optional)

MAKE the sauce and keep it warm.

PREHEAT the oven to 375°F.

RINSE the fish under cold running water, inside and out, being sure to remove all traces of gills and blood. Blot dry with paper towels, inside and out. Lightly sprinkle inside and out with salt and pepper.

RUB a light film of vegetable oil over the bottom of a roasting pan. Pour half the sauce into the pan. Place the fish on the sauce. If desired, tuck the bay leaves, thyme, and onion into the cavity. Pour the rest of the sauce over the fish. Bake for 30–40 minutes, or just until the flesh flakes when tested with a knife. To serve buffet-style, lift the fish onto a platter with two large spatulas and spoon the sauce and cooking juices over it. Or remove the fish from the bone and serve on individual plates, with the sauce spooned over it.

Pescado al Ajillo

GARLICKY PANFRIED FISH

Makes 4 servings

*F*ISH GIVEN THE SPANISH-DERIVED *AL AJILLO* TREATMENT (fried with a lot of succulent garlic) is especially popular in the Lake Catemaco area. At Restorán Julita, one of my favorite spots in Catemaco, chef and owner Elia Pretelín Moreno uses astronomical amounts of whole garlic cloves, skin and all. But you won't duplicate her magic by just throwing in a matching quantity of any garlic you can get your hands on. There are crucial differences between the garlic that comes to markets in Mexico and in the United States. Mexicans not only like varieties that produce small, thin-skinned cloves but also eat garlic much fresher from the ground than we do. Their garlic is young and sweet, more like a vegetable. You may be able to find thin-skinned pinkish garlic in Southeast Asian markets, or ask for new garlic still on the stalk at farmers' markets around midsummer. At my restaurant, we generally offset the harshness of common garlic by cooking the dish in olive oil (Elia uses safflower oil) and sometimes even add a little butter at the end to mellow the flavor.

4 small (8–12 ounces) fish (ocean perch, sea bass, Pacific rockfish, red snapper), scaled and cleaned

1 teaspoon salt, or to taste
  Freshly ground black pepper

40 garlic cloves (about 2 heads garlic, preferably from a thin-skinned variety with small cloves), unpeeled

1 cup olive oil or safflower oil

2 tablespoons butter, cut into bits (optional)
  Lime wedges for garnish

RINSE the fish, inside and out, under cold running water, removing all traces of gills or blood. Blot thoroughly dry, inside and out. Season the cavity and skin with the salt and pepper to taste.

WITH the flat of a heavy knife blade, crush the garlic cloves just enough to release some of the juices, leaving the skin almost intact.

CHOOSE a skillet (two if necessary) large enough to hold the fish comfortably. Add the oil and heat over medium-high heat until rippling. Add the garlic and cook, stirring and tossing constantly, for about 3 minutes. Lift out with a skimmer onto a plate.

ADD the fish to the pan and cook, turning several times with two spatulas, for 5–7 minutes. Scatter the garlic cloves around the fish and continue cooking for another 5 minutes, or until the garlic is golden and crunchy. The fish should be just done enough to flake when pierced near the backbone with a knife tip. Remove the pan from the heat and swirl in the butter, if desired.

SERVE the fish with lime wedges, and tell your guests not to be shy about picking up the garlic cloves and slipping them out of their skins.

Pescado al Mojo de Ajo

FRIED FISH WITH FRIED SLIVERED GARLIC

*I*F THERE IS ONE BASIC FISH DISH EQUALLY AT HOME ALL over Mexico, this is it. The crucial points are that the fish must be lightly crisp, not greasy, and that the garlic should be golden brown, neither underdone nor burned. In Veracruz, I've encountered other kinds of seafood given the same treatment, and at my restaurant, we often serve mushrooms *al mojo de ajo*. I especially like the effect of the pan-browned garlic slivers or slices with fish.

Makes 4 servings

- ½ cup all-purpose flour
- 1 teaspoon salt
- 1 teaspoon freshly ground black pepper
- 4 6-ounce fillets firm white-fleshed fish such as red snapper, sea bass, or Pacific rockfish, skin left on
- ½ cup olive oil
- 2 tablespoons butter
- 6 garlic cloves, slivered
- 2 tablespoons chopped fresh Italian parsley
- 2 tablespoons freshly squeezed lime juice
  Lime wedges for garnish

ON a large plate, combine the flour, salt, and pepper. Lightly coat the fillets in the mixture, shaking off the excess.

IN a large skillet, heat the oil and butter over medium-high heat. When the mixture foams, add the garlic and cook, stirring frequently, until golden and just a bit crisp, about 3 minutes. Add the parsley and cook, stirring, for 1 minute. Add the fish fillets, skin side down, and cook, turning once, until golden and delicately crisp, about 2 minutes per side.

TRANSFER the fish fillets to a platter. Add the lime juice to the pan and deglaze by scraping up the browned bits on the bottom with a spatula. Pour the garlic and pan juices over the fish. Serve at once, with lime wedges.

Jaibas al Mojo de Ajo

CRABS IN GARLIC SAUCE

Makes 4 servings

I HAD THIS VIBRANT DISH AT EL QUELITE IN MISANTLA. Like Fried Fish with Fried Slivered Garlic (page 187), it depends on mighty quantities of garlic, this time in pureed form. It's a good light lunch or supper dish, and it also makes an elegant appetizer.

8 large garlic cloves
1/4 cup water
8 blue crabs, cleaned and cut in half
1 teaspoon salt
1/2 cup olive oil
Lime wedges for garnish

IN a blender or food processor, thoroughly puree the garlic with the water. Set aside.

IN a mixing bowl, toss the crabs with the salt. Set them aside to absorb the flavor while you heat the oil in a large, heavy skillet over high heat until rippling. Add the crabs and cook, turning once, until they are bright red and cooked through, about 2 minutes per side. Add the garlic puree. It should sizzle and spatter lustily. Turn out the crabs and garlic at once onto a platter and serve piping hot, with lobster crackers and picks to dig out the meat. A squeeze of lime juice is the ideal condiment.

Camarones con Chile Chipotle

SHRIMP WITH CHIPOTLE CHILES

I CAN'T CLAIM THIS IS A PEDIGREED VERACRUZAN RECIPE, but the idea for it came from my Veracruz travels. The inspirations were a seafood marinade I loved at Brisas del Mar and a magnificent dish from Restaurant Daría in Zempoala that featured *acamayas* (a huge, murderous-looking kind of river shrimp) in a chipotle sauce. Back in New York, I tried combining the two and developed a shrimp dish that quickly became a favorite entrée on the menu at my first restaurant. (It also makes a great appetizer.) I adore it with toasted country bread, preferably sourdough.

Makes 4 servings
as a main course,
6–8 as an appetizer

1 pound medium shrimp (sold as 16–20 count), peeled and deveined

Tomasita's Seafood Marinade (page 302)

6 canned chipotle chiles in adobo (see page 49), with the sauce that clings to them

6 large garlic cloves

1/2 teaspoon crumbled dried Mexican oregano

1/3 cup extra-virgin olive oil

Salt (optional)

PLACE the shrimp in a bowl, cover with the marinade, and let stand, covered, at room temperature for 5 minutes. Drain well.

IN a blender or food processor, puree the chipotles with their sauce, 1 of the garlic cloves, the oregano, and 2 tablespoons of the oil. Add the mixture to the shrimp, tossing to coat well.

CUT the remaining 5 garlic cloves into thin slivers.

IN a large skillet, heat the remaining oil over medium-high heat until fragrant. Add the garlic and cook for 1 minute, until lightly golden. Add the shrimp mixture. Taste for salt (there will be some from the marinade) and stir in a pinch, if desired. Cook, stirring occasionally, for 3–5 minutes, or until the shrimp are firm but not at all overcooked. Serve at once.

Camarones a la Pimienta

PEPPERED SHRIMP

Makes 4 servings

O NE OF THE STANDARD VERACRUZAN TREATMENTS FOR any kind of seafood is *a la pimienta*— briefly pan-cooked with onion, garlic, fresh green chiles, and a hefty dose of black pepper. With a few little adjustments in timing, the same general formula works equally well for crabmeat, shucked oysters or scallops, squid cut into bite-sized pieces, or virtually any seafood variety I can think of. Use this recipe as an overall model for all kinds of raw seafood. For 1 pound of any seafood, use roughly the same amounts of oil and other seasonings.

Do not scorn the finishing touch of mayonnaise, which I at first thought was unnecessary. It really does mellow and round out the dish. In Veracruz, people also like to add a slug of Maggi sauce, which I usually omit.

These make a great and very quick meal with Fried Plantains (page 278) and Pilaf-Style White Rice (page 291).

- ½ cup olive oil
- 1 large onion, finely sliced or chopped
- 3 garlic cloves, slivered
- 3–4 jalapeño or serrano chiles, stemmed, seeded if desired, and sliced or julienned
- 1 pound shrimp (any size), peeled and deveined (or left in the shell)
- 1 teaspoon salt (optional)
- 1 tablespoon freshly ground black pepper, or to taste
- 2 tablespoons mayonnaise

IN a large skillet, heat the oil over medium heat until rippling. Add the onion and garlic; cook, stirring occasionally, until the onion is translucent and a little wilted but not browned, 3–5 minutes. Add the chiles and cook, stirring, for another 5 minutes, or until softened.

ADD the shrimp, salt (if desired), and pepper and cook for about 3 minutes, or until they are just cooked through. Swirl in the mayonnaise and serve at once.

Camarones o Langostinos Enchipotlados

SHRIMP OR LANGOUSTINES IN CHILE SAUCE

*J*UMBO SHRIMP OR IMPORTED LANGOUSTINES ARE MY preferred substitute for Veracruzan *langostinos* in this simple, bold-flavored classic based on a combination of dried chiles.

At Casa Bonilla in Coatepec, the sauce is flavored with the fresh leaves of allspice trees, which grow all around the area. The flavor is close to that of allspice berries, so the substitution doesn't distort. The original also has fresh *hoja santa*, but in this case the dried leaf will do. Serve with Pilaf-Style White Rice (page 291).

Makes 4 servings

2 ancho chiles, stemmed and seeded

2 guajillo chiles (see page 49), stemmed and seeded

5 dried chipotle chiles, preferably morita-type (see page 48), stemmed and seeded, or 3 canned chipotle chiles in adobo (see page 49)

4 large ripe tomatoes (about 2 pounds)

5 garlic cloves, coarsely chopped

1/4 teaspoon ground allspice, preferably freshly ground

3–4 fresh *hoja santa* leaves or 6 large dried leaves (see page 42)

1 1/2–2 teaspoons salt, or to taste

1/4 cup olive oil

About 2 pounds jumbo shrimp (sold as 10–12 count) in the shell, preferably with heads on, or langoustines, thawed if frozen

2 tablespoons butter, cut into bits (optional)

PLACE all the dried chiles in a medium bowl, cover with boiling water, and let stand for 30 minutes. (If using canned chipotles, reserve them until later.)

WHILE the chiles soak, griddle-roast and peel the tomatoes following the directions on page 58.

DRAIN the soaked chiles and place in a blender with the tomatoes, garlic, allspice, and 2 of the fresh or dried *hoja santa* leaves. If using canned chipotles, add them to the blender. Process to a puree. Taste for seasoning and add the salt.

IN a large saucepan, heat 2 tablespoons of the oil over medium-high heat until rippling. Scrape the pureed mixture into the pan, reduce the heat to medium-low, and cook, partly covered, for 15 minutes, until the fat begins to separate from the sauce.

MEANWHILE, cut the remaining fresh *hoja santa* leaves into fine julienne.

IN a large skillet, heat the remaining 2 tablespoons oil over high heat until rippling. Add the shrimp and cook, turning, for about 2 minutes, until they start changing color. Add the julienned *hoja santa* to the shrimp, or crumble the remaining dried *hoja santa* directly into the pan. Pour the sauce over the shrimp and cook for another 5 minutes, or until just cooked through. Swirl in the butter, if using, and serve at once.

Pulpos a las Brasas

GRILLED OCTOPUS

Makes 4 servings

Glistening-fresh octopus is always one of the most striking sights in Veracruz fish markets. In this country, it's more likely to be frozen than fresh, but octopus survives freezing and thawing better than almost any other kind of seafood. Grilling brings out its depth.

I usually have octopus cleaned when I buy it. If you have to do this job yourself, pick up the octopus by the central bag—the head—and turn it inside out. Cut or pull out the eyes, beak, and viscera; rinse well under cold running water. If you must buy octopus before it is cleaned, 6–7 pounds of octopus will yield 4–5 pounds of usable meat. Cook for about 45 minutes and let it cool in the cooking liquid. If you buy it frozen, defrost it completely before cooking.

4–5 pounds cleaned octopus, thawed if frozen, cooked following the directions on page 82 (to yield about 1½ pounds cooked meat)

½ cup olive oil

2 medium-sized white onions

3 garlic cloves

4 serrano or jalapeño chiles

Coarse salt and freshly ground black pepper

Lime wedges for garnish

CUT the octopus into 3-inch chunks and brush a little of the olive oil over each chunk, using 2–3 tablespoons in all. Set aside.

PREPARE a grill, preferably with hardwood charcoal. While it is heating, cut the onions, garlic, and chiles into ⅛-inch slices. In a medium heavy skillet, heat the remaining 5–6 tablespoons oil over medium-high heat until fragrant. Add the onions, garlic, and chiles and cook, stirring frequently, for 3 minutes, or until the onions are just translucent but still have a little crunch. Set aside.

WHEN the grill is hot, arrange the octopus on the rack about 4 inches above the source of heat and grill, turning once, for 1–2 minutes per side. Transfer to a platter, season to taste with salt and pepper, and top with the reserved onion mixture. Serve with lime wedges.

YOU MAY KNOW that turkey was the original domestic fowl of Mexico, though the indigenous peoples also caught small game birds as well as the many different migratory waterfowl that fly south to spend the winter in Veracruzan rivers and lakes. Chicken arrived only with the Spanish, but over the centuries it became the main kind of poultry eaten by most people.

Today turkey recipes are strangely elusive in many parts of Mexico. In the villages, they are reserved for special celebrations. It makes sense when you remember that turkey parts cannot be casually picked up from supermarkets in Mexico and that cooking a whole turkey is a great investment of time and money. I had a stroke of luck when I found that El Gran Café de la Parroquia, one of the

POULTRY AND EGGS

most important restaurants in the port city, has made roast turkey an everyday specialty — something highly unusual for a Mexican restaurant. I don't know which is better, the turkey itself or the splendid consommé that is prepared from it and served at breakfast with a hearty Spanish-style omelet.

Chicken is *the* modern Mexican poultry choice, just as pork is *the* meat. Despite some signs of change, in most Veracruz village markets, you still see people happily buying the same skinny, flavorful free-range Mexican chickens that I like to think of when I hear the word "chicken." They take longer than ours to become tender, but they have character. I have (reluctantly) written these recipes with our supermarket chickens in mind, but if at all possible, look for free-range chickens and expect to add a few minutes (or up to 15) to the cooking times. They really do taste better.

The chicken recipes I brought back from Veracruz cover virtually the whole spectrum of cooking approaches that exist in the state today. There are chile-based dishes with very old roots such as *mole huasteco* (a pureed chile-tomato sauce with aromatic seasonings), and *pollo con chile seco* (sprinkled with tiny hot chiles ground to a powder). Later, more European influences were the driving force behind dishes using the fruit liqueurs of Xico or the unusually seasoned *pebre de pollo* (chicken stew) from Tuxpan. And today we have cooks like Inés Pavón Contreras bringing a cosmopolitan style to bear on elegant preparations like boned chicken legs wrapped around a filling of ground meats, nuts, and seasonings (*piernas de pollo rellenas*) — it shows the process of culinary-cultural *mestizaje* (commingling) entering a whole new phase.

I HAVE ALSO INCLUDED a small section of Veracruzan egg dishes that are just too good to leave out. In Veracruz, great things are done with scrambled eggs — for example, combining them with shrimp or cooked black beans. The local omelets are frittata-like delicacies enriched with ingredients like plantains or glorified with edible blossoms. And then there is the fabulous omelet in turkey broth as served at La Parroquia. I've never tasted a more delectable lesson in the art of reimagining simple materials.

Chuletas de Pollo al Limón

CHICKEN CUTLETS
MARINATED IN LIME JUICE

I FIRST TASTED THIS LIGHT BUT WINNING DISH AT La Troje restaurant in Orizaba. As you doubtless know by now, soy and Maggi sauce are as Mexican as chutney is English. Serve with Pilaf-Style White Rice (page 291).

Makes 4 servings

4 skinless, boneless chicken cutlets (about 1 pound in all), pounded to ¼-inch thickness
Juice of 2 limes
2 teaspoons soy sauce
1 teaspoon Maggi sauce
⅓ cup olive oil
Lime wedges for garnish

PLACE the chicken in a bowl or shallow dish, add the lime juice, soy sauce, and Maggi sauce, and turn to moisten evenly with the marinade. Cover the dish and refrigerate for 1 hour, turning the chicken occasionally.

REMOVE the chicken from the marinade, drain well, and blot dry with paper towels. Reserve the marinade.

IN a skillet large enough to hold the cutlets in one layer, heat the oil over medium-high heat until rippling. Add the chicken and sauté, turning once, for about 3 minutes per side, or until just cooked through. If desired, transfer the cutlets to a heated platter, add the marinating liquid to the skillet, and boil over high heat for 1 minute. Pour over the chicken. Serve at once, with lime wedges.

Pollo Asado al Chiltepín

GRILLED CHICKEN WITH CHILTEPÍN CHILES

Makes 4 servings

WALKING BY THE ROSTICERÍA BERNAL IN PAPANTLA, WE were pulled to a stop by the smell of chicken grilling over coals. Ordinarily *rosticería* refers to a rotisserie, but there was none in sight. This establishment had only a small charcoal grill by the door with butterflied chickens in progress. It offered a choice of different flavors, of which this simple lime-and-chile version was my favorite.

At home, I adapted the original by cutting the chicken into quarters. This eliminates the usual problem with grilling them whole — having the breast meat dry out before the legs are done.

This is one case in which a supermarket substitute for a particular chile is acceptable. If you can't find chiltepines, add ½–1 teaspoon cayenne pepper to the marinade.

Serve with Steamed Potatoes (page 279).

1	teaspoon chiltepín chiles (see page 48; or substitute cayenne pepper — see above)
1	teaspoon cumin seeds
2	garlic cloves, coarsely chopped
1	teaspoon salt, or to taste
1	teaspoon freshly ground black pepper
1½	tablespoons cider vinegar
	Juice of 3 limes
1	3½-to-4-pound chicken, quartered

PLACE a small heavy skillet over very low heat and let it get hot. Add the chiles and toast, shaking the pan constantly, for 5 minutes, or until fragrant and slightly brittle but not scorched. Transfer to a small bowl and set aside.

RETURN the pan to medium heat, let it heat thoroughly, and add the cumin. Toast, shaking the pan constantly, until fragrant, about 1 minute. Add to the chiles in the bowl and let cool slightly, then grind the toasted chiles and cumin to a powder in an electric spice or coffee grinder or with a mortar and pestle.

IN a small bowl or mortar, mash the garlic to a paste with the salt and pepper. Add the vinegar, lime juice, and cumin-chile mixture.

Place the chicken in a bowl or dish, add the seasoning mixture, and turn the pieces to moisten evenly. Let sit, covered, in the refrigerator for 1 to 3 hours, turning occasionally.

ABOUT 30 minutes before you are ready to cook, light the grill.

REMOVE the chicken from the marinade and pat dry. Build a fire to one side of the grill. Position the chicken pieces so they are not directly over the coals. Grill about 6 inches from the fire, turning once or twice, for about 20 minutes per side for the legs and 15 minutes per side for the breast pieces. The juices should run clear with no trace of pink when a sharp knife is inserted into the thickest part. Serve hot.

Pollo con Naranja

ORANGE-FLAVORED CHICKEN

Makes 4 servings

$\mathcal{T}$HE FRUIT WINES AND LIQUEURS OF THE XICO AREA (SEE page 16) are one of the glories of the Veracruzan table. María del Carmen Virués de Izaguirre, the matriarch of Xico's foremost liqueur-manufacturing family, gave me this recipe, along with the following one.

In this country, fruit liqueurs tend not to stand in high culinary esteem, because they often don't taste natural — many are nothing more than commercial essences or concentrates combined with massive doses of high-proof alcohol and sugar syrup. The authentic ones from Veracruz are naturally distilled from fruits and keep more of their taste with less of an alcoholic kick. I have had good results here with low-alcohol brands such as Colonial Club. If you can't find it, substitute an orange liqueur like Cointreau or Triple Sec diluted half and half with water. Serve with Pilaf-Style White Rice (page 291) and pickled jalapeños, if desired.

1	3^1/₂-to-4-pound chicken, cut into 6 serving pieces
1–1^1/₂	teaspoons salt, or to taste
^{1}/₂	cup Garlic Vinegar with Black Pepper (page 301), or to taste
2	tablespoons vegetable oil
2	cups freshly squeezed orange juice
1	cup low-alcohol orange liqueur or ^{1}/₂ cup standard-brand orange liqueur plus ^{1}/₂ cup water (see above)
1	medium-sized white onion, sliced into paper-thin half-moons
1–2	tablespoons butter (optional)

SEASON the chicken with ^{1}/₂ teaspoon of the salt and place in a bowl or deep dish. Add the garlic vinegar and turn to moisten the pieces all over. Let sit at room temperature for 30 minutes, turning once or twice.

LIFT out the chicken, draining it well, and blot dry with paper towels. Discard the marinade.

IN a Dutch oven or large pot, heat the oil over medium-high heat until rippling. Add the chicken and sauté, turning once, until lightly browned, about 3 minutes per side. Transfer to a bowl and set aside.

WITH a wooden spoon or spatula, loosen the flavorful browned bits from the bottom of the pan. Add the orange juice and orange liqueur. Return the chicken to the pot (I like to start the leg pieces about 5 minutes before the breast pieces). Bring to a boil over medium heat. Taste for salt and add up to 1 teaspoon, if desired. Cook, covered, for 25–30 minutes, or until the cooking liquid has a glossy sheen and the chicken is tender.

ADD the onion and cook just until it is wilted, 2–3 minutes. For an optional enrichment, gently whisk in the butter just until it melts into the sauce. Serve hot.

Pollo en Mora

SHREDDED CHICKEN
IN BLACKBERRY LIQUEUR SAUCE

*T*HIS RECIPE SHOWCASES THE FRUIT-LIQUEUR TRADITION of Xico, home of the Virués family, who gave me this dish. It features shredded chicken with classic Spanish accents, like green olives and almonds. Use a brand of liqueur close to the fairly low-alcohol, not terribly sugary original (Colonial Club is my usual choice).

Pollo en mora makes an excellent appetizer as well as a main dish. For the former, follow the directions below and serve with crisp-fried flour tortillas.

Makes 6–8 servings
as an appetizer,
4 as a main course

1	3¹/₂-to-4-pound chicken
2	medium-sized white onions, 1 unpeeled
2	garlic cloves, unpeeled
2	teaspoons salt, or to taste
¹/₂	teaspoon black peppercorns
3	cups water
1	cup low-alcohol blackberry liqueur (see above)
2	tablespoons olive oil
¹/₂	cup pimiento-stuffed green olives, minced
¹/₂	cup slivered blanched almonds, toasted (see page 64) and finely chopped

PLACE the chicken in a deep saucepan or medium pot with the unpeeled onion, garlic, salt, and peppercorns. Add the water and blackberry liqueur. Bring to a boil over high heat. At once reduce the heat to maintain a low rolling boil and skim off any froth that rises to the top. Cook, partly covered, for 30–40 minutes, until the chicken is tender. Lift the chicken out into a bowl, letting it drain well. Strain the cooking stock and discard the solids.

WHEN the chicken is cool enough to handle, remove and discard the skin. Pull the meat from the bones and tear it into fine shreds. Set aside.

FINELY chop the remaining onion. In a large wide skillet or sauté pan, heat the oil over medium-high heat until fragrant. Add the onion and cook, stirring occasionally, until translucent, about 3 minutes. Add the shredded chicken, olives, and almonds. Cook, stirring to distribute the ingredients, until heated through, 2–3 minutes.

STIR in about 1 cup of the strained cooking stock, or enough to moisten the chicken without swamping it. (You can freeze the rest and use it to make the dish on another occasion.) Cover and cook, stirring occasionally, over low heat until the liquid has almost evaporated, about 10 minutes. Serve hot.

VARIATION

For *Puerco en Mora* (Pork in Blackberry Liqueur Sauce), replace the chicken with a 2-pound piece of pork butt. Follow the directions above, but cook the pork for 1 hour 20 minutes, then shred it.

Pollo con Chile Seco

CHICKEN WITH TINY DRIED CHILES

Makes 4–5 servings

THROUGHOUT MEXICO, EVERY REGION HAS ITS VARIETY OF miniature chiles, usually used dried. They tend to be among the hottest of chiles. So I expected real fireworks at Rancho La Unión, a delightful Papantla-area ranch-cum-family-museum, when I heard that its version of a traditional Totonac chicken dish uses 50 grams (close to 2 ounces, or about ½ cup) of the local small dried chiles. To my surprise, the sauce had only a pleasant bite, not a white-hot sting.

A few years later I was served the same dish at the home of the Papantla vanilla growers Victor and Gloria Vallejo. Or almost the same dish — it had received the wonderful additions of vanilla bean and fresh, fragrant orange juice. Now I make it either with or without.

The *chile seco* of the Papantla region is about the size of a raisin and the chiltepín chiles available in many parts of the United States aren't a bad match, though they are usually smaller and hotter. Look for larger ones, not the tiniest.

The technique used here is a good way to make the most of flavor: you start the cooking in a small amount of water that's allowed to evaporate before the chicken finishes browning in its own rendered fat. At the end, a splash of vinegar and a little good lard (or butter) turn the pan juices into a simple but irresistible, not at all greasy sauce.

Serve with Rice with Roasted Tomatoes (page 294).

1 3½-to-4-pound chicken, cut into 6 serving pieces
1 cup water
2 teaspoons salt
¼–½ cup (or to taste) large dried chiltepín chiles (see page 48)
½ teaspoon freshly ground black pepper
¼ cup cider vinegar or other mild-flavored vinegar
2 tablespoons home-rendered lard (see page 66) or butter
2 large garlic cloves, finely chopped
  Juice of 2 oranges (optional)
1 vanilla bean (optional), split

PLACE the chicken and water in a large Dutch oven or wide heavy saucepan. Add the salt and bring to a boil over medium-high heat. Cook, uncovered, until the water has evaporated and the chicken is beginning to cook in its own fat. (Supermarket chickens will take about 20 minutes; free-range chickens may take much longer.) Continue cooking, turning once or twice, until the skin is lightly browned on all sides, 5–7 minutes.

AS soon as you have started the chicken, place the chiles in a medium heavy skillet over very low heat. Let them toast, stirring constantly, until they make a hollow sound, 12–15 minutes. They should be brittle but only faintly darkened, not burned. Let cool slightly, then grind to a fine powder using an electric spice or coffee grinder (or if you have one, a Mexican stone *molcajete*).

WHEN the chicken is browned, pour off any excess fat from the pot and return to medium heat. Sprinkle the ground chiles and black pepper over the chicken, turning the pieces to coat evenly. Add the vinegar, lard or butter, garlic, and orange juice and vanilla bean, if using; cook, uncovered, for 10–15 minutes more, or until the sharpness of the vinegar is mellowed. Serve hot.

Mole *Huasteco*

Makes 4 servings

THE CUISINE OF THE NORTHEASTERN AREA CALLED THE
Huasteca is an important link between Veracruz state and the rest of
central Mexico (for example, the states of Puebla, Hidalgo, and San
Luis Potosí). Much of what I've learned about the cooking of the
Huasteca comes from Santa María de Guadalupe Armenta Guzmán
("Lupita"). Her method of soaking dried chiles in chicken stock in-
stead of water before cooking has become almost standard practice
with me.

Moles are a hugely varied tribe of dishes defying most generaliza-
tions, except that the meat or poultry plays second fiddle to a large
volume of flavorful sauce. They seldom demand terrific kitchen
skills, but they usually involve a large number of separate steps,
which can be split up in many possible ways. Read through the recipe
before embarking on it. The order of battle I've suggested makes
sense to me, but the sequence of steps up to the pureeing of ingredients in the blender can be done in any way you find convenient. Serve
with rice and freshly made corn tortillas.

- 1 3½-to-4-pound chicken, quartered
- 3–4 large mint sprigs
- 2 small white onions, 1 unpeeled
- 1 tablespoon salt, or to taste
- 6–7 cups water
- 4 large ripe tomatoes (about 2 pounds total)
- 5 garlic cloves, unpeeled
- 1 teaspoon black peppercorns
- 1 1-inch piece *canela* (see page 44)
- 10 cloves
- 5 large ancho chiles, stemmed and seeded
- ¼ cup vegetable oil
- 1 tablespoon sugar

PLACE the chicken in a pot or large saucepan with the mint, the
unpeeled onion, and 1½–2 teaspoons of the salt. Add enough water
to cover and bring to a boil over high heat. At once reduce the heat to

maintain a low rolling boil. Skim off any froth that rises to the top and cook, partly covered, for 25–30 minutes. Lift out the chicken and set aside. Strain the stock; you should have 5–6 cups. When the chicken is cool enough to handle, remove and discard the skin. Remove the meat from the bones and dice or shred; set aside.

WHILE the chicken is cooking, griddle-roast and peel the tomatoes and garlic following the directions on page 58.

WHILE the vegetables are roasting, heat a small heavy skillet over medium heat and toast the peppercorns, *canela*, and cloves for 1–2 minutes, shaking the pan constantly. Turn out into a small bowl and set aside.

WHEN the stock is done, place the chiles in a medium bowl and cover with 2 cups hot stock. Let stand for 15–20 minutes.

WHILE the chiles soak, slice the remaining onion into thin half-moons. In a small heavy skillet, heat 2 tablespoons of the oil over medium heat until rippling. Add the onion and cook until translucent, about 3 minutes. Scrape into a blender and add the tomatoes with their juices, garlic, toasted spices, and softened chiles with their soaking liquid. Puree thoroughly, stopping occasionally to scrape down the sides with a rubber spatula. If necessary, add a little more of the chicken stock to help the action of the blades. With a wooden spoon or pusher, force the puree through a medium-mesh sieve into a bowl.

IN a large saucepan, heat the remaining 2 tablespoons oil over medium heat until rippling. Add the pureed tomato mixture, cover, and cook, stirring occasionally, for 15 minutes, or until the sauce is a little concentrated and the fat is starting to separate.

ADD the reserved chicken and cook to heat through. If desired, thin slightly with a little more of the stock (save the rest for another purpose) and adjust the salt to taste. In Lupita's own words, "Ah! and something very important, add a tablespoon of sugar."

VARIATION

For *Mole Huasteco de Puerco* (Huasteca-Style Pork in *Mole*), replace the chicken with 1 pound boneless pork shoulder butt, cut into 2-inch chunks. Proceed as directed above, allowing about 45 minutes cooking time for the pork.

Tesmole Rojo de Pollo

CHICKEN SOUP-STEW
WITH CHILE-TOMATO SAUCE

*I*N THE INCREDIBLY VAST, VARIED FAMILY OF MEXICAN
central Gulf coast soup-stews, *tesmole* was one of the more exciting
revelations for me. The name first crossed my path in the warm
coastal areas via a glorious vegetable stew with green herbs and but-
tery-tender beef shin, served at Las Brisas del Mar in Boca del Río
(see *tesmole verde,* page 257). In the cool mountain heights of Orizaba,
I later came upon this simpler red *tesmole* at La Fuente, the restaurant
of the Hotel Pluviosilla. The chef, Gamaliel Nicolás Lara, accents the
broth with tomatoes and gives the whole a good flavor kick with dried
chiles.

Makes 4–6 servings

8–10 árbol or 12–15 dried serrano chiles (see page 47)
1 3¹/₂-to-4-pound chicken, cut into serving pieces
2 teaspoons salt
Freshly ground black pepper
2 tablespoons vegetable oil
4 large or 6 medium-sized ripe tomatoes (about 2 pounds total),
coarsely chopped
1 small white onion, coarsely chopped
3 garlic cloves, coarsely chopped
6 large epazote sprigs (see page 41) or 20 cilantro sprigs (1 small
bunch), tied together with kitchen twine
1–2 teaspoons powdered chicken stock base (Gamaliel uses Knorr
Swiss) or 1 chicken bouillon cube
About 2¹/₂ cups chicken stock, preferably homemade (page
142), or water
Corn Masa Dumplings (page 131)
8 ounces fresh green beans, cut into 1-inch lengths
2 chayotes, peeled and pitted (see page 55), cut lengthwise into
eighths

PLACE the chiles in a small saucepan, cover with water, and
bring to a boil over high heat. Cook for 5 minutes, remove from the
heat, and let soak for 10–15 minutes.

MEANWHILE, season the chicken with the salt and a few

grindings of black pepper. In a medium wide Dutch oven, heat the oil over medium-high heat until rippling. Add the chicken and brown lightly, about 2 minutes per side. Transfer to a platter or dish; pour off and discard all but about 2 tablespoons of fat from the pot. Scrape up any browned bits from the bottom (leaving them in the pot) and set aside.

DRAIN the soaked chiles. Place in a blender with the tomatoes, onion, and garlic and process to a puree. Return the pot to medium-low heat. Add the pureed mixture and cook, covered, for about 15 minutes, or until you see the fat starting to separate. Add the chicken stock base or bouillon cube, the chicken pieces (with any cooking juices), the epazote, and enough stock or water to cover them by 2 inches. Bring to a boil over high heat. At once reduce the heat to maintain a low rolling boil and cook, partly covered, for 20 minutes.

WHILE the chicken cooks, make the dumplings. Add them to the broth, along with the green beans and chayotes. Cook for another 7–8 minutes, or until the vegetables are just tender. Remove the herb bundle and serve in soup bowls.

Pollo en *C*acahuate

CHICKEN IN PEANUT SAUCE

Makes 4 servings

*L*OOKING THROUGH MARÍA STOOPEN AND ANA LAURA Delgado's important work *La Cocina Veracruzana*, I found a pork-based version of this dish that I've followed with good results. But I think the sauce works even better with chicken.

Like *moles* and *pepianes*, this is one of those Mexican dishes with a modest amount of meat or poultry swimming in a large volume of sauce. People in Veracruz usually roast raw peanuts for sauces, as directed here (or toast them in the oven, or fry in hot fat). I confess that when I make the dish at home, I use store-bought roasted peanuts and have never seen any problem with the flavor. Serve with Pilaf-Style White Rice (page 291) and Fried Plantains (page 278).

2 ancho chiles, stemmed and seeded

1 cup shelled and skinned raw peanuts or roasted peanuts (see above)

1 3¹/₂-to-4-pound chicken, cut into 6 serving pieces

1¹/₂–2 teaspoons salt, or to taste

1 teaspoon freshly ground *canela* (from a 1¹/₂-to-2-inch piece; see page 44)

2 tablespoons vegetable oil

1 French roll (about 3 ounces), cut into ¹/₂-inch slices, or four ¹/₂-inch slices French baguette

2 large ripe tomatoes, coarsely chopped

1 large fresh *hoja santa* leaf or 2–3 dried leaves (see page 42)

1 small white onion, coarsely chopped

2 garlic cloves, coarsely chopped
Freshly ground black pepper

1 teaspoon sugar

2 Pickled Chipotle Chiles (page 269) or canned chipotles in adobo (see page 49)

2 cups chicken stock, preferably homemade (see page 142)

2 tablespoons cider vinegar

¹/₃ cup dry red wine

PLACE the ancho chiles in a small bowl, cover with boiling water, and let sit for 20 minutes. Drain and set aside.

IF using raw peanuts, place them in a small heavy skillet over medium-low heat and dry-roast, stirring constantly and shaking the pan, until golden, about 15 minutes. *Do not let them scorch!* Set aside to cool. (If using commercial roasted peanuts, omit this step.)

LIGHTLY sprinkle the chicken all over with salt (about ½ teaspoon) and the ground *canela*.

IN a Dutch oven or large heavy skillet, heat the oil over medium-high heat until rippling. Add the chicken pieces and cook, turning once, until lightly browned, about 3 minutes per side. Lift out the chicken and set aside. Add the bread slices and fry, turning, until golden, about 1 minute per side. Lift out onto paper towels to drain. Pour off all but 2 tablespoons of fat from the pot. With a wooden spoon, scrape the flavorful browned bits from the bottom. Set the pot aside.

WORKING in batches as necessary, puree the peanuts, fried bread, and drained ancho chiles in a blender with the tomatoes, *hoja santa*, onion, garlic, 1–1½ teaspoons salt, pepper to taste, the sugar, and chipotles. The consistency will be heavy and pasty; add up to ½ cup of the chicken stock if necessary to help the action of the blades.

RETURN the pot to medium heat. When the fat ripples, add the pureed mixture and cook over medium-low heat, stirring constantly to keep it from scorching, for 15 minutes to deepen and meld the flavors. Stir in the remaining chicken stock with the vinegar and wine.

ADD the chicken legs and thighs and cook for 5 minutes, then add the breast pieces and cook until the meat is tender, about 25 minutes in all. Serve hot.

VARIATION

For *Puerco en Cacahuate* (Pork in Peanut Sauce), replace the chicken with a 2½-to-3-pound center-cut pork loin roast. Rub as directed with salt and *canela*. Brown it well on all sides in the oil, and allow 45–50 minutes' cooking time in the sauce.

Pebre de Pollo

CHICKEN IN SWEET-TART SAUCE

Makes 4 servings

WHEN I'M IN MEXICO EXPLORING A SPOT NEW TO ME, I always start by asking people who's the best cook in town. I tried it in Tuxpan, a Huasteca-area river town that I always think of as the city of spectacular sunsets. The invariable answer was "Angelita" — Doña Ángeles Juárez Molina. This gracious, efficient woman, a former president of the city restaurant association, runs a *rosticería*, a place specializing in rotisserie-broiled chickens. (Yes, rotisserie shops are as popular in Mexico as in the United States — and a lot older.) Angelita is also a champion of traditional local dishes like this richly flavored stew with its accent of fruit.

The Spanish influence is obvious in the caper-olive-raisin-sherry combination. But the dish has nothing in common with the sauce called *pebre*, or *pebrada*, in Spanish cooking, a mixture of vinegar with black pepper (hence the name) and garlic. I wonder if the brined olives and capers in Angelita's *pebre* are a later stand-in for the original vinegar. The large amount of black pepper is a stronger link. I've taken the small liberty of sautéing the tomatoes and onion, which Angelita boils (sautéing offsets the blandness of our tomatoes and restores a little edge of freshness to our frequently elderly onions). I've also taken to serving the dish with pickled jalapeños on the side — I find them a perfect complement to the flavors.

1	teaspoon black peppercorns
4–5	cloves
1/4	cup olive oil
1	medium-sized white onion, coarsely chopped
3	garlic cloves, coarsely chopped
3	large ripe tomatoes (about 1 1/2 pounds total), coarsely chopped
1	4-pound chicken, quartered
1–1 1/2	teaspoons salt, or to taste
	Freshly ground black pepper
1/3	cup capers, rinsed, patted dry, and spread out on paper towels to dry completely
2	cups chicken stock, preferably homemade (page 142)
15–20	pimiento-stuffed green olives
1/2	cup dark raisins

2 tart crisp green apples, unpeeled, cored and cut into eighths
¼ cup dry sherry (I use *fino*)
Pickled jalapeño chiles (optional)

IN an electric spice or coffee grinder, or using a mortar and pestle, grind the peppercorns and cloves to a coarse powder. Set aside.

IN a medium heavy skillet or wide saucepan, heat 2 tablespoons of the oil over medium-high heat until rippling. Add the onion and garlic and cook, stirring occasionally, for 3–5 minutes, or until the onion is translucent. Add the tomatoes and pepper-clove mixture. Reduce the heat to medium and cook, covered, for 12–15 minutes, until the mixture is lightly thickened. Let cool slightly, then process to a puree in a blender. Set aside.

SEASON the chicken with salt and a good grinding of black pepper. In a Dutch oven or large pot, heat the remaining 2 tablespoons oil over medium-high heat until rippling. Add the chicken pieces and cook, turning once, until light golden, about 3 minutes per side. Transfer the chicken to a plate and set aside. Pour off all but 2 tablespoons of the fat from the pot. With a wooden spoon or spatula, scrape the bottom to loosen the flavorful browned bits.

RETURN the pot to medium heat. When the fat ripples, add the capers and stir-fry for 2–3 minutes, until they puff slightly and become brown and crisp. Scoop out and set aside. Add the reserved tomato puree and cook, covered, for 15 minutes, or until the flavor is concentrated and the fat is starting to separate. Stir in the chicken stock, olives, raisins, apples, and all but about 1 tablespoon of the fried capers.

ADD the chicken, with any cooking juices, bring to a boil, and cook, covered, over medium heat for 20–25 minutes, or until the chicken is just done. (You'll get best results if you add the leg pieces first, wait 5 minutes, and then add the breast pieces.) Taste for salt and add up to 1 teaspoon, if desired. Stir in the sherry and cook for about 5 minutes longer, until the raw alcohol taste is gone. Serve at once, with the remaining fried capers scattered over the dish. If you like, serve pickled jalapeños on the side.

Piernas de Pollo Rellenas

STUFFED BONED CHICKEN LEGS

Makes 6 servings

ALMOST EVERY BOOK I'VE SEEN ON VERACRUZAN FOOD has at least one recipe from Inés Pavón Contreras of San Andrés Tuxtla. After spending a delightful afternoon talking about food with her, I can see why. This modest, dignified, gray-haired woman is one of the real presences in Tuxtlas-area cuisine. Although today she is partly retired except for her work as a catechism teacher, she has been greatly in demand as a baker and cook for nearly all her life.

This dish, Doña Inés's own creation, won first prize in a statewide and later a national recipe contest. It does take some effort, especially if you bone the chicken legs yourself, but it's guaranteed to become one of the stars in your repertoire. Pilaf-Style White Rice (page 291) is the best accompaniment.

Please note that each of the little chicken-leg packets has to be thoroughly enclosed in its own skin, so you must take great care to leave the skin intact as you work. Do not cut away any skin from the edges.

6 whole chicken legs (thigh and drumstick), with skin, boned (have the butcher bone them, if possible)
2 teaspoons salt, or to taste
Freshly ground black pepper
Juice of 1 lime
4 garlic cloves, minced
1 ounce boiled ham, minced (¹/₄–¹/₃ cup)
¹/₄ pound ground beef
¹/₄ pound ground pork
¹/₂ cup homemade bread crumbs (from day-old bread)
1 large egg, lightly beaten
¹/₂ small white onion, minced
2 tablespoons finely chopped toasted pecans (see page 64)
¹/₄ cup finely chopped toasted pine nuts (see page 64)
1 canned pimiento, finely chopped
2 tablespoons minced fresh Italian parsley
1 ancho chile, stemmed and seeded
2 bay leaves

About $^1/_2$ cup water

6 tablespoons ($^3/_4$ stick) butter

2 cups dry white wine

RINSE the chicken legs and blot dry with paper towels.

IF you did not have them boned by the butcher, do it as follows: Using a very sharp small thin-bladed knife, make an incision down to the bone all along the inside of each leg from the top of the thigh down to the joint. You should feel the knife tip touching the bone as you work. Continue from the joint down to the end of the drumstick. With the knife tip, cut and probe deeper and deeper around the bone and joint until the flesh is worked clear of the bones except at the lower part of the drumstick. Pull on the bone to tug it free as much as you can, then cut through the stubborn last bit of drumstick skin to release the bone entirely. (You can freeze the bones to add to a chicken stock.) As you work, be careful not to pierce or tear the skin.

PLACE the chicken legs in a bowl and season with about 1 teaspoon of the salt and a generous grinding of black pepper. Add the lime juice and half the minced garlic; turn the pieces to coat well on all sides. Let sit while you make the stuffing.

IN a mixing bowl, combine the minced ham and ground meats with the bread crumbs and egg. Add the onion, half the remaining garlic, the pecans, pine nuts, pimiento, and parsley. Season with salt (about 1 teaspoon) and pepper. With your hands, mix to distribute all the ingredients evenly.

REMOVE the chicken legs from the marinade and blot dry with paper towels. Divide the ground-meat mixture into 6 parts and stuff each chicken leg, folding the skin over to make a pillow-shaped package. Secure with toothpicks. (The chicken can be prepared ahead to this point and refrigerated for up to 3 hours.)

RINSE and griddle-dry the ancho chile following the directions on page 50. Place in a small bowl, cover with boiling water, and let sit for 20 minutes.

PREHEAT the oven to 350°F.

DRAIN the soaked chile and place in a blender with the bay leaves, the remaining garlic, and enough water to facilitate blending. Process until as smooth as possible. With a wooden spoon or pusher, force the puree through a medium-mesh sieve into a bowl. Set aside.

IN a large Dutch oven, heat 3 tablespoons of the butter over medium heat until it foams. Add the stuffed chicken packets and cook, turning once, until lightly browned, about 2 minutes per side. Add the wine, cover the pot tightly, and bake for 30 minutes.

MEANWHILE, melt the remaining 3 tablespoons butter; set aside.

REMOVE the pot from the oven. Lift out the chicken packets onto a plate and brush on all sides with the reserved chile paste, then with the melted butter. Return to the pot and bake, uncovered, for another 10 minutes, or until the chicken is lightly browned.

SERVE with a generous amount of the wine sauce over each portion.

NOTE: It isn't part of the original recipe, but I love to serve this dish with Pickled Chipotle Chiles (page 269) on the side. Allow 1 or 2 per serving.

Pato con Salsa del Cura

DUCK WITH THE CURÉ'S SAUCE

$\mathcal{M}$Y INSPIRATION FOR THIS RECIPE — ONE OF THE BEST duck dishes I know—was a recipe by Débora Íñiguez de Vives published in a wonderful book, *La Cocina Veracruzana*. She uses the true *canate* (a kind of migratory wild duck that winters in the Papaloapan River Basin), cuts it into serving pieces and braises it in a flavorful tomato sauce. (Doña Débora thinks the name *salsa del cura* goes back to a time when many dishes were named for their real or fanciful religious links.) This approach doesn't work for our Long Island (white Pekin) type with its heavy layer of fat. So I throw tradition to the winds and roast the duck in the conventional European way. I make the sauce separately, to be served on the side, using a little of the duck fat to enrich the flavor. It's become my absolutely favorite recipe for entertaining—I serve it over and over, and even dinner guests who have already had it three times at my house are just as crazy about it the fourth time.

Makes 4–6 servings

2	Long Island ducklings (about 5 pounds each)
	Salt and freshly ground black pepper
2	small white onions, unpeeled, plus 1 medium onion, peeled
14	garlic cloves, 8 unpeeled
12	bay leaves
6	large ripe tomatoes, chopped (2½–3 pounds total)
6–8	large fresh thyme sprigs or 2 teaspoons crumbled dried thyme
2–3	fresh marjoram sprigs or ¾ teaspoon crumbled dried marjoram
10	black peppercorns, crushed in a mortar
12	green (California-type) olives, pitted
2	pickled jalapeño chiles, seeded
¼	cup dry sherry (I use *fino*)

PREHEAT the oven to 400°F.

RINSE and thoroughly dry the ducks, inside and out. Pull out any loose fat from the cavities or around the tail vents and set aside. (If your ducks have been ruthlessly trimmed of loose fat, don't worry.) Season the ducks inside and out with salt and pepper. Put 1 of the unpeeled onions, 4 of the unpeeled garlic cloves, and 4 of the bay leaves

in each of the cavities. Firmly close the skin of the cavities (and, if necessary, the necks) with small wooden skewers. Prick the skin all over with a fork to help release the fat in cooking.

PLACE the ducks on a rack in a large roasting pan (or use two smaller pans with racks), and roast for 1¹/₂–2 hours, or until golden. Remove from the oven and let stand for 15 minutes.

WHILE the duck is roasting, make the sauce: Chop the reserved duck fat into pea-sized bits and place in a small saucepan. (If your ducks have no loose fat to work with, wait until some of the body fat has started to render into the roasting pan but is still clear and un-browned, spoon off about 3 tablespoons, and proceed as directed.) Set the pan over low heat and let cook, uncovered, for 20–25 minutes, or until you have a handful of crisp (not burned) cracklings in clear rendered fat. Strain the fat into a small bowl. Either discard the cracklings or quietly nibble on them, depending on your temperament.

CUT the remaining onion and 6 garlic cloves into chunks. In a large Dutch oven or wide saucepan, heat 3 tablespoons of the rendered duck fat over medium-high heat until rippling. Add the onion and garlic chunks and cook, stirring frequently, for about 5 minutes, until the onion is translucent. Add the tomatoes, thyme, marjoram, crushed peppercorns, remaining 4 bay leaves, and about 1 teaspoon salt, or to taste. Bring to a boil, reduce the heat to medium-low, and cook, covered, for 15 minutes, or until the consistency is that of a loose sauce. You should have 4–5 cups. Remove from the heat and let cool slightly.

WORKING in at least 2 batches, thoroughly puree the sauce in a blender, occasionally stopping to scrape down the sides with a rubber spatula. Return the mixture to the pot, add the olives, pickled jalapeños, and sherry, and bring to a boil over medium heat. Cover, reduce the heat to maintain a simmer, and cook, stirring occasionally, for 10 minutes, or until the flavors are nicely melded.

CARVE the duck into serving pieces and serve accompanied with the sauce. I like to spoon a pool of the sauce onto each serving plate, place a portion of duck on it, and pass the remaining sauce in a small bowl or pitcher.

Pavo Horneado y Jugo de Pavo La Parroquia

LA PARROQUIA'S OVEN-ROASTED TURKEY
AND TURKEY GRAVY

TURKEY DISHES DON'T SHOW UP ON A REGULAR BASIS IN many Mexican restaurants. But El Gran Café de la Parroquia, a much-loved institution in the port city of Veracruz, is the exception. Roast turkey is always on the menu there, served on its own or in enchiladas or sandwiches.

La Parroquia's roast turkey is one of the best main dishes I know for a hearty dinner for family or friends. Because it's accented with but not overwhelmed by the chiles and herbs, it even works well with an otherwise non-Mexican menu. By all means serve it as the centerpiece of a small-scale Thanksgiving or Christmas dinner. Do not try this recipe with a monster Thanksgiving turkey. The optimum size is under 12 pounds.

Makes 8–10 servings
(6–8 cups gravy)

1 10-to-12-pound turkey, with neck and giblets
1 small white onion, unpeeled, plus 1 large white onion
1 head garlic, separated into cloves and peeled, except for 2 cloves
1 tablespoon salt, or to taste
1 teaspoon black peppercorns
12 bay leaves
8–9 cups chicken stock, preferably homemade (page 142), or water
3 large ancho chiles, stemmed and seeded
3 guajillo chiles (see page 49), stemmed and seeded
2 large or 3–4 medium-sized ripe tomatoes (about 1 pound total), griddle-roasted and peeled following the directions on page 58
4 large fresh oregano sprigs or 2 teaspoons crumbled dried oregano
4 large fresh thyme sprigs or 2 teaspoons crumbled dried thyme

TO make the stock for the gravy, chop or break the turkey neck into manageable pieces. Place in a large saucepan with the giblets (leave out the liver) and any other available trimmings. Add the unpeeled onion, the 2 unpeeled garlic cloves, 1 teaspoon of the salt, 1/2 teaspoon of the peppercorns, and 2 of the bay leaves. Add enough chicken stock or water, or any combination of the two, to cover the ingredients. Bring to a boil over high heat, then reduce the heat to maintain a low rolling boil. Skim off any froth that accumulates on top and cook, partly covered, for 1–1½ hours, or until the meat is falling off the bones and the onion has given up all of its flavor. Strain the stock through a medium-mesh sieve, discarding the solids, and set aside.

WHILE the stock cooks, rinse and griddle-dry the ancho and guajillo chiles following the directions on page 50. Place in a bowl, add boiling water to cover, and let stand for 30 minutes.

DRAIN the soaked chiles and puree in a blender with the tomatoes, the remaining ½ teaspoon peppercorns, 1 teaspoon of the salt, 2 of the garlic cloves, and 1 sprig (or ½ teaspoon) each of the oregano and thyme. With a wooden spoon or pusher, force the mixture through a medium-mesh sieve into a bowl.

THOROUGHLY rinse the turkey, inside and out, under cold running water. Blot dry, inside and out, with paper towels and slather with the chile-tomato paste. Let stand for 30 minutes.

MEANWHILE, preheat the oven to 350°F.

SLICE the large onion into thin half-moons.

ARRANGE the onion, the remaining garlic cloves, and the remaining oregano, thyme, and bay leaves to make a bed on the bottom of a large roasting pan. Place the turkey breast side down on the bed of aromatics. Roast for 2½ hours, turning the turkey every 30 minutes. (I use two pairs of large kitchen tongs or two very large cooking spoons for this; an alternative tool would be a pair of kitchen mitts too old to matter.) When done, the turkey will have reached an internal temperature of 175°–180°F in the thickest part of the thigh. Lift out the turkey onto a platter and cover loosely with foil while you prepare the gravy.

PLACE the roasting pan on the stovetop, over two burners if necessary. Add the reserved turkey stock and bring to a boil over high heat. With a wooden spoon or spatula, scrape up any browned bits that cling to the bottom of the pan. Reduce the heat to maintain a low rolling boil and cook for 20 minutes to concentrate the flavors. Strain through a fine-mesh sieve; discard the solids. You now have an incomparable consommé-like broth or pan gravy. Pour some of it into a gravy boat to accompany the roast turkey. Save the surplus for La Parroquia's Special Omelet in Turkey Gravy (page 227). Carve the turkey and serve with the gravy.

Tortilla a La Parroquia

LA PARROQUIA'S SPECIAL OMELET
IN TURKEY BROTH

*F*OR ME, THIS OMELET, INVENTED AT EL GRAN CAFÉ DE la Parroquia in the city of Veracruz, sums up the boldness, depth, and simplicity of Veracruzan cooking. It starts with a basic onion-and-potato omelet much like the classic *tortilla española*, but sets it off with a garnish of rapidly cooked onion and green chile, then transposes everything to a totally unexpected key by immersing the finished omelet in the superbly savory turkey gravy-broth-consommé of La Parroquia. Yes, it does sound weird to serve an omelet in something that looks like soup, but the instant I tasted it, I knew that this was a dish I'd kill for. Serve for breakfast or brunch.

Makes 2 servings

1	large waxy potato (preferably Red Bliss)
1–2	teaspoons salt, or to taste
1	medium onion, halved
2–3	jalapeño chiles, stemmed
1	garlic clove
3	tablespoons olive oil
4	large eggs
1	cup Turkey Gravy (see page 224), heated

PEEL the potato and cut it into thin slices (about ¼ inch). Drop into a saucepan of boiling water, add the salt, and cook over medium-high heat for 6–7 minutes, until cooked but not mushy. Drain and set aside.

WHILE the potato is cooking, cut one of the onion halves, the chiles, and garlic into thick slivers. In a small skillet, heat 1 tablespoon of the oil over medium-high heat until rippling. Add the slivered vegetables and cook, stirring constantly, until the onion is translucent but still has some crunch, 2–3 minutes. Set aside.

CUT the remaining onion half into thin half-moons.

IN a nonstick or well-seasoned 9-inch omelet pan or skillet, heat the remaining 2 tablespoons oil over medium heat until fragrant. Add the sliced onion and cook until translucent, about 3 minutes.

IN a mixing bowl, lightly beat the eggs with 1 teaspoon salt. Pour the mixture into the pan with the sliced onion, reduce the heat to low,

Huevos con Camarones

EGGS SCRAMBLED WITH SHRIMP

OVER BREAKFAST AT THE HOTEL DOÑA LALA IN Tlacotalpan, I had a stimulating conversation about the regional food with the dignified and beautiful seventy-eight-year-old *patrona*, Doña Débora Íñiguez de Vives, and Tlacotalpan's handsome young mayor, Hilario Villegas Sosa. Our meal included a deep-flavored dish of scrambled eggs and shrimp that I instantly knew I had to have the recipe for. I came back later in the day to watch Rosa María Castro Chisanto, the chef at Doña Lala, demonstrate this splendid dish. Here in the United States, it would be equally good for breakfast, brunch, or lunch.

Makes 4–6 servings

¼ cup olive oil

1 large onion, cut into thin half-moons

6 ripe plum tomatoes (about 1 pound in all), finely chopped

2 large jalapeño chiles, stemmed and sliced into rounds

6–8 large Italian parsley sprigs, minced (¼ cup)

10 large pimiento-stuffed green olives, cut into thick slices

10 large capers, drained

1 pickled jalapeño chile, seeded and chopped (optional)

1 pound shrimp (any size, though I generally use small), peeled and deveined

10 large eggs, lightly beaten

¼–½ teaspoon salt (optional)

IN a large skillet, heat the oil over medium-high heat until rippling. Add the onion and cook, stirring occasionally, until translucent, about 3 minutes. Add the tomatoes, chiles, parsley, olives, capers, pickled chile (if using), and shrimp. Cook for 2 minutes, stirring to combine thoroughly.

STIR in the eggs and cook, stirring and scrambling vigorously, until fairly well cooked, 2–4 minutes. (I like them quite firm, but follow your own taste; they should still be a little moist from the tomato.) Taste for seasoning and add salt, if desired. (I usually don't find it necessary since the olives and capers contribute quite a lot.) Serve hot.

Huevos Tirados

SCRAMBLED EGGS WITH BLACK BEANS

HUEVOS TIRADOS ARE, LITERALLY, "THROWAWAY EGGS" —
why, I'm not sure, since no one in his or her right mind would apply
a term like "throwaway" to anything so delicious.

Makes 4–5 servings

The general idea of the dish is a combination of scrambled eggs
and some form of well-seasoned cooked beans (they can be mashed,
pureed, or refried). The proportion of eggs to beans is not fixed, and
the dish can be as dry or soupy as the cook wants. My version is
adapted from the excellent *huevos tirados* that Carmina Gutiérrez
Pontón serves at La Fuente restaurant in the Hotel Pluviosilla, her
family's respected hotel in Orizaba.

4–6	árbol or dried serrano chiles (see pages 47 and 51)
¼	cup lard, preferably home-rendered (see page 66), or vegetable oil
1	garlic clove, minced
1	large white onion, sliced into thin half-moons
2	cups Cooked Black Beans (page 283), drained
3–4	cups chicken stock, preferably homemade (page 142)
8	large eggs
1–1½	teaspoons salt, or to taste

PLACE the chiles in a small saucepan, cover with water, and
bring to a boil over high heat. Cook for 5 minutes, or until somewhat
softened; drain and set aside.

IN a nonstick or well-seasoned skillet, heat 2 tablespoons of the
lard or oil over medium-high heat until rippling. Add the garlic and
about three-quarters of the sliced onion. Cook, stirring occasionally,
for 5 minutes, or until the onion is wilted and just starting to color.
Scrape into a blender; set the skillet aside.

ADD the drained chiles, beans, and 3 cups of the chicken stock
to the blender; process to a puree about the consistency of a thin
cream soup, adding a little more stock if necessary (the beans will absorb a bit more or less, depending on their age and degree of dry-
ness). You should have about 5 cups of the mixture.

POUR the bean mixture into a medium saucepan and bring to a boil over fairly high heat. Reduce the heat to low and cook for 5 minutes, stirring occasionally.

MEANWHILE, in a mixing bowl, lightly beat the eggs with the salt. In the same skillet, heat the remaining 2 tablespoons lard or oil over medium-high heat until rippling. Add the remaining sliced onion and cook, stirring, for about 3 minutes. Add the beaten eggs and cook, stirring, until barely set, about 3 minutes (or until done to your taste).

SERVE immediately in bowls, with about 1 generous cup of the hot bean puree ladled over each portion.

Tortilla de Flor de Calabaza

SQUASH BLOSSOM FRITTATA

Makes 4 servings

*V*ERACRUZANS ARE VERY FOND OF OMELETS MADE WITH blossoms such as *izote* (yucca flowers) or *gasparitos* (the brilliant red flowers of the graceful *colorín* tree). Unfortunately, these are scarce or nonexistent in the United States—unlike squash blossoms, which appear in happy abundance in farmers' markets every summer. (Mexicans can get them the year round.) This is a lovely breakfast omelet, also perfect for a light lunch.

Try to find large squash blossoms with no sign of wilting. Sometimes the female ones have the developing baby squashes attached; I usually detach these and use them for another purpose—for example, as a vegetable side dish or as an addition to vegetable soup. I also sometimes like to add a little shredded *queso blanco* to the omelet.

20 small or 12 large very fresh squash blossoms
¼ cup olive oil or vegetable oil
1 medium-sized white onion, sliced into thin half-moons
6 large eggs
1 teaspoon salt, or to taste
4 cilantro sprigs, leaves only, or 1 large epazote sprig (see page 41), leaves only, chopped
2 ounces *queso blanco* (see page 67), shredded (to make ½ cup; optional)
Thin Tomato Sauce, heated (page 317; optional), or other tomato-based sauce

RINSE the squash blossoms under cold running water. Place in a steamer basket set over boiling water or in a microwave oven set on high power; cook for 2 minutes. Drain well, blot as dry as possible, and set aside on paper towels to continue drying.

IN a 9-inch omelet pan or nonstick or well-seasoned skillet, heat 2 tablespoons of the oil over medium heat until fragrant. Add the onion and cook, stirring frequently, until very soft and nicely caramelized, about 20 minutes. Watch carefully and adjust the heat as necessary to keep it from scorching. Remove the pan from the heat. Lift out the onion with a slotted spoon, letting as much oil as possible drain back into the pan, and transfer to a plate. Set the pan aside.

IN a large bowl, beat the eggs lightly with the salt. Stir in the sautéed onion, squash blossoms, and chopped cilantro or epazote.

RETURN the omelet pan to medium heat and add the remaining 2 tablespoons oil. When it is hot but not quite rippling, add the egg mixture and cook for 4–5 minutes, frequently shaking the pan and loosening the edges of the omelet with a spatula to let the uncooked egg trickle to the bottom of the pan. Scatter the *queso blanco* over the eggs, if desired. When the bottom is lightly browned and shrinking from the pan and the top is almost set, run a spatula around the edges and slide the omelet out onto a plate. Invert by holding the pan over the plate and flipping the omelet back into the pan. Cook for another 2–3 minutes, until firmly set but not dry.

SLIDE out onto a plate. Serve either hot or at room temperature, cut into wedges. If desired, accompany with the tomato sauce.

Tortilla con Plátano Macho

FRITTATA WITH PLANTAIN

PEOPLE IN MEXICO AUTOMATICALLY KNOW WHEN *tortilla* means a thin corn or flour tortilla and when it means a frittata-like omelet (as it always does in Spain). I make this one with a rich-flavored ripe plantain (yellow heavily overlaid with black). A green plantain would not be as sweet and mellow. The acidity of the cultured cream is a pleasing contrast.

I was given this recipe by Ana María Capitaine Collinot, the chef-owner (with her husband, Carlos Rubio Novales) of Los Brujos, the restaurant of the Hotel El Palmar on the Costa Esmeralda north of Veracruz city.

Makes 4 servings

- 3 tablespoons butter
- 2 large ripe plantains, peeled (see page 60) and cut into ¼-inch slices
- 1 small white onion, sliced or chopped
- 4 large eggs
- 1 teaspoon salt, or to taste
- 1 cup Refried Beans with Butter (page 285) or other homemade refried beans, heated
- ½ cup Mexican *crema* (see page 67) or crème fraîche

IN a 9-inch omelet pan or nonstick or well-seasoned skillet, melt the butter over medium heat. When it foams, add the sliced plantain and cook until golden on the underside, about 3 minutes (you may need to work in batches). Turn the slices, add the onion, and cook until the onion is translucent, about another 3 minutes.

IN a mixing bowl, lightly beat the eggs with the salt. Pour the mixture over the plantains and immediately reduce the heat to low. Cook, running a spatula around the edges to let the uncooked egg trickle to the bottom of the pan, for 3–4 minutes, or until almost set. Run the spatula around the edges to loosen the omelet and slide it out onto a plate. Invert by holding the pan over the plate and flipping the omelet back into the pan. Cook for another 2–3 minutes, until golden and firmly set.

SLIDE the omelet out onto a serving plate, spread the refried beans over it, and top preferably with *crema*, or with crème fraîche. Serve at once, cut into wedges.

$\mathcal{M}$EAT IS A POST-CONQUEST ADDITION to the Mexican diet that started out as the food of Spanish aristocrats. It took a while to become affordable to all—and, in fact, most European meats never did filter down to popular use. The one that eclipsed all others was the most Spanish of meats, pork. When not eaten freshly butchered, it was turned into a range of cured products and sausages, based on Spanish originals with varying degrees of Mexicanization. In the form of rendered lard, it became Mexico's everyday cooking fat.

Beef comes in a very distant second. Strangely, this holds true even in Veracruz, which is the largest cattle-raising state of the Mexican south. Everywhere in the state, from the torrid coastal plains to

PORK

AND

BEEF

the cool hill country, you see grazing lands—not usually epic-scale ranches, but lots of small ones with perhaps a mixture of steers and dairy cows. Yet most of the beef is destined for export, and at markets in the butcher stalls, you generally

see the same limited selection of scrawny stewing-beef cuts as in other states of central-southern Mexico. Beef is, however, definitely more prominent in Veracruzan cuisine than in that of neighboring Oaxaca. I found several delicious surprises including an excellent hash with potatoes and chayotes, a simple and savory version of braised oxtail, and a celebratory dish from Los Tuxtlas (*tatabiguiyayo*).

Most kinds of meat and poultry are cooked by moist-heat methods (usually braising) and the amounts used are often modest, with other ingredients supplementing the meat. But there are a few great specialties for carnivores, including the Catemaco-area wood-smoked pork loin disconcertingly called "monkey meat" (*carne de chango*) and *longaniza*, a first-class pork sausage that's often smoked in the same way.

Among Veracruz's meat dishes, probably the ones with the oldest pre-Hispanic roots are *tesmole verde* (a soup-stew with beef and assorted fresh vegetables) and *barbacoa de puerco* (a modern pork version of *barbacoa*, the ancient Mexican technique of pit-cooking food wrapped in fragrant leaves). The African influence is evident in the use of ingredients like plantain and West Indian pumpkin in braised pork dishes.

Barbacoa de Puerco

FRAGRANT OVEN-STEAMED PORK

*I*N SOME VERSIONS OF VERACRUZAN *BARBACOA*, THE MEAT is wrapped in individual packets and steamed over boiling water. Teresa Pérez Cabrera, a former chef at Las Brisas del Mar, gave me this alternative version, in which the meat cooks in a large lidded casserole or Dutch oven, lined with a double thickness of banana leaves and *hoja santa* to keep in the perfumed steam. The pot must be very tightly closed to keep the steam from escaping; in Veracruz, cooks sometimes seal the edges with a moist masa-water paste. I prefer to wrap the pot very securely with several layers of heavy-duty aluminum foil. Use whatever method works best for you.

Banana leaves are frequently used in Veracruz and the other central Gulf coast states. Cooks there can simply cut one of the mammoth leaves — a small one might be three feet long — and trim it into rectangles of any desired size. In this country, Latin and Southeast Asian ethnic markets carry packages of frozen banana leaves cut into large pieces. It's a great convenience, or would be if the frozen leaves didn't tend to split on thawing. Sometimes you have to sort through a whole 1-pound package to find a few usable pieces. (I usually buy a second package for insurance.) You can sometimes patch one piece with a strip from another. All this is worth it, however, because of the lovely fragrance they impart to anything wrapped in them.

Makes 8–10 servings

4 pounds boneless pork butt, cut into large (3-inch) chunks
2 teaspoons coarse salt
6 ounces ancho chiles (10–12 chiles), stemmed and seeded
1 teaspoon cumin seeds
1/2 teaspoon allspice berries
10 bay leaves
5 large fresh thyme sprigs or 2 teaspoons crumbled dried thyme
1 large white onion, coarsely chopped
10 large garlic cloves, coarsely chopped
1 1-pound package banana leaves (see above), thawed if frozen, gently wiped clean
12 large fresh *hoja santa* leaves or 24 dried leaves (see page 42)
12 dried avocado leaves (see page 41)

IN a large mixing bowl, toss the pork chunks with the salt. Refrigerate for 1 hour. (Presalting helps develop the flavor of meat.)

PLACE the chiles in a large saucepan and add enough water to cover by 1 inch. Bring to a boil over high heat and cook for 10 minutes. Drain, reserving the cooking liquid.

HEAT a small heavy skillet over medium-low heat. Add the cumin, allspice, and 5 of the bay leaves and toast, shaking the pan, for 1–2 minutes, or until fragrant. Let cool slightly, then grind to a powder in an electric coffee or spice grinder or with a mortar and pestle.

PLACE the spice mixture in a blender with the drained chiles, thyme, onion, and garlic. Working in batches as necessary, process to a puree, adding enough of the reserved cooking liquid to help the action of the blades (³/₄–1 cup per batch).

USING a wooden spoon or pusher, force the pureed chile mixture through a medium-mesh sieve into a bowl. Rub the paste over the meat to coat thoroughly. Cover and refrigerate for at least 1 hour or (preferably) overnight.

WHEN you are ready to assemble the *barbacoa*, preheat the oven to 350°F.

CHOOSE a very large deep casserole or Dutch oven. Cut the banana leaves into pieces large enough to hang over the sides of the casserole by 6 inches and line the bottom and sides of the casserole with them, overlapping generously. Arrange half of the *hoja santa* leaves on the bottom over the banana leaves. Scatter the avocado leaves and the remaining 5 bay leaves over the *hoja santa*. Add the meat, with the chile marinade, and cover with the rest of the *hoja santa*. Fold over the ends of the banana leaves to enclose the meat very snugly. Cover the pot as tightly as possible (see headnote).

BAKE until the meat is falling-apart tender, 2–2¹/₂ hours. To serve, unfold the banana leaves and spoon out portions of the meat with the rich sauce.

Adobo *H*uasteco

CHILE-BRAISED SPARERIBS
FROM THE HUASTECA

*T*HE WELL-LOVED MEXICAN TECHNIQUE OF COOKING MEAT by starting it in a small amount of liquid and letting it brown in its own rendered fat after the water evaporates isn't familiar in this country. But it ought to be. It's really a type of braising-in-reverse. Short of roasting, nothing concentrates the meat flavor more directly, as shown in this easy but robust dish from Santa María de Guadalupe Armenta Guzmán ("Lupita").

Makes 4 servings

Adobo can mean several different things in Mexican cooking, but in this case it's a very simple chile-based sauce added to the meat partway through cooking. The chiles have the extra flavor that Lupita Armenta always gives them by soaking them in good homemade stock rather than water. Serve the spareribs with Rice with Roasted Tomatoes (page 206), Steamed Potatoes (page 279), or refried beans.

> 2 pounds meaty pork spareribs, chopped into 2-inch lengths
> 1½–2 teaspoons salt, or to taste
> 1 cup boiling water
> 4 ancho chiles, stemmed and seeded
> 4 cups Basic Pork or Chicken Stock (page 144 or 142), heated
> 5 garlic cloves
> 5 cloves

SEASON the spareribs with about 1½ teaspoons of the salt. Pour the boiling water into a heavy medium Dutch oven or large heavy saucepan set over medium-high heat. Add the meat, reduce the heat to medium, and cook, uncovered, stirring occasionally, for about 30 minutes. During the last 5–10 minutes, start checking carefully as the last of the water boils off. At this stage, the meat will be starting to render out some of its fat. Keep cooking, stirring frequently to prevent scorching, until it is literally frying in its own fat, 5–10 minutes longer. It should be deep golden but not overbrowned.

AS soon as you've started the meat, begin the chile sauce. Rinse and griddle-dry the chiles following the directions on page 50. Place in a medium bowl and cover with the hot stock; let sit for 20 minutes.

MEANWHILE, griddle-roast and peel the garlic following the

directions on page 58; set aside. Place a small heavy skillet over medium-high heat, add the cloves, and toast until fragrant, about 1 minute. Grind the cloves using a mortar and pestle.

PLACE the chiles and their soaking liquid in a blender along with the garlic and cloves. Puree very thoroughly.

POUR the chile sauce over the browning spareribs. Cook, covered, over medium-low heat for another 20 minutes, or until the ribs are very tender. Taste for salt, add a little if desired, and serve.

Carne en Salsa de Licores

PORK IN FRUIT LIQUEUR SAUCE

Makes 8–10 servings

ℰNRIQUETA IZAGUIRRE DE VIRUÉS, OF THE FAMOUS LIQUEUR-making families Virués and Izaguirre in Xico, borrowed the idea for this dish from the well-known *carne enpulcada*, or pork in *pulque* sauce. Given her heritage, it was a natural switch to use fruit liqueurs instead. The combination of liqueurs and vinegar produces a vividly flavored sweet-and-sour sauce.

In Xico, the meat would be pork loin, but in the United States, this cut is so lean that it comes out like baked cardboard. I've opted for a fresh ham, a cut that I like to use for party dishes (a whole carved fresh ham is great in a buffet). Fresh ham is the *uncured* leg of pork. In many places, it will be necessary to special-order this cut from your butcher; do *not* confuse it with smoked or brine-cured ham.

9 garlic cloves, 5 coarsely chopped, 4 left whole
6 fresh thyme sprigs, leaves only, or 2 teaspoons crumbled dried thyme
6 fresh oregano sprigs, leaves only, or 2 teaspoons dried crumbled oregano
10 Italian parsley sprigs
2 teaspoons salt, or to taste
2 teaspoons freshly ground black pepper
1/2 fresh ham, preferably butt half (bone-in); about 6 pounds (see above)
2–3 tablespoons lard, preferably home-rendered (see page 66)
1 large white onion, sliced into thin half-moons
6 scallions, green tops only, coarsely chopped
1 1/2 cups orange liqueur, preferably a low-alcohol brand such as Colonial Club (see page 202)
1 cup blackberry liqueur, preferably a low-alcohol brand
1 cup cider vinegar

USING a mortar and pestle or a food processor, grind the chopped garlic to a paste with the herbs, 1 teaspoon of the salt, and the pepper. With the tip of a sharp knife, pierce shallow incisions all over the ham, and push a little of the paste into each. Refrigerate, covered, for at least 4 hours, or overnight.

PREHEAT the oven to 375°F.

RUB a light film of lard all over the meat and season with the remaining 1 teaspoon salt. Scatter the onion, scallions, and whole garlic cloves over the bottom of a large deep baking pan. Place the ham on this bed of aromatics. Combine the liqueurs and vinegar in a medium bowl and pour over the meat. Cover the pan tightly (wrap snugly in several layers of aluminum foil if it has no lid) and bake for 3 hours, turning twice, until tender. Uncover the ham and bake until browned, about another 20 minutes. Transfer the ham to a platter and let sit for a few minutes before carving.

MEANWHILE, set a medium-mesh sieve over a bowl and pour the contents of the roasting pan into it. Use a wooden spoon or pusher to force through as much as possible of the flavorful solids.

CARVE the ham and pass the pan sauce in a gravy boat.

Carne de Chango

SMOKED PORK LOIN STRIPS

Makes 4–6 servings

CARNE DE CHANGO, OR *CARNE DE MONO*, LITERALLY MEANS "monkey meat." Some say that at one time this famous smoked specialty of the Catemaco area was made from local monkeys. That may be—the only monkeys now left in the region are a colony of Asian macaques imported from Thailand by University of Veracruz behavioral scientists, who supervise them on an island in the lake. Today the "monkey meat" is pork. Even the name has turned into just *carne ahumada* (smoked meat) on most restaurant menus.

I kept thinking of this delicacy as we explored the wooded hills around jewel-like Lake Catemaco, periodically getting haunting whiffs of the wood fires that most local families still routinely build to cook breakfast and dinner. At certain hours, the whole area smells like a gigantic fireplace. But the arrangements for smoking *carne de chango* are a little more complex. Some people position the slabs of marinated meat on racks over a fire made with green wood (to produce more smoke) and aromatic leaves and seasonings. Others smoke the meat in special adobe ovens. *Carne de chango* can be held for a week or more after cooking. To serve, you then flash-fry it in hot lard and dish it up with a lively local salsa like the chile-lime sauce on page 305.

I fell in love with *carne de chango* as soon as I tasted it, and I longed to re-create that evocative flavor at home. I expected much trial and error, but it was surprisingly easy. The procedure certainly wasn't identical to the way they do it in Catemaco, but the result was remarkably close.

The necessary equipment is not terribly hard to assemble. The only unusual item I had to find was a very sharp long thin-bladed knife for whittling the meat into sheets. I ended up with a meat-filleting knife (not the same as one for fish fillets, which would be too flexible for this purpose). A straight-bladed slicing knife with a pointed tip would also work; a boning knife might do, although the curved shape is not ideal. I heated my kettle grill (I don't have a special smoker-grill) with good hardwood charcoal from a local gourmet shop and used soaked mesquite wood chips for smoking. (If you don't like the aggressiveness of mesquite—I happen to love it, especially with these flavors—I suggest apple or cherry wood chips.) I used a medium-sized metal container (a 9-x-5-inch aluminum loaf pan) to hold water for steam and a candy thermometer to measure the temperature inside the grill.

2 pounds boneless pork loin in one piece, trimmed of nearly all surface fat
1 teaspoon coarse salt
1 teaspoon freshly ground black pepper
3/4 cup freshly squeezed lime juice
3/4 cup freshly squeezed orange juice
10 garlic cloves, crushed
3 tablespoons lard, preferably home-rendered (see page 66), or vegetable oil

CUT the meat crosswise into sections about 3 inches long (the number of pieces will depend on the shape of the meat you start out with). With a very sharp thin-bladed knife (see headnote), score a shallow cut (about 1/4 inch deep) lengthwise into one piece. Then, holding the blade lengthwise and rotating the meat as necessary, begin to cut as if you were peeling an apple or potato — but instead of removing only an outer layer, you should carve the entire piece into one long, sheet-like strip about 1/4 inch thick. Repeat with the rest of the meat pieces.

RUB the strips of meat all over with the salt and pepper. Combine the lime juice, orange juice, and garlic in a large glass baking dish or other shallow dish. Add the meat strips, turning to moisten them on all sides. Cover and refrigerate, turning the meat occasionally, for 2–3 hours.

ABOUT 30 minutes before you are ready to smoke the meat, soak about 3 cups wood chips in 1 quart of water (you may need to add a little more water from time to time). If you have a smoker-grill, set it up according to the manufacturer's directions. Otherwise, do as I did with a standard kettle grill: Mound about 15 large pieces of good hardwood charcoal (commercial briquettes will not do) on the left side of the grill and place a medium-sized metal container (see above) on the right side. Position the rack about 6 inches above the coals. Light the coals, preferably using an electric coil starter, chimney starter, or compressed solid starter. (Lighting fluids are the means of last resort — most leave an awful kerosene smell.)

LET the coals burn until red-hot all over. Close the lid and open a top vent just enough to insert a candy thermometer 5 inches into the chamber. Pull it out at frequent intervals to check the temperature: when it reaches 200°F, add about 1 cup of soaked wood chips to the coals. Remove the meat from the marinade and blot dry with paper towels. Open the lid, quickly place the meat on the rack over the water dish, and close the lid. (Any meat drippings will fall into the water rather than making a lot of acrid smoke as they hit the hot coals.) The meat must smoke for about 40 minutes at a temperature between 185°F and 200°F. Watch carefully, pulling out the thermometer periodically to check and occasionally feeding in another handful of wood chips. If you see the thermometer dipping below 185°F, add another coal to the fire. If it starts getting too hot, open another vent for 2–3 minutes. Turn the meat halfway through the cooking. It is done when it takes on a light reddish tint. The *carne de chango* can be fried at once or stored, covered, in the refrigerator for up to a week.

WHEN you are ready to serve the meat, heat the lard or oil in a large heavy skillet over medium-high heat. When it ripples, quickly flash-fry the meat on both sides, 1–2 minutes in all. The strips can be cut into large individual serving pieces to be eaten with a knife and fork or into 1/2-to-1-inch pieces to be used as a taco filling.

Longaniza

CHILE-SPICED PORK SAUSAGE

THE LONGANIZA OF VERACRUZ IS ESSENTIALLY IDENTICAL to sausage mixtures I've eaten in other parts of Mexico as chorizo. The one distinction that seems to hold true (most of the time) in Veracruz is that the meat for chorizo generally has a finer texture; that for *longaniza* is coarser, with visible bits of meat and fat.

In any case, *longaniza* is a vital part of the Veracruzan kitchen. People stuff it into long skinny casings and sell it coiled up like a garden hose or make it into short, thick links that can be sliced or crumbled. Or the mixture can be used on its own, shaped into patties like small thin hamburgers. I also find it convenient to pack the loose mixture into small plastic bags, in 1-cup portions, and freeze it for future use as, say, a topping for any of the tortilla-like masa specialties described in the corn dishes chapter.

Veracruzans love *longaniza* as a breakfast dish or an appetizer — it's wonderful fried in chunks and rolled up in tortillas with refried beans, as we saw the people at the next table eating it at Restaurant Daría in Zempoala. My version of *longaniza* comes from Doña Daría herself — Daría Muñoz, the founder of this forty-five-year-old dining spot.

Before you embark on this recipe, make sure of the quality of your meat. Let the butcher know in no uncertain terms that you do not want unfortunate bits of gristle and tendon in the meat. You must decide whether to have it ground at the store or chop it yourself for a more interesting texture (gristly bits will be painfully conspicuous if you choose the latter). In either case, you will need a 3:1 ratio (by weight) of meat to fat. Ask the butcher to grind the meat and fat together *coarsely* (very important), or take them home and get out your sharpest, heaviest chopping knife.

If you plan to stuff all of the mixture into casings, buy about 25 feet of 1/2-inch hog casings. Use the stuffing attachment of a meat grinder or kitchen mixer, following the manufacturer's directions. I often make part of the mixture into sausage links and use the rest loose.

Makes about 4 pounds

3 pounds boneless pork, preferably shoulder meat
1 pound unsalted pork fat
8 ounces ancho chiles (22–25 small chiles), stemmed and seeded
6 dried (*not* canned) chipotle chiles, either meco- or morita-type (see page 48)
8 garlic cloves
1 teaspoon cumin seeds
6 cloves
1/2 teaspoon black peppercorns
1/4 cup cider vinegar, or to taste
1 tablespoon salt, or to taste
Hog casings for sausages (optional; see headnote)
Lard, preferably home-rendered (see page 66), or vegetable oil, for frying

IF you have not had the meat and fat ground, cut them into manageable-sized chunks and chop them together on a large cutting board using a large heavy knife or Chinese cleaver. The pieces should be no larger than 1/4 inch, and the fat should be evenly distributed. Set aside in a large mixing bowl.

RINSE and griddle-dry the anchos and chipotles following the directions on page 50. Place in a bowl, cover with boiling water, and let stand for 20 minutes.

DRAIN the soaked chiles. Place in a blender with the garlic, cumin, cloves, peppercorns, and vinegar and process to a paste. (You can add a little water if needed to help the action of the blades, but the mixture should be quite thick.) Work the chile paste and salt into the meat. Check the seasoning by frying a small bit of the mixture for a minute or two and tasting; add a little more vinegar or salt if desired.

IF USING SAUSAGE CASINGS

RUN cold water through them to rinse thoroughly and check for leaks, then tie the end or ends securely with kitchen twine and stuff them with the mixture (see headnote). You can either fill the casings in long, continuous lengths or tie into links of any desired size, but be sure to pack in the meat very tightly so that the *longaniza* will be firm enough to slice. Hang them up to air-dry for about 4 hours in as cool and airy a spot as you can find (I've used a clothes rack or a string stretched between two corners of a room); then refrigerate.

The sausages will keep well in the refrigerator for up to 1 week or in the freezer for up to 1 month.

THERE are several ways of cooking the sausage links. If panfrying, first prick the skin in several places and simmer them, barely covered with boiling water, until they release a little of the fat. Then lift them out and finish browning them in a skillet with 1–2 tablespoons lard or oil. Allow about 5 minutes per side over low heat. They can also be grilled over hot coals for 10 minutes. And I have had great success smoking them; follow the directions for *carne de chango* (page 243), turning once and allowing about 10 minutes per side.

IF USING THE SAUSAGE MIXTURE LOOSE

EITHER pack 1-cup portions into small plastic bags for freezing or shape into 3-x-1/2-inch patties and wrap well. In either case, it will keep in the refrigerator for up to 1 week or in the freezer for up to 1 month. To use, panfry the 1-cup portions in a little lard or oil over medium heat until just done, 3–4 minutes, or the patties for 3–4 minutes on each side. Like the sausage links, the patties are also very good smoked (allow about 10 minutes per side). Serve warm.

Costillas con Longaniza

SPARERIBS WITH
CHILE-SPICED PORK SAUSAGE

Makes 4–5 servings

THE TOWN OF OTATITLÁN, ON THE PAPALOAPAN RIVER only a few miles from the Veracruz-Oaxaca state border, is an out-of-the-way site renowned for nothing except the image of the Black Christ in the church of San Andrés Apostol. The striking jet-black figure is visited by pilgrims from all over Mexico. But we were amazed at the wealth of unusual dishes that people there were eager to share with us. Almost as soon as we walked into the Restorán Don Pepe, I found myself deep in conversation with the founder's daughter and principal chef, Paty (Patricia Prieto Contreras). Not only did she bring out her handwritten *recetario* (collection of recipes) in order to explain the ins and outs of various dishes, but she generously let me take away a photocopy of that priceless record.

Paty told me that *costillas con longaniza* is one of the most popular dishes at Don Pepe. The spareribs are marinated in one of those versatile bottled-condiment and lime-juice mixtures that later turn into finishing sauces. The pairing of ribs and spicy, toothsome sausage is inspired. Links of homemade *longaniza* are the best choice, but if you have to use commercial sausages, look for Spanish-style chorizo.

1 cup freshly squeezed lime juice

3 tablespoons Maggi sauce

3 tablespoons Worcestershire sauce

1 tablespoon coarsely ground black pepper

1 2-pound slab baby back pork ribs, cut into individual ribs

2 tablespoons lard, preferably home-rendered (see page 66), or vegetable oil

1 pound Chile-Spiced Pork Sausage (see page 246) or commercial Spanish-style chorizo, in links

IN a small bowl, whisk together the lime juice, Maggi sauce, Worcestershire sauce, and pepper. Place the ribs in a deep bowl and pour the mixture over them. Cover and let sit, turning occasionally, for 3–4 hours at room temperature or (preferably) overnight in the refrigerator.

WHEN you are ready to proceed with the cooking, lift the meat

from the marinade, letting it drain well, and blot dry with paper towels. Reserve the marinade.

IN a large heavy skillet, heat the lard or oil over medium heat until rippling. Add the ribs and cook, turning occasionally, until golden brown (not darkened) on both sides, about 15 minutes total. The residue of the bottled condiments will tend to stick to the bottom of the pan; adjust the heat as necessary to prevent scorching. With a slotted spoon or spatula, lift out the ribs, letting them drain well, and set aside on a platter. Pour off all but about 1 tablespoon fat from the pan. Return the pan to the stove and heat briefly.

CUT the sausage into 1-inch chunks, or if using Spanish-style chorizo, cut it on the bias into 1/3-inch slices. Add to the pan and cook, turning once, until lightly browned, about 2 minutes per side. With a slotted spoon or spatula, lift out the sausage and set aside on the platter with the ribs. Pour the reserved marinade into the pan, bring to a boil over high heat, and reduce the heat to medium. Let cook for about 2 minutes. Return the cooked ribs and sausage to the pan and stir-fry for about 2 minutes. Serve the meats with the pan sauce poured over them.

VARIATION

For *Pollo* (Chicken) *con Longaniza*, substitute a 3½-to-4-pound chicken for the pork ribs. Make the marinade as directed above. Cut the chicken into serving pieces and marinate in the refrigerator for about 2 hours, turning three or four times. Preheat the oven to 350°F. Remove the chicken from the marinade, reserving the marinade, and blot dry. Brown the chicken as above, for about 3 minutes per side, then transfer to an ovenproof casserole. Pour off all but 1 tablespoon of fat from the skillet; slice and brown the sausage links as directed above. Scatter the sausage over the chicken in the casserole. Add the marinade to the pan and bring to a boil over high heat; reduce the heat to medium and cook for 2 minutes. Pour the sauce over the chicken and sausage.

Cover the pan tightly, using several layers of aluminum foil to wrap it if there is no lid, and bake for about 35 minutes. (For best results, remove the breast pieces from the casserole after 30 minutes and keep warm; bake the leg and thigh pieces for an extra 10 minutes.)

Puerco con Calabaza

PORK WITH MASHED PUMPKIN

PUMPKIN-MEAT COMBINATIONS ARE A HALLMARK OF THE Afro-Caribbean heritage in Veracruz. This tradition is still being superbly upheld by Santiago Careaga and his wife, Elena Gutiérrez, at Santiago's Club in Tamiahua, where I tasted this dish with its unexpected North African accents of cumin and coriander seeds. Not surprisingly, their daughter, Dora Elena Careaga Gutiérrez, is a noted expert on African culinary contributions in Veracruz and co-author (with Raquel Torres) of an excellent recipe collection titled *La Cocina Afromestiza en Veracruz*. This is a meal in itself; you may want to add just a green salad.

Be sure to choose a winter squash or pumpkin with very firm, dense flesh. The Japanese kabocha squash is highly suitable, as are Hubbard and butternut squash. Probably the best kind of pumpkin is that sold as "cheese pumpkin." Or, if you want to be really authentic, go to a Latin American or Caribbean market and buy a wedge from one of the huge, meaty West Indian squashes.

Makes 4–6 servings

2	pounds boneless pork butt, cut into 1–inch chunks
2	small onions, 1 unpeeled
4	garlic cloves, 2 unpeeled
1	teaspoon salt, or to taste
1	teaspoon black peppercorns
4–5	árbol or dried serrano chiles (see page 47)
1	2½-to-3-pound pumpkin or winter squash, or a chunk of the same size cut from a West Indian squash (see above), unpeeled
¼	cup pumpkin seeds
¾	teaspoon cumin seeds
¾	teaspoon coriander seeds
2	medium-sized ripe tomatoes, coarsely chopped
3	tablespoons lard, preferably home-rendered (see page 66), or vegetable oil
2	tablespoons cider vinegar

PLACE the meat in a large pot or small Dutch oven with the unpeeled onion, unpeeled garlic, 1 teaspoon of the salt, and ½ teaspoon of the peppercorns. Add water to cover by about 1 inch. Bring to a boil over high heat; at once reduce the heat to maintain a low rolling boil and skim off any froth that rises to the surface. Cook, partly covered, for 45 minutes or until the meat is tender. Lift out the meat into a bowl, letting it drain very well. Set aside. Strain the stock through a mesh sieve. You should have 3–4 cups. Wipe out the pan and pour the stock back into it; set aside.

MEANWHILE, bring 2–3 cups of water to a boil in a small saucepan. Add the dried chiles and cook, uncovered, for about 5 minutes, or until softened. Drain and set aside.

CUT the unpeeled pumpkin or squash into 8 equal chunks, removing any seeds and strings. Add the chunks to the stock and bring to a boil over high heat. Reduce the heat to maintain a low rolling boil and cook for about 30 minutes, or until tender. Lift out the chunks, place in a colander to drain well, and let cool to room temperature. (You can freeze the stock for soup.)

SCRAPE the flesh into a bowl and discard the skin. Mash thoroughly with a potato masher or pestle. Set aside.

PLACE the pumpkin seeds in a small heavy skillet over medium-low heat. Toast, stirring and shaking the pan, until they begin to swell up and pop, 3–5 minutes. Set aside.

GRIND the cumin, coriander, and the remaining $1/2$ teaspoon peppercorns to a powder using an electric coffee or spice grinder or a mortar and pestle. Coarsely chop the remaining onion and 2 garlic cloves. Puree in a blender with the pumpkin seeds, ground spices, chopped tomatoes, and drained chiles.

IN a medium saucepan, heat 2 tablespoons of the lard or oil over medium-high heat until rippling. Add the pureed mixture, reduce the heat to medium, cover, and cook, stirring occasionally, until the fat starts to separate, about 15 minutes. Add the reserved mashed pumpkin or squash and the vinegar, stirring to mix well, and cook, covered, for 10 minutes. Taste for salt and add more if necessary.

WHILE the pumpkin mixture cooks, heat the remaining 1 tablespoon lard or oil in a large skillet over medium-high heat. Add the meat and brown lightly for about 5 minutes, letting it get a little crisp but not dried out.

SPOON the seasoned pumpkin mixture onto a platter and top with the meat. (At Santiago's, they simply combine the puree and the meat, but I like to set off the flavors more distinctly).

Picadillo de Pobre

POOR MAN'S HASHED MEAT

Makes 4 servings

ιιιιι

*A*LL MEXICANS ARE FAMILIAR WITH *PICADILLO*, WHICH IS something like our version of hash but infinitely more versatile. The fanciest kind, a favorite filling or topping for all kinds of chiles, tacos, or *antojitos*, features chopped or ground pork or beef (or sometimes shredded cooked meat or chicken) with wonderful Mediterranean-inspired accents that often include olives, almonds, raisins, cumin, *canela*, and/or cloves. (The filling for Stuffed Jalapeño Chiles in Vinaigrette, page 104, is one of the simpler *picadillos*.) This "poor man's" version is based on a recipe from the Restorán Caperucita in San Andrés Tuxtla.

The reason for the name is obvious: the meat is thriftily stretched with diced potato and chayote, while luxurious ingredients like the olives, almonds, and "sweet" spices are left out. The main seasoning comes from everyday fresh herbs that people in the region grow or cheaply buy at market as *hierbas de guisar* (stewing herbs): oregano, parsley, mint, and cilantro. Some cooks color the dish with achiote paste, an authentic and pretty regional touch that I have mixed feelings about because the earthy flavor tends to overpower the subtler beef and fresh herbs. Use or omit it as you prefer. Most *picadillos* are cooked until fairly dry, but *picadillo de pobre* should remain a little soupy. Serve it with Pilaf-Style White Rice (page 291).

Be sure to use best-quality beef without any annoying gristly bits, which stand out conspicuously in hand-chopped meat.

1	pound boneless beef chuck, trimmed
1	large Red Bliss or other waxy-type potato
1	large chayote
1½	teaspoons salt, or to taste
2	tablespoons vegetable oil
1	medium-sized white onion, finely chopped
1	large garlic clove, minced
1	large or 2 medium-sized ripe tomatoes, finely chopped
½	teaspoon ground cumin, preferably freshly ground
½	teaspoon crumbled dried Mexican oregano
1	teaspoon freshly ground black pepper

6 large mint sprigs, leaves only, finely chopped

6 cilantro sprigs, finely chopped

3 large oregano sprigs, leaves only, finely chopped

6 Italian parsley sprigs, finely chopped

1 Ping-Pong-ball-sized lump fresh masa or 2 tablespoons masa harina (see page 51)

1 cup chicken stock, preferably homemade (see page 142)

2 teaspoons commercial or homemade achiote paste (see page 43; optional)

WITH a large heavy sharp knife or Chinese cleaver, cut the meat into chunks. Chop into tiny dice, not quite as fine as ground meat. Set aside.

PEEL the potato. Peel and pit the chayote, following the directions on page 55. Cut them both into 1/4-inch dice. Place in a medium saucepan and add water to cover. Add 1 teaspoon of the salt, bring to a boil over high heat, and cook for 3 minutes. Drain and set aside.

IN a large skillet, heat the oil over medium-high heat until rippling. Add the onion and garlic and cook until the onion is translucent, about 3 minutes. Add the tomatoes and cook for about 5 minutes, to evaporate most of the juices. Stir in the chopped meat, cumin, oregano, and pepper, reduce the heat to medium, and cook, stirring, for about 3 minutes, or until the beef has changed color. Stir in the diced potato and chayote, together with the herbs.

DISSOLVE the masa or masa harina in the stock, along with the achiote paste, if using, and add to the skillet. Taste for salt and add up to 1/2 teaspoon more, if desired. Cook, stirring occasionally, for 3 minutes, or until the liquid has reduced to a medium-thick gravy. Serve hot.

Tesmole *Verde*

SOUP-STEW WITH GREEN HERBS AND VEGETABLES

*F*RESH GARDEN VEGETABLES ARE STRANGELY ABSENT FROM the offerings of Mexican restaurants or home cooks proudly trotting out their best dishes for the benefit of visitors. So as a vegetable lover, I was in heaven when I encountered this soupy, aromatic stew at Las Brisas del Mar restaurant in Boca del Río. The rich brothy sauce, or saucy broth, can be made with either beef or chicken.

Tesmoles belong to the big family of soup-stews so beloved in the central-southern areas of Mexico and invariably seem to include minute and toothsome masa dumplings (*bolitas*). The medley of green vegetables used in this version can be varied according to what's good in the market. The cooks at Brisas del Mar used large mature fresh lima beans that stood up well to cooking. In this country, it's not always easy to find a good equivalent. I've successfully used frozen Fordhook limas or fresh green fava beans. I suggest avoiding baby limas — the vegetables in this dish should be full-sized and sturdy, not tiny and super-delicate. If you have to use baby limas, add them only at the end, after the other vegetables and just before the *bolitas*.

Note that the cilantro is used partly for flavor and partly for body. Use the smaller amount if you can get fresh *hoja santa*, the larger amount if you can find only dried *hoja santa*.

Makes about 6 servings

4 pounds beef shin with marrow bones, sawed into 2-inch sections by the butcher

2 medium-sized white onions, 1 unpeeled

6 garlic cloves, 4 unpeeled

3 teaspoons salt, or to taste

6–7 cups cold water

Corn Masa Dumplings (page 131)

6 large fresh *hoja santa* leaves or 10 dried leaves (see page 42)

10–20 cilantro sprigs (¹⁄₂–1 small bunch; see above)

4 jalapeño chiles

1 cup shelled fresh large lima beans (see above)

2 ears corn, fresh or frozen, husked if fresh, and cut into 2-inch rounds

8 ounces mature green beans, topped and tailed
2 chayotes, peeled and pitted (see page 55), and cut lengthwise into 1¹/₂-inch slices
2 medium zucchini, halved lengthwise and cut into 1¹/₂-inch slices

PLACE the meat in a large saucepan or small pot with the unpeeled onion, the unpeeled garlic cloves, and the salt. Add enough cold water to cover the meat and bring to a boil over high heat. Quickly reduce the heat to maintain a low rolling boil; skim off any froth that rises to the top. Cook, partly covered, until the meat is tender, 2–2¹/₂ hours.

WHILE the meat is cooking, make the dumplings. Set aside, covered with a damp towel, while you prepare the other ingredients.

WHEN the meat is tender, lift it out, letting it drain well, and set aside. Strain the stock and return it to the rinsed-out pot; set aside.

COARSELY chop the remaining onion and the remaining 2 garlic cloves. Place the onion and garlic in a blender with half the *hoja santa*, half the cilantro, 2 of the jalapeños, and about 1 cup of the strained stock, or enough to facilitate blending. If using fresh *hoja santa*, add the smaller amount of cilantro and process the ingredients to a puree. If using dried *hoja santa*, add half the larger amount of cilantro. Pour the mixture into the remaining stock (set the blender container aside) and bring to a boil over high heat. Quickly reduce the heat to maintain a low rolling boil. Taste for seasoning and add a pinch or two of salt if desired.

RETURN the meat to the soup. Add the lima beans and cook for 3 minutes. Notch a small cross in the tops of the remaining 2 jalapeños to release some of their spiciness and add to the soup, along with the corn, green beans, chayotes, and zucchini. Cook for 7–8 minutes, or until the vegetables are just crisp-tender. Add the dumplings to the soup and cook just until they float to the top, 3–5 minutes.

MEANWHILE, place the remaining *hoja santa* in the blender. If using the fresh herb, puree with a few tablespoons of stock or water. If using the dried *hoja santa*, add the remaining half of the cilantro and process in the same way.

STIR into the soup and serve immediately.

Tatabiguiyayo

BEEF STEW FOR FIESTAS

Makes about 6 servings

ONE OF MY BIGGEST FRUSTRATIONS WAS NOT BEING ABLE
to witness the making of authentic *tatabiguiyayo,* a kind of beef stew
that is de rigueur at village celebrations around Los Tuxtlas — wed-
dings, baptisms, and processions of holy images. Anthropologist and
historian Fernando Bustamante Rábago thinks the custom may have
sprung up in cattle-raising areas where providing a massive communal meal was a way of displaying prestige. (Maybe not all that different from a Texas whole-steer barbecue.) In any case, a traditional
tatabiguiyayo is an outdoor meal on a grand scale.

I make no claims for the authenticity of my small-scale version,
which is loosely based on different accounts I've heard or read of this
unique dish. (After all, you wouldn't say a stovetop version of a clam-
bake was "authentic"!) But I certainly can claim that it's delicious and
that the ingredients are those of an authentic *tatabiguiyayo.*

For best results, it's worth searching out a thick, solid piece of
best-quality beef chuck and cutting it into cubes yourself. The cubes
of stewing chuck sold in most markets are often gristly. Serve with
freshly made corn tortillas.

About 6½ cups water

2 teaspoons salt, or to taste

2 pounds beef chuck, trimmed and cut into largish (about
1½-inch) cubes

1 pound beef marrow bones, sawed into 1½-to-2-inch pieces by
the butcher

½ teaspoon cumin seeds

½ teaspoon black peppercorns

10–12 cloves

12–13 ounces ripe currant tomatoes (see page 61), grape tomatoes,
or very small, sweet cherry tomatoes

1 medium-large white onion, coarsely chopped

1 garlic clove, coarsely chopped

2 tablespoons masa harina (see page 51)

1 tablespoon commercial or homemade achiote paste (see
page 43)

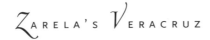

1 medium-sized red onion
20 large Italian parsley sprigs, leaves only
15 cilantro sprigs, leaves only
10 large mint sprigs, leaves only
6 oregano sprigs, leaves only
1 large bunch chives

IN a large saucepan or Dutch oven, bring 6 cups of the water to a boil with the salt. Add the meat and bones, reduce the heat to medium-low, and cook, partly covered, for 1–1½ hours, or until half-tender.

COMBINE the cumin, peppercorns, and cloves in an electric coffee or spice mill and grind to a fine powder. Puree the tomatoes with the onion and garlic in a blender or food processor. Add the spice and tomato mixtures to the cooking stock (you don't need to wash out the blender or food processor) and cook for another 30–40 minutes.

ADD the masa harina and achiote paste to the blender or processor (you don't need to wash it) and process with enough of the remaining water to make a paste. Scrape the mixture into the pot. Stir well to dissolve and cook, stirring occasionally, for another 30 minutes, or until the stock is lightly thickened and the achiote has lost its raw taste.

CHOP the red onion and herbs very fine. Add to the stew and cook for about 5 minutes longer. Remove the marrow bones, skim off the fat, and serve.

Tlaxhuayajú

STEWED OXTAILS

Makes 4 servings

THIS IS ONE OF SEVERAL FINE RECIPES THAT I WAS GIVEN at the Papantla chapter of INSEN, Mexico's National Institute for Old Age (*Instituto Nacional de la Senilitud*), a remarkable organization that, among other projects, has a program which allows a disappearing generation to pass on local cooking traditions. Noemí Castro Domínguez demonstrated this traditional Totonac Indian dish with the characteristic local accent of mint.

For best results, start the cooking a day ahead. This will give you time to remove the large amount of fat that even carefully trimmed oxtails always release in cooking. Serve with freshly made corn tortillas.

2 pounds oxtails, sawed into 1¹/₂-to-2-inch sections by the butcher and carefully trimmed of fat

1 medium-sized white onion, unpeeled

2 garlic cloves, unpeeled

1¹/₂–2 teaspoons salt, or to taste

1 teaspoon black peppercorns

8–10 cups water

2 dried (*not* canned) chipotle chiles, preferably morita-type (see page 48), stemmed and seeded

5 large mint sprigs

AT least 8–10 hours before serving time or, preferably, the day before, place the oxtails in a medium pot with the onion, garlic, salt, and peppercorns. Add enough of the water to cover by about 2 inches. Bring to a boil over high heat; at once reduce the heat to maintain a low rolling boil. Cook, covered, until the meat is tender, about 3 hours.

LIFT out the meat, let cool, and refrigerate. Strain the stock, discard the solids, and let the stock cool to room temperature, then refrigerate, uncovered, until the congealed fat is hard enough to be lifted out and discarded. You should have about 6 cups of stock.

WHILE the meat cooks, place the chiles in a small heavy skillet over very low heat. Toast, shaking the pan and stirring constantly, until they are very dry and brittle, but not scorched, about 10 minutes. Let cool, then grind to a powder in a food processor or mortar.

WHEN you are ready to finish the dish, return the oxtails and stock to the (clean) pot and bring to a boil over high heat. Reduce the heat to medium-low, add the ground chipotles and the mint, and cook until the flavors are well blended, about 15 minutes. Taste for seasoning, add more salt if desired, and serve.

$\int$IDE DISHES AS SUCH are not as deeply ingrained in the Mexican meal structure as they are in the United States. Mexicans cook a lot with vegetables, but that doesn't usually translate into a big selection of vegetable accompaniments to a meat entrée. Things are starting to change a little with the increase in travel. But the major vegetable dishes of Mexico — for example, beans — have traditionally been much more than accompaniments. In Veracruz, as everywhere else in Mexico, beans are the pillar of the meal, not a little something to go with it. Since pre-Hispanic times, they have been a more fundamental part of the diet than *verduras* (garden vegetables), and they are almost always black beans.

Rice, too, is more of a basic staple than an accompaniment. It arrived later with the Spanish, who knew that the tropical wetlands of

VEGETABLES
AND
SIDE
DISHES

the New World were the perfect growing environment and that the slaves had grown at least one variety in Africa. Since rice and beans complement each other nutritionally when eaten together, the pairing of the New World legume and Old World grain became the staff of life everywhere throughout the Afro-Caribbean plantations. (See my version of *moros y cristianos* for a richly sensuous modern interpretation of this historic favorite.)

Another African contribution that links Veracruz, Cuba, and the Caribbean islands is a passionate fondness for *viandas*, a Cuban term for inexpensive starchy foods — mostly tubers — that any peasant or slave with a tiny patch of soil could grow to feed a family. The first one of them, which Columbus found the Taino Indians eating in the islands, was yuca. It grows readily in Veracruz, along with the very similar malanga, and later introductions, such as potatoes, sweet potatoes, taro from the Pacific, and African plantains, which, of course, aren't tubers but are always considered honorary *viandas*. The dense West Indian–type pumpkin (a New World native that went to Africa and then returned with the slaves) is often included in the tribe as well.

Originally the slaves ate these vegetables just boiled and mashed, perhaps with some scraps of pork. But people kept the taste for *viandas* long after slavery ended and the races had intermarried. They began mashing them with seasonings (*machuca de plátano*), frying them in oil with or without garlic (*yuca al ajillo* and *plátanos fritos*) and turning them into batter-dipped fritters (*tortitas de yuca*).

*I*N VERACRUZ, I ALSO FOUND a number of dishes that fit comfortably into the category of vegetable side dishes — more than I generally expect to find when eating in Mexico. I was delighted to encounter fresh salads, something I always crave after I've been in Mexico for a week. I would like to awaken everyone to the pleasures of hearts of palm turned into a creamy puree. And I invite all pasta lovers to sample a beautiful Christmas dish of spaghetti with green poblanos.

Ensalada de Palmitos

HEARTS OF PALM SALAD

THIS SIMPLE BUT UNIVERSALLY POPULAR MIXTURE IS equally good as a side dish or an appetizer spread. It's one of many dishes made on the home ground of several palm varieties resembling the Florida "swamp cabbage," with a tender, delicious artichoke-like core at the center of the young trunks. Because the whole tree must be cut down to obtain a small yield of palm heart, it remains a highly limited crop in ecologically fragile areas like Florida, and I have never seen it sold fresh in this country. Suitable palm trees are much more abundant in Veracruz and are used for many purposes such as building materials, so harvesting the fresh hearts of palm is not such a wasteful practice. Even in Veracruz, however, cooks are known to resort to canned hearts of palm. I visited a factory in Pánuco where they are put up, though I doubt that that the brand is available in the United States. Most of the ones sold here come from Brazil or Costa Rica. Can or jar sizes vary confusingly from brand to brand; don't worry as long as you end up with roughly 26–30 ounces in all.

2 garlic cloves
1 28-ounce or two 14-ounce cans hearts of palm, drained
1/3 cup olive oil (preferably extra-virgin), or as needed
1/2 cup finely chopped whites of scallions
Dash of salt (optional)

PROCESS the garlic to a paste in a mini-processor. Add the hearts of palm and process to a rough puree. With the motor running, add the oil in a thin stream until you see the mixture coming together in a velvety puree. The absorbency of palm hearts can vary; any one batch may take a bit less or more than 1/3 cup.

TRANSFER to a serving bowl and stir in the scallions. Taste for salt and add a little if desired (some canned brands have more salt than others). Serve within a few hours or hold in the refrigerator for up to a day. (In that case, reserve the scallions and stir them in just before serving.)

Ensalada de Lechuga con Aderezo de Cilantro

ROMAINE LETTUCE SALAD WITH CILANTRO
DRESSING

I RECEIVED THIS RECIPE FROM THE ELEGANT LOLITA FUSTER
de Isla, the eighty-five-year-old grande dame of fine cooking in San
Andrés Tuxtla. I spent a lovely afternoon listening to her recollections
of living and cooking at La Isla, the ranch where she and her husband
raised cattle and grew pineapples for many years. In Mexico, to serve
a green salad like this marks a cook as having sophisticated, cosmopolitan taste.

Makes 6–8 servings

1	large head of romaine lettuce, ragged outer leaves discarded
1	cucumber (any type), peeled, seeded, and julienned
4	large celery stalks, trimmed and julienned
20	cilantro sprigs, leaves only
1/2	cup olive oil
1/4	cup cider vinegar
1/2	small white onion, finely chopped
1	teaspoon salt, or to taste
	Freshly ground black pepper to taste

HAVE ready a large bowl of ice water. Rinse the lettuce under
cold running water, tear into bite-sized pieces, and let stand in the ice
water to crisp for 10–15 minutes. Drain well and dry very thoroughly
in a salad spinner.

IN a salad bowl, combine the lettuce, cucumber, and celery.

IN a blender, combine the cilantro and olive oil; process to a
puree. Add the remaining ingredients and blend until smooth. Toss
with the salad and serve.

Ensalada de Germen

SPROUTS SALAD

Makes 4 servings

PEOPLE WHO REGULARLY TRAVEL IN MEXICO KNOW HOW hard it is to find salads — or other dishes, for that matter — featuring *any* kind of raw fresh vegetables or greens on restaurant menus. Usually you must implore someone to bring you anything corresponding to our idea of a simple salad. So I was overjoyed to find this refreshing exception to the national rule when I dined at Restorán Romanchú in Orizaba. It was a treat all the better for being completely unexpected; generally speaking, sprouts have yet to make it onto the Mexican table. When I knew more about Orizaba, I realized that the local concentration of industries draws a lot of foreign business travelers, which may be why Romanchú was offering something so strange by Mexican standards. It was made with alfalfa sprouts, which I like the best.

4 cups (2 pints or about 1 pound) alfalfa or other sprouts
2 garlic cloves
1 teaspoon salt, or to taste
  Juice of 1 large lime
1/4 cup olive oil
1 Mexican-type avocado (Hass or Fuerte)
  Cilantro leaves for garnish (optional)

RINSE the sprouts thoroughly under cold running water. Shake off as much water as possible and let drain for 2–4 hours in a colander. Blot dry with paper towels to remove the last traces of moisture.

IN a large mortar or small mixing bowl, crush the garlic to a paste with the salt. Whisk in the lime juice and oil.

PEEL and pit the avocado. Cut it into 1/4-inch dice.

PLACE the sprouts in a serving bowl and pull apart the strands with your fingers. Add the avocado and the garlic dressing; toss to combine well. Serve at once, garnished with the cilantro if desired.

Chiles Secos Curtidos

PICKLED CHIPOTLE CHILES

Makes about 2 quarts

*I*N XICO, THIS VERSION OF *CHILES SECOS CURTIDOS* IS SO popular that you find housewives setting up little tables on the doorsteps and selling pickled chiles to passersby. The *chile seco* of the title refers to the particularly bright-flavored variety of chipotles more commonly called *chile morita*. If you can find them, you will find the flavor of these pickled chiles especially fresh and floral.

This recipe is from Odilia Suárez Hernández, the wife of Xico's mayor. It's a time-consuming dish to prepare, not because the cooking is difficult but simply because removing the seeds and veins from several dozen chiles does take a while. But oh, how useful and versatile the pickled chipotles are! I love them as a relish or side dish. I've also found that they are a perfect accompanying touch for richly sauced dishes with seasonings on the delicate side. One of these chiles used to garnish each serving of Stuffed Boned Chicken Legs (page 217) adds a charming fillip without overpowering the dish. Or add one or two when grinding the ingredients for a nut-based sauce like the one in Chicken in Peanut Sauce (page 212) or Rolled Filled Tortillas in Peanut Sauce (page 124).

8 ounces dried (*not* canned) chipotle chiles, preferably morita-type (see page 48)

10 ounces *piloncillo* (Mexican brown loaf sugar; see page 70), broken into large pieces, or 1½ cups packed dark brown sugar

2 teaspoons salt, or to taste

3 quarts water

2 cups cider vinegar

⅓ cup olive oil

3 large carrots, peeled and sliced into ⅛-inch rounds

2 large white onions, sliced into thin half-moons

4 heads garlic, cut crosswise in half

6 bay leaves

1 teaspoon crumbled dried Mexican oregano

¼ teaspoon black peppercorns

CAREFULLY remove the stems, seeds, and veins from the chiles, trying to tear the skin as little as possible. Place in a large saucepan with the *piloncillo* and salt. Add the water and bring to a boil over high heat. Reduce the heat to medium-low and cook until the chiles are rehydrated, about 5 minutes for morita-type or 10–15 minutes for regular chipotles. They should be somewhat softened but not falling apart. Add the vinegar and bring back to a boil; remove from the heat and let the chiles cool to room temperature in the cooking liquid. Drain, reserving the liquid.

IN a large skillet, heat the oil over medium-high heat until rippling. Add the carrots, onions, and garlic and cook, stirring, until the onions are translucent and the carrots are crisp-tender, about 5 minutes.

MEANWHILE, place the bay leaves, oregano, and peppercorns in a small heavy skillet over medium heat. Toast, shaking the pan occasionally, just until fragrant, 1–2 minutes. Remove from the heat.

CHOOSE a 2-quart glass or ceramic jar or crock (or other non-reactive container) and add the chiles, the sautéed vegetable mixture, and the toasted spices. Add enough of the chile cooking liquid to cover them plentifully. Taste for salt and add more if desired. Let sit, tightly covered, in the refrigerator for at least 2 days before using. The chiles will keep for 2–3 months.

Champiñones a la Galera

MUSHROOMS A LA GALERA

Makes 4 servings

SPANISH MANCHEGO CHEESE TURNS UP A LOT IN Veracruzan cooking, especially for melted toppings. (Some of it is actually a manchego-style cheese made in Mexico.) Manchego is now increasingly available in the United States; you even find it in some supermarkets. I wouldn't try to substitute anything else in this simple, spirited dish from the Restorán Galera in Xico.

This dish could also be turned into an appetizer—a quesadilla-like filling for folded tortillas (freshly made, if possible). The flavor of epazote is preferable, but you can substitute 10 cilantro sprigs, if you have to.

1 pound cultivated white mushrooms
3 thick slices bacon, diced
1 medium-sized white onion, finely chopped
2–4 jalapeño chiles, stemmed, seeded, and finely chopped
4 large epazote sprigs, leaves only, finely chopped, or 2 teaspoons crumbled dried epazote (see page 41)
4 ounces manchego cheese, shredded (about 1 cup)

WIPE the mushrooms clean with a slightly damp cloth or paper towels; trim the bottoms of the stems and cut the mushrooms lengthwise into slices. Set aside.

IN a medium heavy skillet, fry the bacon over medium-high heat until crisp but not overbrowned. Lift out the bacon onto paper towels, letting as much fat as possible drain back into the pan. Pour the bacon fat into a large wide skillet and heat over medium-high heat until rippling. Add the onion and cook, stirring occasionally, until translucent, about 3 minutes. Add the mushrooms, chiles, and epazote and cook, stirring, for 10 minutes, or until the juices released by the mushrooms have nearly evaporated. Remove from the heat.

PREHEAT the broiler. Transfer the mushrooms to a wide broilerproof baking dish and scatter the bacon and the shredded cheese over the top. Run under the broiler for a few minutes, until the cheese is melted and bubbling. Serve at once.

Setas a la *V*inagreta

WILD MUSHROOMS IN HERBED
VINAIGRETTE

Makes 4–6 servings

*W*HEN I FIRST STARTED DEVELOPING A PASSION FOR
Veracruzan food, my best source of information in between trips was
the splendid illustrated cookbook *La Cocina Veracruzana* by María
Stoopen and Ana Laura Delgado, published in 1992 under the aus-
pices of the state government. (In my opinion, it is the finest general
work on the food of *any* Mexican state—an indispensable aid to all
who love Veracruzan cooking.) Even now that I've combed the state
from end to end, feeling my way to a very personal concept of the Veracruzan kitchen, I go back to some of these delightful and thought-
provoking recipes. My understanding of *setas a la vinagreta* was deepened after I visited the Veracruzan hill country and saw how the
misty climate ensures plentiful seasonal supplies of many wild
mushrooms. I asked about the kind locally called *setas* and was
shown something that I'd call oyster mushrooms. Try to use something similar, or any preferred mixture of exotic kinds with the always
useful shiitakes. The balance of flavors in the recipe in *La Cocina Veracruzana* seems to match many kinds of mushrooms.

2 pounds oyster mushrooms or a combination of varieties
   (see above)
1/2 teaspoon cumin seeds
10 black peppercorns
2 large thyme sprigs, leaves only
2 large oregano sprigs, leaves only
1 head garlic, separated into cloves and peeled
2/3 cup olive oil
2 large white onions
2 medium carrots, peeled
2 jalapeño chiles
1/4 cup cider vinegar, diluted with 1/4 cup water (see note,
   page 375)
4 bay leaves
2 teaspoons salt, or to taste

WIPE the mushrooms clean with a damp cloth or paper towels if
they appear dusty or gritty. Trim away any ragged or spoiled-looking
bits. Set aside.

*V*EGETABLES AND *S*IDE *D*ISHES

MAKE the seasoning paste as follows, using either a large mortar and pestle or an electric coffee or spice mill and food processor: Grind the cumin and peppercorns to a powder. Either add the thyme, oregano, and garlic to the spices in the mortar and pound to a paste, or puree them together in a food processor and add the ground spices. In a small heavy skillet, heat about 2 tablespoons of the oil over medium-low heat until rippling. Add the garlic-herb paste and fry, stirring, for 2–3 minutes. Set aside.

CUT the onions and carrots into thin slices. Stem and seed the chiles and cut into fine julienne. Choose a skillet large enough to hold all of these and the mushrooms (or plan on dividing the ingredients between two skillets). Heat the remaining oil over medium-high heat until fragrant. Add the onions, carrots, and chiles and cook, stirring, for 2 minutes, or until the onions are just about translucent. Add the mushrooms and half of the diluted vinegar. Cook, stirring and tossing to distribute evenly, for 5–7 minutes, or until the mushrooms have released their juices.

STIR in the reserved garlic-herb paste, the remaining diluted vinegar, and the bay leaves. Season with the salt and cook, uncovered, over low heat for 15 minutes, or until the juices have nearly evaporated and the flavors are well blended. Serve hot, at room temperature, or cold. These will keep in the refrigerator, well covered, for a week to 10 days.

NOTE: It's not at all Veracruzan, but I have become captivated by a flavored vinegar from Switzerland that makes absolutely wonderful *setas a la vinagreta*. If you are lucky enough to find it (Kressi brand, sold in specialty food shops), use 1/2 cup, undiluted, instead of the diluted cider vinegar.

Machuca de Plátano

SEASONED MASHED PLANTAINS

Makes 6–8 servings

*T*HIS IS A DISH WITH DEEP AFRICAN AND AFRO-CARIBBEAN roots, cousin to the *fufu* of West Africa and the West Indies. In Cuba today, they make something very close to this under the name *machuquillo*. The big variable in *machuca de plátano* is the ripeness of the plantains. The dish is most suave and unctuous when made with ripe plantains. Green plantains (which would traditionally have been cheaper and more available in slave days) produce a very starchy mash that tends to become leaden if not eaten quite hot. I have seen it made with either or a combination of both. Experiment if you like, trying to remember that plantains go through more stages of stubbornness and tenderness than can be exactly timed in any recipe. My own preference is to choose them on the semi-ripe side, yellow without a lot of black spots.

My recipe is adapted from a version of *machuca de plátano* in Raquel Torres and Dora Elena Careaga Gutiérrez's important collection *La Cocina Afromestiza en Veracruz*.

3 large yellow plantains (see above), unpeeled
2 garlic cloves, coarsely chopped
2–3 jalapeño chiles, stemmed and coarsely chopped
1 medium-sized white onion
3 tablespoons lard, preferably home-rendered (see page 66), or vegetable oil
1 teaspoon salt (optional)

CUT the tips off the plantains; cut each crosswise into 3 chunks. Place in a medium saucepan with water to cover by at least 1 inch. Bring to a boil over high heat. Cover the pot, reduce the heat to low, and cook for 20–30 minutes, or until a knife easily pierces the skin and flesh. (If you are using less ripe plantains, the cooking time must be increased. Green ones, which will not be as sweet as yellow ones, may take about 1 hour.) Drain well and peel, using a knife tip if necessary to help detach the skin. Return to the pan and mash as smooth as possible with a wooden spoon or potato masher.

WHILE the plantains are cooking, crush the garlic and chiles to a paste using a mortar and pestle, or puree in a mini-processor. Chop the onion.

IN a small skillet, heat the lard or oil over medium-high heat until rippling. Add the garlic-chile mixture, onion, and salt, if using, and cook, stirring occasionally, until the onion is translucent, about 3 minutes.

STIR the mixture into the hot mashed plantains. (Alternatively, if you prefer a denser texture, heat the lard and cook the aromatics in a large skillet, then add the hot mashed plantains.) Cook, stirring, until the flavors are well melded, 3–5 minutes. Serve at once. (If your schedule is rushed, you can make the dish several hours ahead, but it will seize up to a most forbidding texture when it cools and should be briefly reheated in a microwave to restore the original consistency.)

Plátanos Fritos

FRIED PLANTAINS

Makes 4 servings

*C*OOKED WHITE RICE AND FRIED PLANTAINS ARE THE backbone of many people's daily meals throughout the Caribbean. These two imports from the Old World go together as naturally as the native Mexican corn tortillas and beans. (There are Veracruzan meals that contain all four.)

Please note that the following recipe is for ripe plantains, black or mostly black with soft, slightly sweet flesh that becomes meltingly luscious in frying. People also cook green or semi-ripe plantains the same way, but the flavor and texture are completely different. See the variation at the end of the recipe.

2 large ripe plantains
4 tablespoons (1/2 stick) butter or 2 tablespoons each butter and vegetable oil
Mexican *crema* (see page 67) or crème fraîche (optional)

WITH a small sharp knife, cut the tips off the plantains. Cut a lengthwise incision through the skin from end to end and work the skin free of the flesh. Cut the plantains into rounds about 1/2 inch thick.

IN a medium heavy skillet, heat the butter or butter-oil mixture over medium-high heat until foaming. Working in batches as necessary, add the plantains and fry until golden and just slightly crisp, 1–1 1/2 minutes per side. Serve hot, preferably with *crema* or with crème fraîche, if desired.

VARIATION

To prepare the dish with green or semi-ripe plantains, it is best to deep-fry them, because their extra starchiness makes them dry and cardboardy if they are shallow-fried. Peel 2 green or semi-ripe plantains as directed above. Cut them into quarters (halve lengthwise, then crosswise). Pour vegetable oil into a heavy medium skillet to a depth of 3/4 inch and heat to 375°F over medium-high heat. Working in batches as necessary, fry as directed above (the timing will be the same). Lift out with a slotted spoon onto paper towels to drain; serve very hot.

Papas al Vapor

STEAMED POTATOES

*T*HIS USEFUL DISH ISN'T "STEAMED" IN THE SENSE OF being put on a steaming rack or in a basket above boiling water. It is called *al vapor* because the potatoes are pan-cooked in a very small amount of liquid, just enough to fill the pot with steam. It's important to use a heavy saucepan that has a tight-fitting lid and is deep rather than wide. The water will take longer to boil off in a narrow pan; in a wide one, the bottom may start to scorch before the potatoes are done.

The recipe is based on one in *La Cocina Veracruzana* by María Stoopen and Ana Laura Delgado. It works with any type of potato, though I marginally prefer a waxy variety. I've increased the amount of olive oil because I like to add an extra dash at the end to enhance all the other flavors. If you prefer, use cilantro in place of the epazote.

Makes 4 servings

1	pound potatoes, peeled and cut into 1½-inch chunks
1–2	jalapeño chiles, stemmed, seeded, and cut into rounds
3–4	fresh epazote sprigs, leaves only, coarsely chopped, or 1 tablespoon crumbled dried epazote (see page 41; or above)
1	tablespoon coarse salt, or to taste
2–4	tablespoons olive oil
1	cup water

PLACE the potatoes in a medium deep, heavy saucepan and toss with the chiles, epazote, salt, and 2 tablespoons of the oil. Add the water, cover the pan tightly, and cook over low heat for 15–20 minutes, or until the potatoes are tender.

SERVE at once, drizzled, if you like, with the remaining 2 tablespoons oil.

Tortitas de Yuca

YUCA FRITTERS

Makes 6–8 servings

*I*N ORIZABA, THEY MAKE WONDERFUL BATTER-DIPPED fritters with *chayotextle*, the potato-like root of the chayote plant. Do you suppose any chayote supplier here has thought of digging up the roots and selling them? Not so far — but I have hopes that the situation will change.

Meanwhile, I make a very good version of the same fritters using yuca root. This is not really a distortion, because people in Veracruz apply the same delicious mashing/batter-coating/frying treatment to all kinds of starchy root vegetables like malanga, taro, and yuca. It would be just as good with sweet potatoes, white potatoes, or plantains. There may be different refinements of seasoning, but the basic formula will always be about 1 to 1¼ pounds of the chosen starchy base, 2 eggs, and ½ cup flour. Yuca has a denser texture than *chayotextle*, but it makes great fritters.

Remember that there can be considerable waste depending on the condition of fresh yuca as it reaches your shopping basket. Today Latin American cooks in this country often opt for the more reliable frozen yuca.

1¼–1½ pounds fresh yuca or 1 pound frozen yuca, thawed (see page 62)

1–1½ teaspoons salt, or to taste

1 tablespoon butter

Freshly ground black pepper

½ cup all-purpose flour, or as needed

2 large eggs, separated

Vegetable oil for frying

Thin Tomato Sauce (page 317), heated

IF using fresh yuca, carefully peel off the thick two-layered skin and cut into 2-inch chunks. Halve the chunks lengthwise and remove the stringy core. Trim away any soft rotted bits. As you work, drop the prepared yuca into cold water to keep it from discoloring.

DRAIN the yuca and place in a medium saucepan with water to cover by 2–3 inches. Add 1 teaspoon of the salt and cook over medium heat for 20–25 minutes, or until tender. If using frozen yuca, cook according to the directions on the package, adding 1 teaspoon of the salt.

DRAIN well and *at once* transfer to a mixing bowl. Before the yuca can cool, add the butter, pepper, and the remaining 1/2 teaspoon salt (or to taste) and start mashing with a potato masher.

WHEN the mixture is as smooth as possible, shape it into 12–15 golf ball–sized balls and press them into flat round cakes about 2 inches across and 1/2 inch thick. (It helps to keep wetting your hands as you do this.) As they are formed, place on baking sheets lined with parchment or waxed paper. (The fritters can be prepared ahead and refrigerated overnight, well covered.)

AT serving time, spread out the flour on a wide flat plate. In a medium bowl, beat the egg whites until very stiff. Add the yolks, one at a time, beating well after each addition. Pour oil into a medium deep skillet to a depth of about 2 inches and heat to 375°F over medium-high heat. Working with 3 or 4 yuca cakes at a time, dredge them in the flour (shaking off the excess), dip into the egg mixture to coat lightly, and fry in the hot oil until golden, turning once, about 1 minute per side. With a slotted spoon, lift out onto paper towels to drain.

THESE are classically served with the tomato sauce. For a buffet presentation, pour the hot tomato sauce onto a deep platter and add the yuca fritters. Otherwise, divide the sauce among wide individual soup bowls and add 2 fritters each. Serve immediately.

Yuca al Ajillo

GARLICKY FRIED YUCA

Makes 4–6 servings

$\mathcal{F}$OR SOME IN THIS COUNTRY, YUCA TENDS TO BE AN acquired taste because of its dense, extra-starchy texture. But when the same doubters taste yuca given this Spanish-Cuban treatment— generously dosed with olive oil and garlic—they are usually converted on the spot. This recipe, a fairly standard one, comes from Inés Pavón Contreras.

2 pounds fresh yuca or 1^1/$_2$–1^3/$_4$ pounds frozen yuca, thawed (see page 62)
2 teaspoons salt
8 garlic cloves
^{1}/$_2$ cup olive oil, or as needed
Coarse salt to taste (optional)

IF using fresh yuca, carefully peel off the thick two-layered skin and cut into large (about 4-inch) chunks. Halve them lengthwise and trim away any spoiled-looking bits. As you work, drop the prepared yuca into cold water to keep it from discoloring.

DRAIN the yuca and place in a large saucepan with water to cover by 2–3 inches. Add the salt and bring to a boil over high heat. Reduce the heat to maintain a low rolling boil and cook, partly covered, for 40 minutes, or until just about tender when tested with a knife tip. If using frozen yuca, cook according to the directions on the package, adding the salt. Drain well and let cool enough to handle.

WITH a sharp knife, remove the stringy core from each chunk and cut into narrow (about ^{1}/$_2$-inch) sticks; place in a bowl. The knife blade may tend to stick; keep dipping it in cold water.

MINCE the garlic and add to the yuca. Add about 3 tablespoons of the oil and toss to coat evenly. Let stand for at least an hour.

IN a large skillet, heat the remaining 5 tablespoons oil over medium-high heat until rippling. Add the yuca-garlic mixture and fry, stirring occasionally, for about 5 minutes, or until golden and slightly crisp. (You may have to add a little more oil, depending on how much the yuca has absorbed from the marinade.) Serve at once, preferably seasoned with coarse salt.

Frijoles Negros Cocidos

COOKED BLACK BEANS

Makes 7–8 cups,
or 6–8 servings

THERE IS NOTHING ESPECIALLY VERACRUZAN ABOUT THIS recipe except the choice of black beans above all other contenders. It's the same as the everyday pan-Mexican way of cooking all dried beans. Remember that for plain boiled beans, the cooking liquid is not considered an irrelevant by-product to be thrown away. It becomes flavorful and concentrated, almost like gravy, and is always included in a bowl of freshly cooked beans.

Epazote, though not absolutely mandatory, is almost inseparable from basic cooked beans in any Mexican kitchen. (There is a firm belief that it alleviates the gas problem.) Otherwise, people are not given to gussying up ordinary cooked beans with seasonings.

Presoaking, so often recommended by experts here, is usually ignored by Mexican cooks, including me. Yet I have come around to using the soaking method for one purpose: when I plan to combine partly cooked beans with other starchy ingredients in a dough like Small Fried Masa Cakes with Bean Filling (page 129). I give this way of treating them as a variation on the basic method (see below).

1 pound (about 2¹/₂ cups) dried black beans, picked over and rinsed

1 large fresh epazote sprig or 1 tablespoon crumbled dried epazote (see page 41; optional)

2–3 teaspoons salt, or to taste

PLACE the beans and epazote, if using, in a large saucepan or Dutch oven. For best results, choose a pan that is deep rather than wide — the best of all is the traditional narrow-necked Mexican clay *olla* (pot). Add enough cold water to cover the beans by at least 2 inches. Bring to a boil over high heat, reduce the heat to low, and cook, partly covered, for 25 minutes. Add the salt.

HAVE a kettle of boiling water in reserve. Continue to cook the beans, checking on them from time to time and adding hot water as necessary to keep them covered by at least 1 inch, for another 20 minutes. Test for doneness by eating a bean or two. If they are softened, remove from the heat; otherwise keep cooking and testing until they are tender, adding more hot water as necessary. Usually it takes

50–60 minutes (total) until the beans are done and the cooking liquid somewhat concentrated. Very old specimens may require more than 1¹/₂ hours.

SERVE the beans hot and fresh, with a little of the cooking liquid. (If using them in another recipe, follow the directions and drain or not as specified.)

VARIATION

For *Frijoles Negros Semicocidos* (Semicooked Black Beans), the object is firmer-textured beans that can be worked into a dough with corn masa, plantains, and/or other starches. Place the beans in a deep bowl or pan, cover well with cold water, and let sit overnight, or for at least 4 hours. Drain the soaking liquid. Proceed as above, but add water just to cover, omit the epazote and salt, and cook for only 25–30 minutes, until a test bean yields a little to the touch but is still somewhat chalky and resistant inside. Drain well and use as directed in the individual recipes. (Feel free to halve or quarter the amount of beans if you don't want to be stuck with a large surplus.)

Frijoles Refritos en Mantequilla

REFRIED BEANS WITH BUTTER

O NE THING I'VE LEARNED WHEN EATING IN VERACRUZ IS to expect the unexpected. I never know when I'll come across some charming original touch that transforms the familiar. It happened to me at La Viuda restaurant in Alvarado when our order arrived with a bowl of refried beans. "What tastes so wonderful in these?" I wondered. Dora Hernández, the manager, supplied the clue to the rich, elusive quality I was picking up on: the beans are refried in a mixture of butter and grated onion. This is one case where pinto beans might be used instead of black beans.

Makes 6 servings

1 large white onion
1 pound dried pinto beans or black beans, prepared as for Cooked Black Beans (page 283) and slightly cooled
6 tablespoons ($^3/_4$ stick) butter
1 teaspoon salt, or to taste

GRATE the onion on the fine side of a box grater, or coarsely chop and grind to a puree in a food processor. Set aside.

DRAIN the beans in a colander, reserving about $1^1/_2$ cups of the cooking liquid. Working in batches as necessary, process the beans to a smooth paste in a blender or food processor, using the reserved cooking liquid as necessary to help the action of the blades.

IN a medium heavy skillet, heat the butter over medium heat. When it foams, add the onion and cook until just lightly golden, about 5 minutes. Add the beans, stir to mix thoroughly, and cook, stirring occasionally, for 10 minutes, until the beans are thoroughly imbued with the butter flavor. Taste for salt and add as desired. Serve hot.

Frijoles en Achulchut

TOTONAC-STYLE BEANS WITH PUMPKIN SEEDS

SOLEDAD GÓMEZ ATZÍN, THE EIGHTY-SEVEN-YEAR-OLD matriarch of the family who run the House of Masks museum in Papantla, taught me this simple version of a traditional dish of the Totonac Indians. It features toasted pumpkin seeds lightly crushed in a mortar rather than ground to a paste as in most versions.

Good pork cracklings (*chicharrones*) are essential to the dish. If you don't make your own—the best way—then buy them fresh from a Latin American butcher. Avoid the factory-processed kind in cellophane bags, which will add all the charm of fried Styrofoam. This dish is delicious with Chicken with Tiny Dried Chiles (page 206) or Grilled Chicken with Chiltepín Chiles (page 199).

Makes 6–8 servings

1 pound black beans, picked over and rinsed

2 teaspoons salt, or to taste

2 ripe plum tomatoes or small globe tomatoes, coarsely chopped

1/2 small white onion, coarsely chopped

2 jalapeño chiles, stemmed and sliced

2 medium chayotes, peeled and pitted (see page 55), and cut into 1/2-inch dice

8 ounces meaty fresh pork cracklings (page 66), chopped into 1/2-inch pieces (about 1 1/2 cups; see above)

2 ounces (about 1/2 cup) hulled pumpkin seeds

FOR GARNISH

12 cilantro sprigs, leaves only, finely chopped

6 fresh epazote sprigs, leaves only, finely chopped, or 1 tablespoon crumbled dried epazote (see page 41)

6 scallions, green part only, finely chopped (about 1/2 cup)

PREPARE the beans as for Cooked Black Beans (page 283) through the stage of adding the salt. While the beans are cooking, puree the tomatoes and onion in a blender or food processor.

AFTER adding the salt to the beans, stir in the puree. Add the chiles, chayotes, and cracklings; cook, tasting the beans occasionally for doneness, for 25–30 minutes longer, or until they are almost tender. Add boiling water as necessary to keep them covered as they cook.

MEANWHILE, place the pumpkin seeds in a small heavy skillet over medium-low heat. Toast, stirring and shaking the pan, until they begin to swell up and pop, 3–5 minutes. They should be only very lightly browned. Turn out the seeds into a mortar and crush them with a heavy pestle until they are broken up but not pasty.

ADD the pumpkin seeds to the almost tender beans and cook for another 8–10 minutes. Serve garnished with the chopped cilantro, epazote, and scallions.

Frijoles de Otatitlán

OTATITLÁN-STYLE BEANS

IN OTATITLÁN, ON THE WEST BANK OF THE PAPALOAPAN River, Luisa Reyna Mortera Aguirre, secretary to the town administration, took charge of us for the afternoon. She brought us to her home and parted with recipes for several unusual Otatitlán recipes, including these sumptuous beans. I'd never heard of beans being cooked with peanuts, which are one of the most important crops around Otatitlán. The combination of bacon and chorizo is an inspired touch. And I love the sprightly accent of the small hot chiles. In Veracruz, they would be comapa chiles, which you still can't get here; I've successfully re-created the dish in New York with árbol chiles. Serve with Smoked Pork Loin Strips (page 243).

Makes 8–10 servings

½ cup lard, preferably home-rendered (see page 66)
1 small white onion, chopped
Cooked Black Beans (page 283), slightly cooled
15 árbol chiles (see page 47)
1 cup (about 5 ounces) roasted peanuts
1 cup milk
6 thick slices bacon, cut into ¼-inch dice
6–8 ounces Chile-Spiced Sausage (page 246), removed from the casings and crumbled, or Spanish-style chorizo, finely chopped (to make about 1 cup)

IN a small skillet, heat about 1 tablespoon of the lard over medium-high heat until rippling. Add the onion and cook, stirring occasionally, until soft and fragrant, about 5 minutes. Set aside.

DRAIN the beans, reserving about 2 cups of the cooking liquid. Set aside.

PLACE the dried chiles in a small heavy skillet over the lowest possible heat. Toast, shaking the pan constantly, until they are brittle and slightly darkened but not scorched, about 5 minutes. In a food processor, grind the toasted chiles to a powder. Add the peanuts and process to a smooth paste. Add the milk, onion, and beans. Process the mixture, adding the reserved cooking liquid as necessary to form a smooth puree. (You may prefer to do this in batches.) Scrape the mixture into a bowl and set aside.

PREHEAT the oven to 350°F.

IN a medium skillet, fry the bacon until fairly crisp but not hard and brittle. Lift out onto paper towels and set aside.

POUR about 2 tablespoons of the bacon fat into a small skillet set over medium heat. (Discard the rest or save it for another purpose.) Add the sausage and cook, stirring to break up any lumps, for about 3 minutes, or until lightly cooked. Stir the chorizo and bacon into the bean puree.

MELT the remaining lard and stir it into the puree. Transfer the mixture to a $2^1/_2$-to-3-quart baking dish. Bake, tightly covered, for 20 minutes. Serve at once.

Arroz Blanco

PILAF-STYLE WHITE RICE

*T*HIS DISH IS CALLED *BLANCO* (WHITE) NOT BECAUSE IT'S
white rice and nothing else, but to distinguish it from rice dishes colored with tomatoes (*arroz rojo*) or green chiles and herbs (*arroz verde*).
All are made by the *sopa seca* (dry soup) method, which is what we
would call the pilaf method: sautéing the rice in oil or lard with seasonings before cooking it in liquid. The liquid in question would be
water in most Veracruzan kitchens, but it could be stock on occasion.
Personally, I never use anything but stock for *arroz blanco*.

I usually seek out imported Spanish Valencia rice because of the
nice way it absorbs liquid without getting waterlogged.

Makes 3–4 servings

1 cup medium- or long-grain white rice (see above)
3 tablespoons vegetable oil or lard, preferably home-rendered
(see page 66)
1 small white onion, sliced or finely chopped
1 small garlic clove, minced
2 cups Basic Chicken Stock (page 142) or water
$^1/_2$–1 teaspoon salt (use the smaller amount if you use stock)

RINSE the rice under cold running water until the water runs
clear. (Be thorough about this— Mexicans hate the stodgy texture of
imperfectly rinsed rice.) Set aside to drain in a sieve or colander for
about an hour. It must be very well drained.

IN a medium heavy saucepan or small Dutch oven with a tight-
fitting lid, heat the oil or lard over medium-high heat until rippling.
Turn down the heat to medium, add the rice, and cook, stirring constantly, until the grains are well coated with the fat and the rice makes
a sound like sand, 2–3 minutes. Stir in the onion and garlic and cook,
stirring constantly, until the onion is translucent, about 3 minutes.
The ingredients must not brown; adjust the heat as necessary.

ADD the stock or water and salt. Reduce the heat to low, cover
the pan tightly, and cook, without stirring, for 15 minutes, or until the
liquid is absorbed. Remove the pan from the heat and let stand undis-
turbed for 5 minutes before serving.

Moros y Cristianos

MOORS AND CHRISTIANS

SPANISH-SPEAKERS FROM VALENCIA TO VENEZUELA KNOW that the Moors of the title are black beans, while white rice stands for their foes, the Christians. This is a picturesque image, but no more so than the name applied to the dish in some parts of Veracruz: *casamiento* (marriage). Other combinations of rice and legumes go back for centuries before Columbus in Arabic and African cooking. Probably *moros y cristianos* was a new version of some dish or dishes already known to the African slaves, their Spanish masters, or each independently. In Veracruz, there seem to be as many different approaches to *moros y cristianos* as there are different cooks. Some people make it by just combining some cooked beans and some cooked rice in a pot. Some like it as dry as pilaf; others want it to resemble one of the soupier Spanish rice dishes. I have found that the most flavorful Veracruzan versions are close to the beloved Cuban *moros y cristianos* and involve making a well-seasoned *sofrito* (a sautéed mixture of aromatics) and simmering the rice together with the partly cooked beans and their cooking liquid. This brings the color of the rice closer to that of the beans—which is just what happened with the mixing of the races in a lot of colonial "marriages."

My version is a freewheeling takeoff with ideas borrowed from Veracruzan and Cuban examples and a few totally unorthodox touches. A lot of it comes from my son Aarón Sánchez, a terrifically gifted young chef. Probably the biggest departure from tradition is sautéing the rice in the hot fat before cooking it with the beans. (Usually the rice is directly cooked in liquid.) I think it's the best *moros y cristianos* I've tasted.

Some people may think that the combination of lard and bacon fat is a bit over the top. Actually, combinations of cooking fats are a strong part of the Spanish culinary heritage. If you like, omit the bacon and simply sauté the onion and garlic in the ¼ cup lard. But you'll be losing a big part of the flavor.

½	pound dried black beans, picked over and rinsed
	About 8 cups water
6	bay leaves
2	teaspoons crumbled dried thyme
2–2½	teaspoons salt, or to taste

¼ cup lard, preferably home-rendered (see page 66), or vegetable oil

6–8 thick slices bacon (12–14 ounces), cut into ¼-inch dice

1 medium-sized white onion, finely chopped

2 large garlic cloves, finely chopped

2 teaspoons ground cumin, preferably freshly ground

2 teaspoons ground coriander, preferably freshly ground

2 cups long-grain white rice

Freshly ground black pepper

1 large piece banana leaf (see page 236), thawed if frozen (optional)

PLACE the beans in a large saucepan with enough water to cover by about 2 inches. Bring to a boil over high heat; reduce the heat to low and add 3 of the bay leaves, 1 teaspoon of the thyme, and 1 teaspoon of the salt. Cook, partly covered, replenishing with hot water as needed to keep the beans covered by 2 inches, for 20–25 minutes, or until the beans are slightly softened but still definitely chalky inside. Drain the beans in a colander, reserving 4 cups of the cooking liquid. Discard the bay leaves and set the beans aside.

IN a large heavy skillet, heat the lard or oil over medium heat until rippling. Add the bacon and cook, stirring frequently, until crisp but not dark, 5–7 minutes. Place the bacon on paper towels, letting as much of the fat as possible drain back into the pan, and set aside.

PREHEAT the oven to 350°F.

POUR about ¼ cup of the fat into a large Dutch oven (discard the rest). Heat over medium heat until rippling. Add the onion and garlic; cook, stirring until the onion is well softened but not browned, about 10 minutes. Add the cumin, coriander, and the remaining 3 bay leaves and 1 teaspoon thyme. Cook, stirring, for 2–3 minutes. Add the rice and cook, stirring, until the grains are well coated with fat.

ADD the beans to the sautéed rice mixture and stir in the reserved bean cooking liquid. Add the bacon; taste for salt and add 1–1½ teaspoons more, if desired. Season generously with pepper.

WITH kitchen scissors, cut 1 or 2 pieces of the banana leaf, if using, into a shape just large enough to fit snugly over the pot. Place a tight-fitting lid over the leaves or wrap well with heavy-duty aluminum foil. (A damp tea towel may be used in place of the banana leaf, but the fragrance will be lost.) Bake for 30 minutes, or until the liquid has been completely absorbed. Serve at once.

Arroz a la Mexicana

RICE WITH ROASTED TOMATOES

Makes 6–8 servings

VERACRUZAN COOKS ARE AS FOND AS EVERYONE ELSE IN Mexico of this tomato-enriched version of basic pilaf-style rice. Don't skip the soaking and rinsing, which really do improve the texture a lot.

2	cups medium- or long-grain rice
1/2	cup vegetable oil
1	medium-sized white onion, coarsely chopped
2	garlic cloves, coarsely chopped
2	large ripe tomatoes, griddle-roasted and peeled following the directions on page 58
5	cups Basic Chicken Stock (page 142), heated, or hot water
1 1/2–2	teaspoons salt
2	cilantro sprigs, leaves only

PLACE the rice in a colander and rinse thoroughly under cold running water until the water runs clear. Let stand until no water is dripping from the rice (it should not be wet when you sauté it).

IN a medium saucepan or small Dutch oven with a tight-fitting lid, heat the oil over medium heat. Add the rice and onion, reduce the heat slightly, and cook, stirring constantly, for about 10 minutes. The rice will turn golden and translucent, and you will hear a difference in the sound it makes (to me it sounds like sand when it reaches the right stage). Drain off as much of the oil as possible.

MEANWHILE, puree the garlic and tomatoes in a blender. Add the mixture to the rice and cook for 5 minutes, stirring frequently.

ADD the hot stock or water, salt, and cilantro. Cover the pan tightly and cook over low heat for about 15 minutes, until the liquid is absorbed and the rice is fully swelled. It will be lighter and fluffier if you let it sit in a warm place off the heat for 5–8 minutes before serving.

Espaguetti Verde

GREEN SPAGHETTI

"WHAT DO YOU MAKE FOR CHRISTMAS?" I ASKED TERESA Pérez Cabrera, a busy grandmother and former restaurant cook who came to meet me and talk about food at her old workplace, Las Brisas del Mar in Boca del Río. I don't know what answer I expected — maybe something exotic reflecting Teresa's Afro-Mexican ancestry — but it certainly wasn't *espaguetti*! Actually, pasta with a green poblano sauce is quite popular in Mexico, but usually in baked versions. It's not too dissimilar (except for some of the flavorings) from macaroni and cheese. Teresa's "green spaghetti," however, has a fresh poblano-cilantro sauce tossed with the cooked pasta, a little closer to the Italian way. Who knows — it could become a favorite Christmas or perhaps Christmas Eve dish in your family!

Any kind of dried pasta will work well in the dish as long as it's not tiny or extra-thin.

Makes 4 servings

2 large poblano chiles
6 large cilantro sprigs, leaves only
1 small white onion, coarsely chopped
1 garlic clove, coarsely chopped
2 tablespoons salt
1/2 pound spaghetti or other dried pasta
2 tablespoons butter
1/2 cup Mexican *crema* (see page 67) or heavy cream
4 ounces white cheddar or manchego cheese, shredded (about 1 cup)

GRIDDLE-ROAST, peel, and seed the chiles following the directions on page 58. Puree in a blender or food processor with the cilantro, onion, and garlic.

BRING a large pot of water to a boil and add 5 teaspoons of the

salt. Add the spaghetti and cook according to the package directions; it should not be al dente.

WHILE the spaghetti cooks, heat the butter in a medium saucepan over medium heat. When it foams, add the chile mixture. Cook, partly covered, for 10–12 minutes. Stir in the *crema* or cream and the remaining 1 teaspoon salt.

DRAIN the spaghetti when almost done to your taste. Return to the pot, pour the sauce over it, and toss to combine well. Scatter the cheese over the spaghetti and serve at once.

*T*HE FAMILY OF VERACRUZAN SAUCES is really several families — plus several important sauce enrichments and one unclassifiable adoptee. One tribe is composed of relish-like table sauces, prepared with great skill from carefully chosen and very fresh ingredients and paired with many kinds of dishes. Table sauces can be either raw or cooked. Those of Veracruz are more varied and imaginative than those of any other region I know. At the same time, most are extremely simple, letting one or two basic ingredients do the talking. You can hardly imagine how much magic there is in a mixture of jalapeño chiles and lime juice (*chile pastor*) or a coarse puree of sweet, intense currant tomatoes with garlic and tiny hot chiles (*tachogobi*). I kept finding new sauces that I was tempted to

serve with *everything* — only there were so many more. My absolute favorite is the Orizaba-style version of *salsa macha*, an inspired mixture of small hot chiles, garlic, and olive oil with peanuts.

Yet another, smaller clan would be composed of sauces meant to be served in something closer to the European fashion — hot, as an accompaniment to other dishes. The chief ones are tomato-based; *caldillo de tomate* (Thin Tomato Sauce) is the most basic and versatile.

Another family would include the rich, elaborate main-dish sauces, a concept that modern Mexico inherited from the pre-Hispanic peoples. The basic principle is that any meat, poultry, or other ingredient like potatoes should be only a simple complement to the sauce, not vice versa. The sauce — for example, *mole de xico* (Xico-Style Mole) or *tlatonile* (Toasted Sesame Seed Sauce) — is entirely the star of the occasion and should be served hot in generous portions, like soup. The main-dish sauces are not as many or as prominent in Veracruz as in Oaxaca (the "Land of the Seven *Moles*"), but they are regarded with just as much honor.

The ever popular *salsa a la veracruzana* defies categorization. It can function either as a cooking medium (traditionally, for oven-poached or stovetop-poached fish) or as a sauce for something cooked separately. It is really very close to the classic Spanish *sofrito* (a sautéed sauce base of onion, garlic, and tomato), but it is also laced with capers, olives, and Mediterranean herbs—and, just to give it Mexican immigration papers, a little pickled chile.

*F*OR FULL FLAVOR, most Mexican cooked sauces must be fried in hot fat until they reach a crucial stage easier to recognize than to describe. People in Mexico call it *chinita*, a word that can be a term of endearment, like "ducky." You know that the sauce has reached the proper texture and flavor when it becomes *chinita*—that is, when the surface has a glistening quality, showing that the fat is starting to separate at the top (usually after 15–20 minutes' cooking). It is something that you should learn to look for if you want to develop the instincts of a Mexican cook.

Ajo Preparado

GARLIC BUTTER ENRICHMENT

Makes about ³/₄ cup

MANY COOKS IN THE PORT CITY AND THROUGHOUT Sotavento — the prime fish and seafood areas of Veracruz state — swear by a sauce enrichment consisting of pureed garlic cooked in butter. Sometimes onion is added as well. People make up the mixture, or buy a prepackaged version that I've seen at street markets, and add it to all sorts of prepared seafood dishes to give an extra dimension.

My recipe is based on a formula used by Tomasita Meléndez at the restaurant Las Brisas del Mar in Boca del Río. Try it in Hashed Fish with Fresh Herbs and Olives (page 84), Garlicky Stir-Fried Shrimp (page 97), or anything else you feel like. I suggest using a tablespoon for a dish to feed 4.

¹/₂ cup garlic cloves (from 2 large heads of garlic)
¹/₂ cup cold water
 2 tablespoons butter

PUREE the garlic with the water in a blender or food processor. In a small saucepan, gently melt the butter over medium heat, not letting it bubble. Add the garlic puree and cook without stirring for about 5 minutes, or until the water has evaporated and the mixture is bubbling up in ploppy craters.

LET the mixture cool to room temperature, then transfer it to a small container. It will keep, tightly sealed, for up to a month in the refrigerator.

Salsa del Sabor Secreto

GARLIC VINEGAR WITH BLACK PEPPER

Makes about 1 cup

THIS SPRIGHTLY SEASONING IS THE SECRET INGREDIENT in many of the dishes made by María del Carmen Virués, one of the best cooks in Xico. It's no wonder I enjoy her food so much—I tend to like a splash of acid in almost anything. She uses this "sauce" as a marinade for chicken dishes (for example, Orange-Flavored Chicken, page 202) or adds 1 or 2 tablespoons to braised poultry or meat dishes like Pork in Fruit Liqueur Sauce (page 241). Try it as the spirit moves you, putting in a dash at the "correct-the-seasoning" stage of cooking, and see how it manages to round out or perk up the other flavors.

6 large garlic cloves, coarsely chopped
1 tablespoon black peppercorns
1 cup distilled white vinegar

USING a mortar and pestle (preferably a Mexican *molcajete*), pound the garlic and peppercorns to a slightly textured paste. (You can also do this in a food processor, but be sure not to make it too fine.) Stir in about half of the vinegar and pour the mixture into a jar.

RINSE out the mortar with the remaining vinegar and add to the jar. This will keep, tightly covered, in the refrigerator for up to a month.

Marinada de Tomasita para Mariscos

TOMASITA'S SEAFOOD MARINADE

*T*HIS IS ANOTHER TRUSTY PREPARATION IN THE KITCHEN of Las Brisas del Mar, Tomasita Meléndez's well-loved seafood restaurant in Boca del Río. Mexicans never see anything un-Mexican about reaching for the *salsa inglesa* (Worcestershire) or *salsa de soya*. Many is the seafood dish at Las Brisas del Mar that owes an extra flavor dimension to this marinade — a mixture of things from jars or bottles. Use as a marinade for whole fish, fish steaks, shrimp, or other seafood; lightly drain the marinade from the food before cooking.

Makes about 2 cups

1 12-ounce bottle of light (lager, not "lite") beer

Juice of 5 limes

1 teaspoon powdered chicken stock base or 1 bouillon cube

1 teaspoon Worcestershire sauce

1 teaspoon Maggi sauce

1 teaspoon soy sauce

1 teaspoon Tabasco sauce

1 teaspoon freshly ground black pepper

6 garlic cloves, minced

PLACE all the ingredients in a small jar and shake to combine. Let sit for at least 1 hour before using. It will keep for a week, tightly sealed, in the refrigerator.

Pasta de Chile Chipotle de Lata

CANNED CHIPOTLE CHILE PASTE

No, THIS IS NOT MEANT AS A SUBSTITUTE FOR ANY OF the preparations using Veracruzan chipotle chiles. It is a very quick, useful basis for a lot of seasoning purposes, from marinating to discreetly adjusting the balance of acid and heat. Not that the adjustment has to be discreet, either—you can add this by tiny dabs to a delicate sauce or by heaping tablespoons to one you want to announce, "SLEEPERS WAKE!" Combined with mayonnaise, it makes a great accompanying sauce for crudités. I like it with nearly anything, from eggs to fish. I've been making the recipe just the same way for many years and am giving it as I gave it in my first cookbook, *Food from My Heart.*

Makes about 1 cup

1 8-ounce can chipotle chiles in adobo (see page 49), with their sauce
4–5 garlic cloves, minced (about 2 tablespoons)
1 tablespoon crumbled dried Mexican oregano
2 tablespoons olive oil or vegetable oil

PROCESS the chiles and their sauce to a puree in a blender or food processor. Add the remaining ingredients and pulse several times to combine thoroughly while keeping a little texture. This will keep in the refrigerator, tightly covered, for 3–4 weeks. I think it loses a lot in freezing.

Salsita Picante con Dos Chiles

TWO-CHILE THIN HOT SAUCE

We TROOPED INTO LA VIUDA RESTAURANT IN ALVARADO expecting to meet a local culinary expert, who turned out not to exist. But La Viuda, set slightly apart from a string of waterfront *pescaderías* (fish houses) in this busy fishing village, had such wonderful food that we couldn't complain. A bottle of this thin sauce sits on every table—a fiery but unexpectedly complex combination of herbs, garlic, and two very different chiles—the fruity and direct fresh habanero and the canned chipotle, with its sharp adobo marinade.

Makes about 3 cups

- 10 habanero chiles (see page 46)
- 1 8-ounce can chipotle chiles in adobo (see page 49), with their sauce
- 10 large garlic cloves, coarsely chopped
- 2 teaspoons salt, or to taste
- 5 bay leaves, ground to a powder in an electric spice or coffee grinder
- 1 teaspoon crumbled dried Mexican oregano
- 1 teaspoon black peppercorns
- 2 cups cider vinegar

WEARING protective gloves, remove the seeds and veins from the habanero chiles. Place in a blender with all the remaining ingredients and process to a smooth, pourable, thin sauce. It will keep almost indefinitely at room temperature.

Chile Pastor

LOS TUXTLAS–STYLE CHILE-LIME SAUCE

SAUCES DON'T GET MUCH SIMPLER THAN THIS MARRIAGE of four or five flavors that accompanies many dishes in the Tuxtlas area. It is great with Masa–Sweet Potato Shells with Filling (page 127) or Large "Pinched" Tortillas (page 118), but I also like it with fish and meat dishes. *Chile pastor* is so basic and unfussy that it suits almost everything, and I find myself using it with specialties from all parts of the state. It is best made with the ingredients chopped very fine by hand and served chilled. The texture should be slightly watery.

Makes 1^{1}/$_{2}$–1^{3}/$_{4}$ cups

2–3	jalapeño or serrano chiles, stemmed and finely chopped
1	tablespoon finely chopped fresh chives
^{1}/$_{2}$	cup finely chopped red onion (optional but good)
1	cup cold water
^{1}/$_{4}$	cup freshly squeezed lime juice
1	teaspoon salt

COMBINE all the ingredients in a small nonreactive container. Refrigerate for at least 1 hour before serving. Serve cold.

Pasta de Chile Seco

CHIPOTLE CHILE PASTE

SALSA MADE WITH DRIED CHILES, A POWERFUL HELLFIRE-and-damnation condiment, appears in different versions on many Veracruzan tables. As I point out elsewhere, Veracruzan morita-type chipotles sing with flavor not always matched by the kind available in this country. However, I find that ordinary chipotles can pack a punch of complexity—not just heat—when handled with skill.

The following formula yields a versatile paste that can be employed either as a flavor adjunct to be used in cooking or as a dipping sauce served with chips. It comes from the restaurateur Tomasita Meléndez. Her *pasta de chile seco* is glorious as a vivid but not overpowering intensifier of seafood and other dishes. Rub it over the skin and the inside of a whole fish or chicken to be baked or poached, or add a tablespoon or two to perk up a simple sauce like Thin Tomato Sauce (page 317). It's a great addition to barbecue sauces. This versatile paste is also the basis of a sauce as heady and many-sided as the Provençal *aïoli*, the seductive and addictive *mayonesa de chipotle* (see variation, page 307).

4 ounces dried (*not* canned) chipotle chiles, preferably morita-type (about 50 small or 30 large chiles; see page 48)

3 tablespoons vegetable oil

3 tablespoons olive oil, plus extra if needed

4 large garlic cloves

2 teaspoons salt, or to taste

REMOVE the stems from the chiles. Either lightly wipe them with a slightly dampened cloth (as is done in Veracruz) or rinse them under cold running water and let them dry thoroughly, at least overnight, to be sure no moisture clings to them.

IN a medium heavy skillet, heat the oils over medium heat. When fragrant, add the chiles. Reduce the heat to the lowest possible setting and cook, stirring constantly, until they are puffed and starting to turn red. Be careful not to let them scorch.

TRANSFER the chiles to a medium bowl, reserving the oil left in the skillet. Cover them with boiling water and let stand for 40 minutes.

DRAIN the chiles, reserving a little of the soaking liquid ($1/4$–$1/3$ cup) if desired, to help in processing.

PUREE the garlic and salt in a food processor. Add the drained chiles and reserved oil; process until smooth, adding a little of the soaking liquid or more olive oil if necessary to help the action of the blades. Scrape the paste into a small container and store in the refrigerator, tightly sealed, for up to 1 month.

VARIATION

For *Mayonesa de Chipotle* (Chipotle Mayonnaise), combine 1 cup homemade or commercial mayonnaise with 1–2 tablespoons of the chipotle chile paste and 1 garlic clove (optional) — either mince the garlic fine and combine with the other ingredients or puree all the ingredients in a food processor.

Salsa Verde con Aguacate

GREEN SAUCE WITH AVOCADO

Makes about 2¹/₂ cups

EVERYONE WHO VISITS VERACRUZ ENCOUNTERS THE famous *picadas*, which resemble thick tortillas with the edges pinched up like the shell of a tart to hold a light topping of salsa and grated cheese (page 121). They usually are brought to the table in both red and green versions, the former topped with a fresh *salsa roja* of roasted tomatoes (page 313) and the latter with some cousin of this lovely tart sauce. Since discovering it, I've taken to using it in various nontraditional ways—for example, to sauce simple grilled foods, or with a bowl of tostadas as a lighter, spicier replacement for guacamole. I've tasted many versions, but none I like better than the one I found in María Stoopen and Ana Laura Delgado's *La Cocina Veracruzana*.

2	garlic cloves, coarsely chopped
1¹/₂	teaspoons salt, or to taste
1	small white onion, coarsely chopped
2–3	serrano or jalapeño chiles, stemmed and coarsely chopped, or to taste
6–8	medium tomatillos (about ¹/₂ pound), husks removed, rinsed and cut into quarters
1	ripe Mexican-type avocado (such as Hass or Fuerte)
12–15	cilantro springs

WHETHER you are using a machine or a mortar and pestle, most of the process is the same: In a food processor or blender or a heavy mortar, process or pound the garlic and salt to a paste. Add the onion, chiles, and tomatillos and pulse to make a slightly chunky paste or pound and mash the ingredients together as fine as possible.

HALVE and pit the avocado and scoop out the flesh. For a smooth machine-finished puree, add it to the other ingredients, along with the cilantro, and process very fine. If using the hand method, chop the avocado flesh fine and mash it into the onion-tomatillo mixture. Chop the cilantro leaves and stems and stir in. Or, for a compromise version, process the onion-tomatillo mixture in the machine until smooth, pour into a bowl, and mix in the chopped avocado flesh along with the cilantro. Serve as soon as possible, certainly within an hour.

Salsa Macha

SHE-MAN SAUCE

Macho (masculine) takes the feminine ending when it goes with a feminine noun like *salsa*, so I guess the literal meaning would be something like "She-Man Sauce." This fierce and fiery condiment is known throughout Veracruz, in widely different versions linked only by the use of small hot dried chiles, garlic, and oil (usually olive oil, but some people prefer vegetable oil). The Orizaba-Córdoba area is an epicenter of excellent *salsa macha*, often featuring ground peanuts.

I've tasted variants of *salsa macha* that were smooth or chunky, swimming in oil or just gently touched by it, mellowed with sautéed or roasted garlic or galvanized with raw garlic, and made according to different local or seasonal chile preferences. Perhaps it's unfair to present only one version of anything so flexible and individual — but I modestly think I've achieved a composite that's the best of all *salsa macha* possibilities.

Once you've tried the recipe, you can, of course, experiment — gently fry the chiles and/or minced garlic in oil, process the sauce until it is as smooth as peanut butter, increase or decrease the garlic, etc. However, I think you'll end up preferring the sauce as I give it here. Note that Veracruzans start with raw peanuts, frying or toasting them until rich and nutty. After much experimenting I can honestly report that commercial roasted peanuts give just as flavorful a result.

No kind of chile available in the United States exactly duplicates any of the varieties preferred on the home territory of *salsa macha* — comapa, dried serrano, Veracruzan chipotles. Probably the best substitute is árbol chiles, which are a bit larger and tougher-skinned than the ones people use in Veracruz. They're also somewhat hotter, which is why I suggest eliminating some of the seeds after toasting.

Makes about 1¼ cups

1/3–1/2 cup árbol, dried serrano, or other small dried chiles (see page 47)
1–2 garlic cloves
1 teaspoon salt, or to taste
1/2 cup roasted peanuts
1/4–1/3 cup olive oil (I use extra-virgin)

PLACE a small heavy saucepan over the lowest possible heat. Add the chiles and let them toast very gently, shaking the pan frequently and listening for the sound they make: at first they will rustle like dry leaves, but when ready, in 15–20 minutes, they will make a slightly higher-pitched hollow noise. They should have a glistening look, and the skins should be slightly darkened and brittle but not scorched. Pour the chiles into a colander to cool slightly, then shake out and discard the seeds, not trying to get them all.

PUREE the garlic and salt in a food processor. Add the toasted chiles and grind fairly coarse. Add the peanuts and pulse to crush them into bits the size of broken rice grains. With the motor running, start adding the oil in a thin stream. It should be not quite completely absorbed but leave just a light film on the surface of the sauce; the exact amount will depend on the starchiness of the peanuts. Taste for salt and add another pinch or two if desired. Serve at once, or transfer to a small container and store in the refrigerator, tightly sealed, for up to a month.

Salsa Macha Verde

GREEN SHE-MAN SAUCE

Makes about 1 cup

*I*N SAN ANDRÉS TUXTLA, WE WERE TREATED TO A MAGNIFICENT luncheon at La Caperucita, a magnet for good eating in the Tuxtlas area. (The restaurant's name refers to the fairy tale of Little Red Riding Hood, "Caperucita Roja," which is also the brand name of a popular cheese.) Elodia Guevara Chávez and Juan Pablo Chávez Guevara, the mother-and-son team who built up the restaurant from its humble beginnings as a hamburger cart, pulled out all the stops to welcome us and introduce us to experts on the regional cuisine. An epic meal featuring at least a dozen excellent seafood, meat, and masa specialties was accompanied by this fresh-flavored variation on the beloved Veracruzan *salsa macha*.

This type of sauce is not difficult to make by hand in a *molcajete* or other large mortar. If using a blender or food processor, try to reproduce the chunky texture of the hand-ground version by stopping before the ingredients turn into a paste.

1/2 small white onion, coarsely chopped

2 garlic cloves, coarsely chopped

6 jalapeño or serrano chiles, stemmed, seeded, if desired, to reduce the heat, and coarsely chopped

1 teaspoon salt, or to taste

Juice of 1/2 lime

USING a mortar and pestle, grind the onion, garlic, chiles, and salt to a rough paste, or place in a blender or food processor and pulse just until roughly combined. Add the lime juice and grind or process just until the mixture forms a coarse-textured sauce. Use at once.

Salsa Roja de Orizaba

RED SAUCE FROM ORIZABA

*T*HIS CENTRAL VERACRUZAN VERSION OF A CLASSIC PAN-Mexican table sauce gets its flavor from the local dried chiles. It's a good multipurpose condiment that is particularly good with Seafood Frittata (page 168), "Swaddled Baby" Seafood Omelet (page 172), or Yuca Fritters (page 280). Aminta Osorio, a distinguished cook of Orizaba, gave me her recipe.

In Orizaba, people would make the sauce with Veracruzan morita-type chipotles (smoky and pungent, but with a wonderful freshness), the small comapa chiles (bright-flavored and slightly acid), the somewhat larger costeño chiles (sweeter, fruitier, and hotter), or dried serranos (thin-fleshed, robust, and not terribly fiery). As explained earlier, these names are absolutely unstandardized from place to place, and you should expect to do some searching among the equivalents available in this country (see suggestions on pages 47–51).

Makes about 2 1/2 cups

3 large or 5–6 medium-sized ripe tomatoes (2–2 1/2 pounds)
1 small white onion, unpeeled
6 garlic cloves, unpeeled
6–8 small dried chiles (see above)
2 tablespoons lard, preferably home-rendered (see page 66), or vegetable oil
1 tablespoon salt, or to taste

GRIDDLE-ROAST and peel the tomatoes, onion, and garlic following the directions on page 58, being sure to save all the tomato juices.

WHILE the vegetables are roasting, bring a small saucepan of water to a boil over high heat. Add the chiles and cook, uncovered, for 10 minutes, or until thoroughly softened. Drain.

PLACE the chiles in a blender with the roasted and peeled vegetables. (Remove the seeds and veins if you want to tone down the heat of the chiles; I leave them in.) Process to a smooth paste, stopping occasionally to scrape down the sides with a rubber spatula.

IN a medium heavy saucepan, heat the lard or oil over medium-high heat. Add the tomato-chile mixture and salt and bring to a boil, stirring. Cover and cook for 15 minutes, or until the puree is slightly concentrated and the surface has the look Mexicans call *chinita* (ploppy and cratered, with the fat starting to separate). Use at once, or let cool and pour into a small container. The sauce will keep in the refrigerator, tightly sealed, for 1 week.

Chile Limón

FRESH LIME AND CHILE DRESSING
FOR FISH

$\mathcal{A}$T THE LITTLE FISH RESTAURANTS AND OUTDOOR CAFÉS around Lake Catemaco, this is a usual accompaniment to panfried or broiled fish or *langostinos*. At its simplest, the original *chile limón* consisted of just grinding hot green chiles with salt in a mortar and pestle and adding freshly squeezed lime juice. Now you find versions with tomatillos, cilantro, and other seasonings. I love them all! Make the sauce as simple or complex as you like. The mortar-and-pestle version is still very good, but nowadays people usually prefer a blender.

I am giving my favorite version of *chile limón* with garlic, onion, tomatillos, and cilantro. If desired, you can omit any of these except the onion. Without the tomatillos, the yield will be 3/4–1 cup.

Makes about 2 cups

6–8	medium tomatillos, husks removed (about 8 ounces), rinsed
2	teaspoons salt, or to taste
2	jalapeño or serrano chiles, stemmed and seeded
4	garlic cloves
1/2	small white onion, coarsely chopped
8	cilantro sprigs
1/2	cup freshly squeezed lime juice
1/4–1/2	cup cold water

PLACE the tomatillos in a small saucepan with a pinch of salt. Cover with water, bring to a boil, and cook over medium heat until they change color, about 5 minutes. Drain and let cool to room temperature.

IF you are using a blender, simply process all the ingredients together, very slowly adding enough water to thin the sauce to a slightly soupy consistency. If making the sauce by hand, first coarsely chop the chiles and garlic, then pound them to a rough paste with about 2 teaspoons salt, using a mortar and pestle. Add the other ingredients and grind to form a chunky sauce; thin with water as necessary. Serve with broiled or fried seafood, using Fish with Fresh Lime and Chile Dressing (page 179) as a general model.

Tachogobi

CURRANT TOMATO SAUCE FOR FISH

*T*HE MANY OPEN-AIR RESTAURANTS AND SMALL EATERIES around Lake Catemaco always bring out a bowl of this lusty, garlicky sauce to eat with grilled or fried lake fish such as the perch-like *mojarra*.

For the authentic *tachogobi* of the lakeside cafés, the miniature tomatoes used to be crushed by hand and all the ingredients pounded or ground together in a stone mortar. I use a blender or food processor, but I make sure to stop while the mixture still has some texture.

In Catemaco, some of the sauce is often used to coat the fish before cooking: you slather each side in turn so that the *tachogobi* becomes a wonderful grilled crust when exposed to the heat. If you're a fan of grilled fish, make a little extra so that you'll have enough for both crusting and serving as a condiment.

Makes about 2 cups

6 large garlic cloves, coarsely chopped

1 tablespoon dried chiltepín chiles (see page 48)

1 teaspoon salt, or to taste

12–13 ounces currant tomatoes (see page 61) or very small, sweet grape or cherry tomatoes

2 tablespoons lard, preferably home-rendered (see page 66)

PLACE the garlic, chiles, and salt in a blender or food processor and process for a few seconds. Add the tomatoes and process just until the ingredients come together in a chunky sauce.

IN a medium saucepan, heat the lard over medium-high heat until rippling. Add the tomato mixture, bring to a boil, and cook, uncovered, stirring occasionally, for 10 minutes to mellow the flavors and concentrate the sauce slightly. Serve hot.

Caldillo de Tomate

THIN TOMATO SAUCE

ALICIA LEYVA TENORIO OF LA TROJE RESTAURANT IN Orizaba seasons this useful cooked tomato sauce with a chicken bouillon cube. Her chiles are comapas; in this country, árbol chiles are the best substitute.

Señora Leyva serves the *caldillo* with root-vegetable fritters like Yuca Fritters (page 280), but it's also a great accompaniment to Seafood Frittata (page 168).

Makes about 2¹/₂ cups

5   medium-sized ripe, juicy tomatoes (about 1¹/₂ pounds)
¹/₄ cup árbol or dried serrano chiles (see page 47)
1   medium-sized white onion, chopped
1   garlic clove
1   teaspoon powdered chicken stock base, 1 chicken bouillon cube, or 1 teaspoon salt
2   tablespoons vegetable oil
1   large fresh epazote sprig or 1 teaspoon crumbled dried epazote (see page 41) or 6–8 cilantro sprigs

GRIDDLE-ROAST and peel the tomatoes following the directions on page 58, being sure to save all the juices. Set aside.

HEAT a small heavy skillet over very low heat. Add the chiles and toast for about 5 minutes, stirring often. When ready, they will sound hollow and should be brittle but not burned. Immediately pour the chiles into a blender and add the tomatoes and their juices with the onion, garlic, and stock base, bouillon cube, or salt. Process until smooth, occasionally stopping to scrape down the sides with a rubber spatula.

IN a medium saucepan, heat the oil over medium-high heat until rippling. Add the tomato mixture and epazote or cilantro. Reduce the heat to maintain a simmer, cover, and cook, stirring occasionally, until craters are bubbling up on the surface and the fat starts to separate, about 15 minutes. Serve hot.

Salsa Roja Ranchera

RANCH-STYLE RED SAUCE

I BLUSH TO SAY THAT I NO LONGER REMEMBER JUST WHERE I encountered this basic salsa, though I think it must have been someplace around Lake Catemaco. The fiery but wonderfully perfumed habanero chile is essential for the right flavor. For the best texture use a mortar and pestle. If you have to use a food processor, be sure to leave the sauce slightly chunky. The texture is a little less easy to control with a blender.

Makes about 1¹/₂ cups

2 habanero chiles (see page 46), seeded, deveined, and coarsely chopped (use rubber gloves for this)

1¹/₂ teaspoons salt, or to taste

2 garlic cloves, coarsely chopped

1 very small or ¹/₂ medium-small white onion, coarsely chopped

2 medium-sized ripe tomatoes (10–12 ounces), peeled, seeded, and coarsely chopped

4–6 cilantro sprigs, chopped

USING a mortar and pestle (preferably a Mexican *molcajete*), mash the chiles to a paste with the salt. (Watch your eyes!) Add the garlic and continue pounding and mashing. When the garlic is thoroughly incorporated, add the onion and mash as fine as possible. Mash in the tomatoes.

POUR the sauce into a serving bowl, sprinkle with the cilantro, and serve at once.

Salsa de Tomate con Chile Chipotle

TOMATO SAUCE WITH CHIPOTLE CHILES

Makes about 3 cups

I'VE HAD SAUCES LIKE THIS IN MANY PARTS OF MEXICO, including Veracruz, so I have to say it's not unique to the state. Veracruzan cooks, however, find it as useful as I do. It makes a great accompaniment to Seafood Frittata (page 168) and the seafood-filled omelet known as "Swaddled Baby" (page 172), as well as fritter-like vegetable dishes. It's also one of those cases where canned ingredients are not just handy but preferred.

- 2 tablespoons lard, preferably home-rendered (see page 66), or vegetable oil
- 1 medium-sized white onion, sliced into thin half-moons
- 2 garlic cloves, minced
- 1 28-ounce can plum tomatoes (preferably San Marzano from Italy)
- 2–3 canned chipotle chiles in adobo (see page 49), with the sauce that clings to them
- 1 teaspoon crumbled dried Mexican oregano
- ½ teaspoon salt, or to taste (optional)

IN a medium heavy saucepan, heat the lard or oil over medium-high heat until rippling. Add the onion and garlic and cook, stirring occasionally, until the onion is translucent, about 3 minutes.

BREAK up the tomatoes coarsely with your fingers and add the tomatoes and their juices to the sautéed onion. Stir in the chiles and oregano. Reduce the heat to medium, cover, and cook, stirring occasionally, for 15 minutes, or until slightly concentrated. Remove from the heat and let cool to lukewarm, about 15 minutes.

PUREE the mixture in a blender or food processor. Taste for salt and add a little if needed. Serve at once or store, tightly covered, in the refrigerator for up to 4–5 days; reheat before serving.

Salsa a la Veracruzana

VERACRUZ-STYLE SAUCE

𝓕OOD LOVERS WHO KNOW NOTHING ELSE ABOUT VERACRUZAN cuisine probably have heard of this sauce through a dish served in restaurants from Mexico to Manhattan: *huachinango a la veracruzana*, red snapper topped with a medley of onions, tomatoes, garlic, capers, pickled chiles, pimiento-stuffed green olives, and some combination of herbs, all gloriously redolent of olive oil. (See the recipe on page 182.) Actually, a wide range of things can be called *a la veracruzana* when blanketed with the sauce during or after cooking. People in Veracruz don't stop at red snapper; they use any suitable firm-fleshed fish steaks or whole fish and call the dish *pescado a la veracruzana*. The sauce (sometimes also enriched with potatoes) is equally popular served with chicken, and I've encountered it with poached beef tongue. I've experimented still further, using it as a sauce with fried squid. At my restaurant, we also use it as a pasta sauce for staff meals.

There are versions of *salsa a la veracruzana* ranging from thin to thick, fussy to minimalist. Some people puree the tomatoes and let everything else simmer in them; others chop all the ingredients rather coarse or very fine and let them cook down to a juicy mixture or a dense paste. For me, the only essential thing is very good tomatoes. The following *salsa a la veracruzana* comes from La Sopa restaurant in Xalapa, known not just for good food but for cultural activities (it's also an art gallery) and good works (at the time of the pre-Christmas procession-pageants called *posadas*, La Sopa feeds homeless children). Lunchtime always finds people lined up around the block waiting to eat the inexpensive *comida corrida* (set menu). Owner/chef Pepe Ochoa has been known to serve his *salsa a la veracruzana* with canned tuna in empanadas.

¹/₄ cup olive oil

5 garlic cloves, 2 minced, 3 left whole

1 medium-sized white onion, finely chopped

4–5 large ripe tomatoes (about 2 pounds), finely chopped, or one 28-ounce can Italian plum tomatoes (preferably San Marzano), coarsely chopped, with their juice

12 pimiento-stuffed green olives, sliced if large

2–3 pickled jalapeño chiles, stemmed, seeded, and cut lengthwise into thin strips

1 teaspoon capers (12–15 large or 24–30 small ones)

2 bay leaves

1/2 cup fresh Italian parsley leaves

2 fresh thyme sprigs or 1/4 teaspoon crumbled dried thyme

2 fresh marjoram sprigs or 1/4 teaspoon crumbled dried marjoram

2 fresh oregano sprigs or 1/4 teaspoon crumbled dried Mexican oregano

1 teaspoon salt, or to taste

1/4 teaspoon freshly ground *canela* (see page 44)

1/2 cup dry white wine

IN a medium heavy saucepan with a well-fitting lid, heat the oil over medium-high heat until rippling. Add the 3 whole garlic cloves and cook, stirring, until deep golden, but not browned, on all sides; remove and discard. Add the 2 minced garlic cloves and the onion. Cook, stirring frequently, until the onion is translucent, about 3 minutes. Stir in the tomatoes. Reduce the heat to medium-low and cook, stirring occasionally, for 15 minutes, or until slightly concentrated.

ADD all the remaining ingredients and cook, covered, for another 15–20 minutes, until the flavors are richly melded and the sauce is as thick as you like. Taste for salt and add another pinch or two if desired. If using whole fresh herbs, fish them out of the sauce and discard before serving.

Pepián Verde Huasteco

HUASTECA-STYLE GREEN PEPIÁN

Makes about 2 cups

THE DISHES OF HUASTECA AND OTHER NORTHERLY parts of Veracruz state are characterized by plain basic seasonings. Since my own instinct is for complex "layered" flavors, I often have to re-attune my palate to appreciate the purity of many of the specialties of the region. Such was the case with this version of a *pepián* (the celebrated pumpkin seed–chile sauce of Mexico) that I encountered at Doña Virginia restaurant in Pánuco. As with some especially good Italian country cooking, there is almost nothing to distract the taste buds from one or two elemental flavors — here, buttery pumpkin seeds and fresh hot chiles.

I have successfully used this brilliant green *pepián* as an accompanying sauce for roast poultry and meats as well as for enchiladas (see Enchiladas with Huasteca-Style Green Pepián, page 120). Don't try to serve it alongside intricately seasoned dishes or rich sweet-tart flavor combinations — it really shines best in a simple meal.

8	ounces (about 2 cups) hulled pumpkin seeds
3	tablespoons lard, preferably home-rendered (see page 66), or vegetable oil
1	medium-sized white onion, thinly sliced
2	garlic cloves, minced
5	serrano or jalapeño chiles
1½–2	teaspoons salt, or to taste
1–1½	cups water

PLACE a medium heavy skillet over medium heat. Add the pumpkin seeds and toast, stirring constantly and shaking the pan, until they puff up and start to pop, 3–5 minutes. Before they can scorch (which would make the whole dish bitter), quickly scoop them out into a bowl.

IN the same pan, heat the lard or oil over medium-high heat until rippling. Add the onion, garlic, and chiles and cook, stirring frequently, until the onion is translucent and the chiles are blistered but still green, about 5–7 minutes. Scoop out into a blender.

ADD the toasted pumpkin seeds and salt. Process until smooth, adding water as needed to help the action of the blades and thin the sauce to about the consistency of heavy cream.

POUR the sauce into a medium saucepan and bring to a boil over medium-high heat. Quickly reduce the heat to maintain a low simmer and cook, uncovered, stirring once or twice, for 5 minutes. Use at once, or let cool to room temperature and transfer to a storage container. The sauce will keep in the refrigerator, tightly covered, for up to 3 days, but it will thicken a lot as it sits. When ready to use, thin it with enough water to restore the original consistency.

Tlatonile

TOASTED SESAME SEED SAUCE

*H*AVE YOU EVER TASTED CHINESE SESAME PASTE? IF SO, you may have a flicker of recognition on trying this classic sauce from Huatusco, in the hills of north-central Veracruz. It took me a while to warm to *tlatonile*. Then I had the version served at the restaurant at Los Cocuyos resort and was converted. What makes that version special is that the seeds are very carefully roasted and that the seasonings really set off the flavor of the sesame.

Tlatonile is one of the Mexican main-dish sauces that is usually made up in quantity as a concentrated paste, then thinned with good stock to an almost soupy consistency and used to cook meat or poultry, generally either a stewing cut of pork (simmered in stock or water until nearly done) or chicken (browned in hot lard or oil and braised until partly done). See the description under Xico-Style *Mole* (page 326). It will keep best if you use water rather than stock for the initial blending.

In Huatusco, the dried chiles would be a combination of anchos and small, fruity-flavored comapas. Since comapa chiles are not yet available in this country, I suggest árbol chiles.

Makes about 4 cups
concentrated paste

3 ancho chiles, stemmed and seeded
1/4 cup árbol or dried serrano chiles (see page 47)
8 ounces (about 2 cups) sesame seeds
1 1/2–2 teaspoons salt, or to taste
About 2 cups water or Basic Chicken or Pork Stock (page 142 or 144)
3 tablespoons lard, preferably home-rendered (see page 66)

TO PREPARE FOR SERVING
Additional stock or water (see below for proportions)
2–3 fresh epazote sprigs or 2 tablespoons crumbled dried epazote (see page 41) or about 10 cilantro sprigs

RINSE and griddle-dry the ancho chiles following the directions on page 50. Place in a medium bowl, cover with boiling water, and let sit for 20 minutes.

ZARELA'S VERACRUZ

WHILE the chiles soak, place half of the árbol or serrano chiles in a small heavy saucepan over very low heat. Toast, stirring occasionally and shaking the pan, for 5 minutes, or until brittle and fragrant but not scorched. Heat 1 tablespoon of the lard in a small skillet over medium-high heat and fry the remaining chiles until crisp but not browned. Set aside on a plate lined with absorbent paper to drain.

PLACE the sesame seeds in a large heavy skillet over medium-low heat. Toast, stirring constantly, until they are golden (*not* dark) brown, 5–7 minutes. Watch carefully, because they can go from light golden to scorched very fast. Quickly scrape the seeds into a food processor and process to a fine paste, stopping occasionally to scrape down the sides with a rubber spatula. The processing may take time, since the tiny seeds tend to elude the blades.

DRAIN the ancho chiles and add to a blender, along with half of the toasted árbol chiles and the salt. Process to a smooth puree, adding the water or stock as necessary to help the action of the blades. The sauce should be just a little thinner than a nut butter.

IN a medium heavy saucepan, heat the remaining 2 tablespoons lard over medium heat until rippling. Add the sesame and chile mixtures and cook, stirring constantly to keep the sauce from sticking, for 15 minutes, or until the color is slightly deepened. Remove from the heat and let cool to room temperature. If you are not ready to use it at once, scoop the paste into small storage containers. (It will keep in the refrigerator, tightly covered, for up to 1 month.)

WHEN you are ready to use the paste, thin it with either stock or water, using 1 cup of liquid per 1 cup of the *tlatonile* concentrate to make a sauce the consistency of a heavy cream soup. Bring to a boil over medium heat. Add the epazote or cilantro and the chosen meat (see headnote). Cook, uncovered, for about 10 minutes, or until the meat is fully done. Garnish the dish with the reserved fried árbol chiles.

VARIATION

Tlatonile is sometimes made using a combination of sesame seeds and pumpkin seeds. If you would like to try this version, use 4 ounces (3/4–1 cup) toasted sesame seeds and the same amount of hulled pumpkin seeds, toasted separately (see page 64). Proceed as directed above, toasting the seeds before blending them with the other ingredients.

Mole de Xico

XICO-STYLE *MOLE*

THIS GREAT REGIONAL SPECIALTY BELONGS TO THE FAMILY of southern and central Mexican main-dish sauces meant to be served in generous soupy portions with some simply poached or braised meat or poultry swimming in them. The *mole de Xico*, or *mole xiqueño*, is not as universally known outside of Mexico as the elegantly balanced *mole poblano* nor as famous inside the country as the super-elaborate *mole negro oaxaqueño* (named for their cities of origin in neighboring Puebla and Oaxaca). But it's equally important in its own right.

Every cook in the town of Xico can point out something a little different about her or his *mole xiqueño*. (My own individual touch is toasting the dry chiles and grinding them to a powder instead of boiling and pureeing them.) The constants are: the sauce must be sweet and almost marmalade-like, a rich concentrate containing a lot of nuts and seeds (preferably many kinds), a combination of dried and fresh fruits, corn tortillas or bread (usually both) for extra thickening, and a not-too-dominant medley of dried herbs and spices. It demands the flavor of good lard (this is not a case where oil would be a proper substitute). And for the right brown-black color, you must use very dark chiles, generally mulatos and/or pasillas.

This is probably the most labor-intensive dish in the book. To me it doesn't seem horribly demanding — perhaps because I've spent so many hours wrestling with some of the most complex Oaxacan *moles*! Yes, it does take patience to keep frying and pureeing each group of ingredients one after another, but the following version — my free interpretation of a recipe shared by Enriqueta Izaguirre de Virués — has one great advantage: virtually all of the heavy-duty pureeing can be done in one machine, the food processor. I've broken down the work into separate parts — the nuts, the fruits, the chiles — that don't always have to be prepared in the same sequence. Indeed, the beauty of the recipe is its flexibility. Not only can you do the important preliminary steps in any order you prefer (or *almost* any order — for best flavor, the spices and aromatics should be left till last), but you can usually take a breather from one process when you want and come back to it later. And any one step — or all of them — up to preparing the spices and aromatics can be done several hours ahead.

Makes about 4 quarts
basic paste

Please note that the recipe makes about 4 quarts of a thick, heavy paste that keeps well for weeks or months. (People in Xico wouldn't go to all that trouble for just one meal's worth!) To use it, take a few cups of the paste and thin it with stock to a slightly loose, pourable consistency, using about 3/4 cup per cup of paste. The Mexican way would be to simmer some chicken or pork until halfway done in a little water, then use some of the cooking liquid to thin the *mole* and finish cooking the meat in the sauce. For 6 servings, use 3 cups of the basic paste thinned with 2½ cups stock.

To make the paste, you must have at least one large and one small heavy skillet for frying and pan-toasting, a food processor, a spice grinder (or mortar and pestle), a medium-mesh sieve, an assortment of bowls, and eventually a large deep saucepan or Dutch oven in which everything will be combined.

FOR THE CHILES

12 ounces mulato chiles or a combination of mulato and pasilla chiles (about 40 chiles; see page 49)

FOR ALL THE FRYING

3/4 cup (approximately) lard, preferably home-rendered (see page 66)

FOR THE NUT-SEED MIXTURE

1 cup slivered almonds

½ cup pine nuts

½ cup pecan halves or pieces

¼ cup hulled pumpkin seeds

¼ cup sesame seeds

½ cup roasted peanuts

½ cup skinned roasted hazelnuts

FOR THE FRUIT MIXTURE

1¼ cups pitted prunes

½ cup dark raisins

3 crisp tart-sweet apples (I use Granny Smith), peeled, cored, and cut into ½-inch slices

1 ripe plantain, peeled (see page 60) and cut into ½-inch slices

FOR THE THICKENING

2 commercial corn tortillas, cut into 1-inch strips

1 French roll, cut into ¹/₂-inch slices, or 5–6 half-inch slices good French or Italian bread

FOR THE SPICE MIXTURE

1 2-inch piece *canela* (see page 44)

¹/₂ teaspoon aniseed

¹/₂ teaspoon crumbled dried oregano

2 cloves

¹/₂ teaspoon black peppercorns

FOR THE AROMATICS

1 large white onion, unpeeled

2–3 large ripe tomatoes (about 1 pound)

8 garlic cloves, unpeeled

FOR FINISHING THE *MOLE*

1 3-ounce Mexican chocolate tablet (see page 69), grated

2 tablespoons grated *piloncillo* (Mexican brown loaf sugar; see page 70) or dark brown sugar

1 tablespoon salt

FOR THE CHILES

LIGHTLY wipe the chiles with a damp cloth or rinse lightly with water, shaking off the excess, and let dry thoroughly overnight.

PREHEAT the oven to 275°F.

PLACE the chiles on baking sheets (do not crowd them) and toast until fragrant and crisp but not browned. Let cool. Remove the stems and seeds; you can use all or part of the seeds for extra heat, or discard them for a milder *mole*. Working in batches as necessary, grind the toasted chiles (and seeds if desired) to a powder in a food processor. Set aside.

TO FRY THE NUT-SEED MIXTURE

IN a large heavy skillet, heat about 2 tablespoons of the lard over medium heat until rippling. Add the almonds and pine nuts and fry, stirring constantly, until golden, 3–4 minutes. With a slotted spoon, scoop into a bowl, letting as much fat as possible drain back into the pan. Add about 1 more tablespoon lard to the pan and let it heat until rippling. Add the pecans and fry in the same way, about 3 minutes, being careful not to scorch them (reduce the heat slightly if necessary). Scoop out into the same bowl; set the skillet aside for later.

HEAT a small dry skillet over medium heat and add the pumpkin seeds. Toast, stirring constantly, just until they start swelling up and popping, 3 minutes or less. Quickly add to the bowl with the other nuts. Add the sesame seeds to the skillet and toast, stirring, until golden, about 2 minutes. Scrape into the same bowl.

ADD the peanuts and hazelnuts to the bowl of nuts and seeds and stir to distribute everything evenly. In the food processor, in 1 or 2 batches, process to a very fine, smooth paste. Scrape into a bowl and set aside.

FOR THE FRUIT MIXTURE

ADD another 2 tablespoons lard to that remaining in the skillet used for frying the nuts. Heat over medium heat until rippling. Add the prunes and raisins and cook, stirring occasionally, for about 2 minutes, or until they've absorbed some of the fat. Scoop out into a bowl. Add another 2 tablespoons of the lard to the skillet. When it ripples, add the sliced apples and plantain. Cook, stirring, until golden and slightly softened, 5–7 minutes. Scrape the sautéed fruit into the bowl with the prunes and raisins. Let cool slightly, then process to a smooth puree. Scrape into a bowl and set aside.

FOR THE THICKENING

RINSE out and dry the large skillet (to remove any scorch-prone residue of fruit). Add another 2 tablespoons of the lard and heat over medium heat until rippling. Add the tortilla strips and fry, stirring frequently, for 3–4 minutes, or until golden. Lift out onto paper towels to drain.

IN the same pan, fry the bread slices until golden on both sides, about 2 minutes per side. Lift out and drain. You have now finished all the major preparations.

FOR THE SPICE MIXTURE

WHEN you are ready to finish cooking the *mole*, heat a small dry skillet over medium heat. Add the *canela* and toast for 1 minute. Add the other seasonings. Shaking the skillet occasionally, toast until fragrant, about 2 minutes. Let cool to room temperature, then grind

very fine using a mortar and pestle or an electric coffee or spice grinder. Set aside.

FOR THE AROMATICS

GRIDDLE-ROAST and peel the onion, tomatoes, and garlic, following the directions on page 58. Place the roasted vegetables in a blender (my preference) or food processor, along with the fried tortillas and bread, and process to a coarse paste.

ADD the remaining 3–4 tablespoons lard to a large Dutch oven or deep heavy saucepan over medium heat. When it ripples, add the onion-tortilla mixture and the ground spices. Cook, stirring occasionally, for about 10 minutes, or until the flavors are mellowed. Stir in the pureed chiles, ground nuts and seeds, and pureed fruits. Bring to a boil and cook, stirring frequently, for 3–5 minutes, or until well combined.

TO FINISH

STIR in the chocolate, *piloncillo* or brown sugar, and salt; cook, uncovered, for another 20–30 minutes, stirring frequently to keep the *mole* from scorching. Remove the *mole* from the heat and let cool to room temperature, then transfer to small containers. It will keep for 4–5 weeks in the refrigerator, or indefinitely in the freezer.

TO dilute the *mole* with stock for use as a sauce, see headnote on page 328.

THE STORY OF SWEET THINGS in Veracruz has sometimes been bitter. On the one hand, the proud Spanish-Moorish tradition of confectionery was brilliantly transplanted there and has been preserved down to modern times. But what it took to supply the sugar for the classic almond- and egg-based sweets was slave labor. Veracruz became a land of sugar plantations that raised a cash crop en masse for export and that were worked by first Indian and then African slaves.

Sugar was king for centuries, the most valued product of Veracruzan soil. Honey, the older sweetener, took a very distant back seat with European honeybees replacing the bee-like insects that the pre-Hispanic peoples had domesticated. The local confectioners could actually perfect their art with better and cheaper supplies of sugar than anybody in Old Spain.

Almonds were introduced to Mexico when the first Spanish missionaries arrived in Veracruz carrying slips and seeds of Old World plants. There's a certain irony in the fact that sweets like marzipan, really a legacy of the "infidel" Moors, became a highly profitable business for orders of nuns both in Mexico and in Spain. This tradition remains today, but the art of sweet making also moved out of the convents into private homes. The lovely town of Tlacotalpan (see page 9) has made a strong effort to preserve some of the old cottage industries through which many wives, mothers, and single women once supported their households. Here you can still find women creating *pasta de almendra* (marzipan) and macaroons that would not have been out of place in Renaissance Spain. Over the centuries, inventive cooks also learned to pair sugar with New World almond substitutes like pumpkin seeds (to make the taffy-like *pepitoria*) and peanuts (in tartlets like *polvorones de cacahuate*).

Veracruz also became an important center for ices and ice creams, because in early days fresh snow and ice from Mount Citlaltépetl and its neighbors were convenient to the growing regions for the state's magnificent tropical fruits. Mexicans in general value a range of ices that amazes visitors from the United States, but I've found some particularly mind-blowing lists of flavors in the *neverías* (ice cream shops) of Veracruz. From one visit to the Centro Nevero in the port city I remember seeing (among others) carrot, prune, fresh corn, mushroom, kiwi, black sapote, currant, litchi, passion fruit, mint, tangerine, melon, banana, jícama with chile, marshmallow, cheese and blackberry, tequila with lime, fig with mezcal, tamarind, sweet potato with pineapple, *jobo* (filled with the small and woody but delicious yellow fruits of *Spondias lutea*), rose petal, and *cajeta* (milk reduced to a caramel — the much better precursor of the Häagen-Dazs *dulce de leche* ice cream). Needless to say, my friends and I could only sample a handful, but we did our heroic best.

WITH INDOMITABLE SPIRIT, the Africans and mixed-blood plantation workers learned to convert the leavings of the sugar-refining process into syrups and loaf sugars that today are universally prized in Veracruz for particular cooking purposes. (My favorite example is the syrup that goes with *buñuelos veracruzanos*, page 340.) And history doesn't stop there — in the twentieth century, butter cakes like those in this country came to Mexico, and in the last few generations, Veracruzan cooks have translated them into super-rich bases for incredible, baroque layer cakes with sumptuous fillings.

Cocoles de Anís

DIAMOND-SHAPED ROLLS WITH ANISE

*C*OCOL (RHOMBUS) REFERS TO THE MOST TRADITIONAL shape of the sweet yeast breads made in the central Veracruzan highlands. Actually, they aren't limited to one geographical area — or even one shape, though most *cocoles* are some variation on a diamond. They can be lighter or darker, plain or cheese-filled, large or small. Many have decorative borders, or at least some token of an ornament. The ones that I lost my heart to were from La Fama bakery in the hill-country town of Coscomatepec.

Panadería La Fama has been in business since 1924 and may be the best-loved institution of Coscomatepec. The first time I visited, one of the current owners, Luz María Castro de Garnica (a granddaughter of the founder), presented me with an official history of the bakery and a poem celebrating the many fanciful nicknames of the different rolls and pastries. (Some of these are immortalized in a possibly apocryphal story of a customer asking to have some items deleted from her order and replaced by others. The Spanish is really untranslatable, but it comes out in English something like "Take off my pants and give me some kisses," and "Remove my horns and give me a few good whacks on the head" — each of the items in question being the name of a particular specialty.)

What drew me to this version of *cocoles* was the depth of flavor given by the combination of *piloncillo* (unrefined loaf sugar) and anise. They are great favorites in Coscomatepec. People plan their daily activities by the bakery's schedule, which starts at 7:00 A.M. with the firing of the wood ovens and reaches its climax shortly after noon, when the long-awaited treasures are ready for sale. Serve with coffee or chocolate.

Makes 16 rolls

12 ounces *piloncillo* (Mexican brown loaf sugar; see page 70), chopped or broken into chunks

$^3/_4$ cup water

1 tablespoon aniseed

2 ounces (or slightly less) compressed yeast, or 4 packages (3 tablespoons) active dry yeast

$1^1/_2$ cups lukewarm water

About $4^1/_2$ cups unbleached all-purpose flour, plus $^1/_2$ cup for kneading if necessary ($1^1/_4$–$1^1/_3$ pounds)

$^1/_2$ teaspoon salt

$^1/_2$ cup vegetable shortening, at room temperature

PLACE the *piloncillo* in a small saucepan with the water. Bring to a boil over medium heat and cook, stirring, until the sugar is completely dissolved. You should have about $1^1/_4$ cups liquid; set aside to cool to lukewarm.

GRIND the aniseed very fine in an electric coffee or spice mill. Set aside.

DISSOLVE the yeast in the lukewarm sugar-water until it foams. Heap $4^1/_2$ cups of the flour in a large bowl or on a work surface and make a well in the center. Put the salt, shortening, and ground anise into the well. Pour in the dissolved mixture. With your hands, quickly push the flour together from the walls toward the center and start mixing it into the liquid until the mixture forms a soft but workable dough. Knead for about 5 minutes, or until the dough is smooth and elastic; add a small amount of flour if necessary to help in kneading, but better too little than too much. (Alternatively, you can mix the ingredients and knead the dough for 5 minutes in the bowl of an electric mixer fitted with the dough hook.)

TRANSFER the dough to a clean bowl and let stand in a warm, draft-free spot, covered with a damp cloth, until nearly doubled in bulk, about $1^1/_2$ hours.

PUNCH down the dough and divide it first in half, then into quarters, eighths, and so forth, until you have 16 equal pieces. Shape each into a ball, then press out with your fingers into a square about 4 x 4 inches. Pull gently on two opposite corners, stretching the square into a diamond. Bring the points of two opposite corners to the center so they meet and pinch them together in the air. Take the other two corners and twist them into a small knob of dough. Place the *cocoles* on ungreased baking sheets 2–3 inches apart as they are shaped and let sit, lightly covered with tea towels, for 1 hour, or until nearly doubled in bulk.

PREHEAT the oven to 375°F.

BRUSH the tops of the rolls with cold water (it improves the finish of the crust) and bake for 15–18 minutes, or until lightly browned. Cool before serving.

Mostachones

ALMOND MACAROONS

THESE ARE ONE OF THE SPECIALTIES THAT REGULARLY proceed from Leticia Alavés's kitchen in Tlacotalpan to a large and delighted clientele.

Makes about 24 macaroons

4^1/$_2$ cups (1 pound) blanched slivered almonds

2 cups plus 2 tablespoons sugar

2 large egg whites, lightly beaten, plus 1 extra white if needed

Vegetable oil for rolling

PLACE the almonds and sugar in a food processor and pulse and process until very finely and evenly ground. This will take about 10 minutes; pulse several times at the beginning and then let the machine run continuously. The mixture should be a packed powder with a consistency like brown sugar. Add the 2 egg whites and process until the mixture comes together in a ball. Lightly beat the extra white and add it gradually if necessary to help the processing.

PREHEAT the oven to 375°F. Line two baking sheets with parchment paper.

MOISTEN your palms with a little oil. Pinch off small (about 1-tablespoon) portions of the mixture and roll each into a ball, then flatten slightly, press out a small indentation on the underside with your index finger, and place on the baking sheets. Re-oil your hands from time to time as necessary.

PLACE a shallow pan of water on the bottom of the oven. Place the baking sheets on the center and top racks and bake for 10 minutes, or until very lightly browned. Let cool in the pans. The macaroons will keep in airtight containers at room temperature for 2–3 weeks.

Polvorones de Cacahuate

PEANUT SAND TARTS

YOU MAY HAVE ENCOUNTERED THE PLAIN VERSION OF *polvorones* as "Mexican wedding cookies." This delicious variation is adapted from a recipe developed at a Xalapa vocational school and published in that superb book *La Cocina Veracruzana*, by Ana Laura Delgado and María Stoopen. For ordinary cooking purposes, Mexicans never use the flavorless commercial hydrogenated lard sold in 1-pound packages. But they do resort to it for some baked desserts, where it gives a needed fluffiness to the dough.

Makes about 48 cookies

1 cup roasted peanuts
1³/4 cups all-purpose flour
1 teaspoon baking powder
¹/2 teaspoon salt
1 cup commercial lard, at room temperature
1 large egg
About ¹/2 cup sugar for rolling

PREHEAT the oven to 375°F. Grease two baking sheets.

COARSELY grind the peanuts in a food processor. Do not process to a paste; you want them to have some texture. They should be a little finer than Grape-Nuts.

SIFT the flour, baking powder, and salt together into a mixing bowl. Make a well in the center and add the lard and egg. With your fingers, work the ingredients lightly but thoroughly to make a soft dough, then work in the ground peanuts.

SHAPE the mixture into walnut-sized balls and place on the greased baking sheets. Bake for 15–18 minutes, or until they are lightly golden. Let cool slightly, then roll in the sugar. Let cool in the pans. The cookies will keep for 3–4 days in airtight containers at room temperature.

Pemoles

CORN MASA COOKIES

Makes about 36 cookies

PEMOLES AS MADE BY THE BEST VERACRUZAN COOKS ARE based on fresh masa, air-dried at home and then ground to a fine flour. It is not exactly the same as the commercial masa harina that I use here, because fresh masa is very perishable and sours slightly in the process of drying. I miss the little acid note, but this version of *pemoles*, adapted from a recipe that Ángeles Juárez Molina gave me in Tuxpan, is still delectable. The cookies have a rich, complex, elusive flavor, with a delightful crunchy texture from the masa harina.

1	tablespoon instant espresso
1	cup hot water
4	cups (about 1 pound) masa harina (see page 51)
1¹/₂	cups sugar
¹/₂	teaspoon baking soda
¹/₂	teaspoon salt
¹/₂	cup vegetable shortening, at room temperature
8	tablespoons (1 stick) unsalted butter, at room temperature
2	tablespoons lard, at room temperature
	Grated zest of 1 lime
1	teaspoon pure vanilla extract

PREHEAT the oven to 375°F.

DISSOLVE the instant espresso in the hot water; set aside. Combine the dry ingredients in a large bowl.

BEAT the shortening, butter, and lard in a large mixing bowl until fluffy. Beat in the dry ingredients and the espresso with a wooden spoon until the mixture forms a firm but pliable dough. Work in the lime zest and vanilla extract.

PINCH off walnut-sized pieces of the dough, shape into balls, and press out with your fingertips into 1¹/₂-inch rounds, leaving the indentation of your fingertips in the center.

PLACE about 1 inch apart on ungreased baking sheets and bake for 10–12 minutes, or until the cookies smell toasty and take on a pale tan color. Let cool on the pans. The cookies will keep for 2 weeks in airtight containers at room temperature.

Gelatina de Rompope

MEXICAN EGGNOG MOUSSE

I LOVE *ROMPOPE*, MEXICO'S NATIONAL VERSION OF EGGNOG, so I was delighted to find it put to a new purpose in this recipe from a cookbook sold by a ladies' volunteer committee for the Coatepec chapter of the Red Cross. The creamy, voluptuous mousse makes a great holiday-season dessert — or, if you want to try it at another time of year, it also goes delightfully with fresh summer berries.

Makes 6–8 servings

- 2 envelopes unflavored gelatin
- ¹/₂ cup cold water
- ³/₄ cup Mexican Eggnog (page 364), with the liquor added before the combined mixture is cooked
- 1 cup Mexican *crema* (see page 67) or sour cream
- 1 teaspoon pure vanilla extract, preferably Mexican
- 2 teaspoons dark rum

LIGHTLY oil a 1-quart mold. (Oiling isn't absolutely necessary, but it helps the mousse unmold more easily.)

IN a small saucepan, soften the gelatin in the water for 15 minutes. Meanwhile, stir together all the remaining ingredients in a small bowl. Set the saucepan over very low heat, stirring constantly, until the gelatin is completely dissolved, about 2 minutes. Add it to the eggnog mixture, stirring to mix thoroughly. Pour the mixture into the mold and chill until completely set, at least 3 hours or (preferably) overnight. It will hold for up to 3 days.

TO unmold, carefully dip the mold into very warm (not hot) water for about 1 minute, being sure not to let any water leak in. Run a thin-bladed knife around the rim; place a platter or plate on top. Invert the mold onto it, remove the mold, and serve.

Buñuelos Veracruzanos con Miel de Piloncillo

VERACRUZAN BEIGNETS WITH BROWN LOAF SUGAR SYRUP

Makes 12–16 *buñuelos*
(8–10 servings)

IN SPANISH, THE NAME *BUÑUELOS* (FRITTERS) IS GIVEN TO various crisp fried things that don't really have much in common. One kind, called *buñuelos de viento* (wind fritters) in Spain, uses the same principle as French *beignets soufflés* made with *pâte à choux* (cream puff dough). You start with a smoothly cooked mixture of flour, water, and melted fat and vigorously beat eggs into it one at a time until the dough has taken as many as it can without becoming too wet. (The description of *pâte à choux* in Madeleine Kamman's *The New Making of a Cook* is very helpful.) Then you form the mixture into doughnut shapes and deep-fry them to produce something like the "French crullers" of New York doughnut shops, only moister and more tender.

My first introduction to the Veracruzan version of these beignets was the sublime, airy, anise-scented *buñuelos* that Tomasita Meléndez serves at Las Brisas del Mar restaurant. Tomasita and her pastry chef, Pilar Sánchez Pérez, gave me a restaurant-sized recipe that I've successfully scaled down for home use.

1	teaspoon aniseed
	Pinch of salt
¼	cup vegetable shortening
1	tablespoon lard, preferably home-rendered (see page 66)
2	cups water
2	cups all-purpose flour (8 ounces)
5–6	large eggs
	Vegetable oil for frying
	Brown Loaf Sugar Syrup (page 342), warmed or at room temperature

PLACE the aniseed, salt, shortening, and lard in a large heavy saucepan. Add the water and bring to a boil over high heat. Remove from the heat and add the flour all at once. Beat in the flour with a wooden spoon or whisk until the dough comes together in a mass. Set the pot over medium-low heat and cook, stirring and beating the mixture to help the water evaporate, for about 1 minute. Stop when you see a hint of film on the bottom of the pan, before the mixture starts to scorch or break.

TURN out the dough into a large mixing bowl or the work bowl of an electric mixer. The eggs must be added *gradually*. Add 1 egg to the flour mixture and beat vigorously with a wooden spoon or an electric mixer set on medium speed, to incorporate completely. Don't worry if the mixture looks stringy. Continue to add the eggs one at a time, beating thoroughly after each addition, until the mixture is smooth, glistening, and just firm enough to shape (gingerly) with your hands. (You may want to beat the last egg separately in a small bowl and add it gradually, since the exact number of eggs will vary depending on the absorbency of the flour. The dough will require a little less egg if made in an electric mixer than if beaten by hand.)

POUR oil into a medium deep skillet to a depth of 2 inches. Heat to 375°F over medium-high heat.

NOW comes the potentially tricky part: handling the soft, moist dough. It will help to keep wetting your hands with lukewarm water. Take about a 1/2-cup portion of the dough and, holding it in your hands, gently flatten it into a 4¹/₂-inch round, then use a finger to hollow out a hole in the center, doughnut-fashion. Drop the *buñuelos* into the hot oil, a few at a time, turning once, until puffy and golden, about 1¹/₂ minutes per side. Lift out onto paper towels to drain. It's best to shape and fry no more than two at a time; as you work, keep checking the temperature of the oil and adjusting the heat as necessary to maintain a constant 375°F. To serve, pour a generous amount of *piloncillo* syrup (¹/₃–¹/₂ cup per serving) into individual bowls and place a *buñuelo* in each bowl.

Miel de Piloncillo

BROWN LOAF SUGAR SYRUP

Makes 4–5 cups

*I*F YOU ARE LUCKY ENOUGH TO EAT *BUÑUELOS* AT LAS BRISAS del Mar (see page 340), the fritters themselves will be only half of the experience. You will also taste a rare piece of Veracruzan history in the exquisite brown syrup that comes with them. It is true *caña* (cane syrup) from a local artisanal sugar mill. In this country I use a syrup made from commercial *piloncillo* (brown loaf sugar) — not so flowery and delicate, but still excellent.

Remember that the size of the loaves sold in Latin American groceries here can be anything from an ounce or two to nearly a kilo. Buy as many as you need to come close to a total of a pound, and don't worry if it's a bit more or less. The flavor is what counts. Break up the loaves if they are very large (bashing with a hammer is inelegant but effective).

1 pound *piloncillo* (Mexican brown loaf sugar; see page 70), broken into pieces

6 cups water

PLACE the *piloncillo* in a medium deep heavy saucepan, add the water, and bring to a boil over high heat, stirring to dissolve. Reduce the heat to medium and cook for 15–20 minutes, or until the syrup thickens enough to coat a spoon. As the sugar dissolves, it may throw off some residue of the unrefined cane juice; remove this with a skimmer. Serve warm or at room temperature with *buñuelos*.

Beso del Duque

THE DUKE'S KISS

WHO WAS THE DUKE, AND WHOM WAS HE KISSING? Spanish and Mexican desserts tend to leave you scratching your head over the meaning of their titles, but you can guess that it was a very *sweet* kiss. Egg-based sweetmeats and cakes bathed in perfumed sugar syrups are part of the Moorish tradition that came from Spain to Latin America and still exists in Mexico to some extent. *Beso del duque* is one of the most unusual members of the large tribe. The basic cake reminds me a little of a Viennese torte raised only with beaten eggs and bound with crushed crumbs instead of flour. In Veracruz, they would use crushed *galletas de María*, a kind of dry biscuit resembling old-fashioned arrowroot biscuits. Animal crackers, believe it or not, are the closest substitute here.

Makes one 13-x-9-inch cake
(10–12 servings)

FOR THE SYRUP

2¹/₃ cups sugar

2 cups water

A strip about 2¹/₂ inches long from the outer layer of a *canela* stick (see page 44)

FOR THE CAKE

2 2¹/₈-ounce boxes animal crackers

1 teaspoon freshly ground *canela* (see page 44)

6 large eggs, separated

¹/₄ cup sesame seeds

¹/₄ cup slivered blanched almonds

¹/₄ cup dark raisins

³/₄ cup dry sherry (I use *fino*)

FOR THE SYRUP

IN a medium saucepan, combine the sugar and water. Add the *canela* and bring to a boil over high heat, stirring to dissolve the sugar. Reduce the heat to medium and cook until the mixture forms a light syrup, about 5 minutes. Remove from the heat and discard the *canela*.

LIGHTLY grease a 13-x-9-inch Pyrex baking dish and pour half the syrup into it; set aside. Preheat the oven to 375°F.

CRUSH the animal crackers very fine with a rolling pin or process in a food processor. You should have about 1 cup.

IN a large mixing bowl, beat the egg whites to glossy peaks. Add the yolks, one at a time, beating well after each addition. The mixture should remain glossy and fairly light. Fold in the crushed crackers and the *canela*. Pour the mixture into the baking dish. It will float on top of the syrup. Scatter the sesame seeds, almonds, and raisins over the top.

BAKE until the batter is set but not browned, 10–12 minutes. Remove the pan from the oven; pierce the top all over with a fork or the tip of a sharp knife. Combine the remaining syrup with the sherry and pour over the cake.

RETURN the pan to the oven and bake for another 8–10 minutes, until the top is pale golden and all the syrup has been absorbed (from both top and bottom). Let cool in the pan.

CUT into 3-x-4-inch rectangles and serve warm or at room temperature.

Pastel de Coco

COCONUT LAYER CAKE

Makes one two-layer
10-inch cake (about
12 servings)

ONE OF MY FAVORITE VERACRUZAN COOKBOOKS, *COCINA Veracruzana de Abolengo*, has a coconut cake recipe that I just *had* to try. And it was fully as delicious as it sounded — except that the original had a whipped-cream filling that would not have been my first preference. I did some experimenting and found that meringue makes not only an excellent icing but a refreshingly light filling that plays against the richness of the cake layers. Remember that it will dry out quickly once spread on the cake, so plan on serving within half a day or (preferably) less.

2¹/₂ cups all-purpose flour

2 teaspoons baking powder

¹/₄ teaspoon salt

1 14-ounce can condensed milk

³/₄ cup freshly squeezed orange juice

1 teaspoon pure vanilla extract, preferably Mexican

¹/₂ pound (2 sticks) unsalted butter, at room temperature

1 tablespoon finely grated orange zest

1¹/₄ cups sugar

6 large eggs, separated

3 cups (approximately) freshly grated coconut (from about three-quarters of a coconut)

Meringue Icing (page 350)

PREHEAT the oven to 325°F. Grease and flour the sides of two round 10-inch pans, preferably with sides 2¹/₂–3 inches high. Cut two 10-inch circles of parchment paper or waxed paper to line the bottoms and place in the pans. Set aside.

SIFT together the flour, baking powder, and salt into a medium bowl. In a small bowl, combine the condensed milk, orange juice, and vanilla extract.

IN a large bowl, beat the butter with the orange zest until very light. Gradually add the sugar, beating until fluffy. Beat in the egg yolks, one at a time.

SWEET BREADS AND DESSERTS

ADD the flour mixture in three batches, alternating with the milk mixture, beating just until smooth. Fold 2 cups of the grated coconut into the batter.

BEAT the egg whites to glossy peaks. Fold into the batter with a rubber spatula.

POUR the batter into the prepared pans and bake for 30–40 minutes, or until a toothpick inserted in the center comes out clean. Remove the pans from the oven and let cool on racks for 10 minutes.

RUN a small knife around the inside of each pan to loosen the edges of the cake. Place a plate over each pan and invert, then lift off the pan, remove the paper, and let cool completely on racks. (The cake layers can be made up to 1 day in advance; store, tightly wrapped, at room temperature.)

WHILE the cake layers are cooling, make the icing and fold in the remaining 1 cup coconut.

SET one layer on a cake plate and spread about 2 cups of the icing over the top. Set the second layer over the first and ice the entire cake with the remaining icing. Cut into slices and serve.

Turrón

THIS TENDS TO DRY OUT RAPIDLY ONCE MADE, SO ALWAYS
plan on using it quickly.

Makes 7–8 cups

1½ cups sugar
½ cup water
4 large egg whites
½ teaspoon fresh lime juice

PLACE the sugar in a small heavy saucepan with the water and
bring to a boil over high heat, stirring to dissolve the sugar thoroughly. Cook, without stirring, until the syrup forms a thick thread
when poured from a spoon, or registers about 230°F on a candy thermometer.

AS soon as the sugar mixture reaches a boil, begin beating the
egg whites with an electric mixer set on medium-high. Beat to soft
peaks (by that time the syrup should be at the right temperature).

REDUCE the speed to medium and start pouring the syrup into
the egg whites in a thin stream, being careful to avoid the beaters.
When all the syrup has been added, raise the speed to medium-high
and continue beating for 4–5 minutes, until the mixture is glossy and
thoroughly cooled. Beat in the lime juice and use immediately.

Helado de Cacahuate

PEANUT ICE

OUR UNFAILINGLY KNOWLEDGEABLE GUIDE, VICTOR AGUSTÍN Benítez, headed like a homing pigeon for one of the best ice cream shops (many would say *the* best) in the port city of Veracruz, the Centro Nevero. It's just off the bustling promenade on the harbor embankment, and for any lover of frozen desserts, it will be paradise — though I have to say that this is true of ice cream shops throughout the length and breadth of Mexico. My favorite of the more than three dozen flavors of ice creams listed on the big board behind the counter turned out to be a peanut ice cream that was really more like a milk sherbet.

Because there's so much fat in the nuts themselves, I like to use skim or low-fat milk. But this is a personal preference of mine, not standard Mexican practice. In most cases people use whole milk or — for extra richness — evaporated milk. Don't try making Mexican ices with fresh cream; the texture will be completely inauthentic.

Helado de cacahuate can be made with freshly ground roasted peanuts, "natural" peanut butter, or — my preference — homogenized peanut butter like the kind familiar to all children in both countries. The first two choices may result in a gritty texture unless the mixture is put through a fine-mesh sieve. I love to serve this with an unorthodox "syrup" — Milk Punch with Peanuts (page 363), which is richer than the *helado* and makes a potent complement.

    ½ cup Syrup for Ices (page 352)
    ½ cup peanut butter (see above)
    3 cups milk (any kind; see above)

THOROUGHLY mix all the ingredients in a mixing bowl or blender. Pour the mixture into an ice cream maker and freeze according to the manufacturer's directions. Transfer to a freezer container and freeze until ready to serve. Or, if you don't have an ice cream machine, use the still-freeze method. Put the mixture in the freezer for 2 hours in a metal bowl; chill electric beaters. Beat to a slush using the chilled beaters. Freeze for another hour (chill the beaters again) and beat again, then freeze until ready to serve.

Miel para *H*elados

SYRUP FOR ICES

1 cup sugar	Makes 1 cup
2 cups water	

IN a small saucepan, heat the sugar and water together over medium heat, stirring to dissolve the sugar thoroughly. Bring to a boil and cook until reduced to about 1 cup. Let cool to room temperature before using. The syrup will keep almost indefinitely in the refrigerator, tightly sealed.

Huevitos de Almendra

"LITTLE EGGS" OF ALMOND PASTE

CARMEN RIVERA DÍAZ OF PAPANTLA GAVE ME THE RECIPE for these little sweetmeats, which make adorable party favors. (Don't be horrified at the number of egg yolks — fourteen is paltry when you look at old recipes for some of the baroque-era Spanish convent sweets that used to be made in Mexico.) In Papantla, the *huevitos* are often made with a soaked prune embedded in the almond paste.

People also make very similar candy eggs using ground peanuts (*huevitos de cacahuate*) or pumpkin seeds (*huevitos de pepita*).

Before beginning the recipe, buy some brightly colored tissue paper (preferably several different shades) for wrapping the "eggs."

Makes about 48 small candies

$4^1/2$ cups (1 pound) blanched slivered almonds
$4^1/3$–$4^1/2$ cups (2 pounds) sugar
2 cups water
14 large egg yolks
$^1/_2$–$^3/_4$ teaspoon almond extract

GRIND the almonds in a food processor until very fine but not greasy: pulse a few times at the beginning, then let the machine run continuously for about 7 minutes. Stop and loosen the ground mass from under the blades, then process for another 2–3 minutes. Set aside.

PLACE the sugar and water in a medium deep, heavy saucepan and bring to a boil over medium-high heat, stirring to dissolve the sugar completely. Cook without stirring until the syrup registers 240°F on a candy thermometer, or until a small bit dropped into cold water forms a soft ball.

WHILE the syrup is cooking, beat the egg yolks in a large bowl until they fall from the beaters in a thick flat ribbon.

ADD the ground almonds to the sugar syrup and cook, stirring constantly, until the mixture thickens enough to come away from the sides of the pan, 5–6 minutes. Stir in the beaten egg yolks and almond extract and cook, stirring constantly, until the mixture comes away from the sides again (less than a minute).

QUICKLY scoop the mixture into a bowl; sprinkle with a little cool water or place a layer of waxed paper over the top to keep the surface from getting crusty as it cools. Let sit, stirring occasionally with a wooden spoon, until it cools to room temperature. If it begins to stiffen so that it can't be worked, sprinkle it with a few drops of water or place briefly in a sealed plastic bag so that condensation can soften it. It should be firm but still shapable when completely cooled.

FORM the mixture into egg-shaped balls a little larger than an almond in the shell. Wrap them in twists of colored tissue paper and store in airtight containers.

NOTE: If you like, roll the candy eggs in sugar before wrapping in tissue paper.

Pepitoria

PUMPKIN SEED–SESAME CANDY

Makes about 48 candies

꜒꜒꜒꜒꜒

CANDY MADE WITH *PILONCILLO*, THE UNREFINED MEXICAN brown loaf sugar, doesn't behave exactly like its counterparts made with white sugar. The sugar syrup will look very different at all the cooking stages. But the flavor of *piloncillo* makes conventional sugar candy seem dull. This delightful example has a caramel-like consistency and an unusual textural interest from the combination of crushed *pepitas* (pumpkin seeds) and sesame seeds.

I first saw *pepitoria* made at the Gómez-Atzín family museum, La Casa de las Mascaras, near Papantla. When Marta Gómez Atzín and her aunt Doña Vero (Verónica) made the recipe for me, they poured the candy rounds onto a freshly cut and rinsed banana leaf that they had just gathered from their garden — much more memorable than our waxed paper!

> 2 pounds *piloncillo* (Mexican brown loaf sugar; see page 70), broken into chunks
>
> 4 cups water
>
> 1 cup (4 ounces) hulled pumpkin seeds
>
> 1 cup (4 ounces) sesame seeds

HAVE ready several long pieces of parchment or waxed paper.

PLACE the *piloncillo* in a large heavy saucepan with the water. Bring to a boil over medium-high heat, stirring frequently, until the sugar is completely dissolved. Continue cooking, without stirring, for another 30 minutes, or until the temperature registers 240°F on a candy thermometer.

WHILE the syrup is cooking, place the pumpkin seeds and sesame seeds in two separate medium heavy skillets. Set the pumpkin seeds over medium-low heat and toast, shaking the pan and stirring frequently, until they puff up and start to pop, 3–5 minutes. At the same time, set the sesame seeds over medium-low heat and toast, shaking the pan and stirring frequently, for about 5 minutes, or until they are light golden. Before they can scorch, quickly scrape out the seeds into a large mortar or a food processor. Grind roughly with the pestle or process just until broken up but not pasty — you want some

texture. (You can also scoop them out onto a baking sheet or clean work surface and crush with a rolling pin.)

WHEN the *piloncillo* syrup has reached 240°F, quickly stir in the crushed seeds. With a large kitchen spoon, drop rounds of the mixture (about 1 tablespoon each) onto the sheets of parchment or waxed paper. Let cool completely. The candy can be stored in the freezer for 7–10 days.

BEVERAGES

*T*HIS CHAPTER BEGINS with true specialties of Veracruz and ends with a drink that I've tasted with pleasure there but that belongs to all of Mexico: rompope, our answer to eggnog. I just happened to find a version from a Veracruz restaurant family that I prefer to any I've encountered elsewhere in Mexico.

The other drinks belong more specially to Veracruz. In my years of living and later traveling in Mexico, I've tasted and loved many of our heavenly fresh-fruit drinks, but never one that surprised me more happily than *agua fresca de chayote*. It's a whole new perspective on something I'd only thought of as a vegetable. Blackberries, one of the best wild fruits in the cool Veracruzan highlands, turned out to be a wonderful flavoring for *atole*, the corn masa drink loved by all Mexicans. As for the sweet but lethal peanut *toritos* (creamy drinks spiced with cane liquor) and the unique local interpretation of a mint julep, travelers can hardly be said to have officially visited Veracruz without having tried them.

I have to mention one other pan-Mexican indulgence: *michelada*, the popular beer-based drink that is particularly enjoyed in the major brewery town of Orizaba. This whoop-de-do invention can't really be reduced to a recipe. But the main requirements for a *michelada* are a beer (dark or lager as you prefer), a good slug of fresh lime juice (¹/₄ cup for 12 ounces of beer is not considered excessive), a salt-rimmed glass, and lots of ice cubes. You can also throw in a dash of hot chile sauce (the bottled kinds are fine) with Worcestershire, Maggi, and/or soy sauce. With these latter additions a *michelada* is often called a *chelada*, though I doubt that there's any hard-and-fast distinction between the two. Now you know enough to go with.

Agua Fresca de Chayote

CHAYOTE-ADE

No ASPECT OF MEXICAN CUISINE GIVES MORE JOY TO Mexicans and visitors alike than the wonderful galaxy of cool, refreshing drinks (*aguas frescas*) made with every kind of fruit. They are like lemonade and orangeade transposed to a dozen different keys. There are even *aguas frescas* made with flowers, herbs, and vegetables. The basic idea is almost always to combine the chosen ingredient with cold water, enough sugar to sweeten it lightly (not cloyingly), and enough lime juice to brighten the flavor. Somehow I had never thought of making an *agua fresca* out of chayotes until I visited Orizaba, where it is almost a citywide obsession to cook with chayotes in every way, shape, and form. Their delicate flavor is pleasantly surprising in a summer-drink context. (See the photograph on page 360.)

Makes about 1 quart
(4–6 servings)

1 large chayote, peeled and pitted (see page 55), coarsely chopped
4 cups very cold water
1/4 cup sugar
Juice of 1 large lime

IN a blender, process the chayote and cold water to a puree. With a pusher or wooden spoon, force the mixture through a medium-mesh sieve into a bowl. Add the sugar, stirring to dissolve well; stir in the lime juice.

POUR into a chilled pitcher and serve immediately.

Atole de Mora

BLACKBERRY ATOLE

I DON'T KNOW ANYTHING MORE TRULY MEXICAN, OR MORE baffling to foreigners, than *atoles*. They're food and drink together, velvety liquid porridges bound with corn masa and flavored with anything from chile peppers to mangoes. Think of a combination of hot cereal, hot beverage, and fruit juice. *Atoles* are much beloved for breakfast, though they are also quite popular with supper.

I had this especially delicious version made with blackberries at a hill-country coffee estate that is the home of María Esther Hernández Palacios, the former director of the Veracruz State Cultural Institute. It is an excellent basic recipe, for which you can use any fruit of your choice. You can vary the proportions of water and masa to make the drink a little thicker or thinner; the amount of sugar will depend on the acidity of the fruit. But for 6 or so servings, you should always count on using about a pint (or a pound) of the chosen fruit.

Makes about 1½ quarts
(about 6 servings)

9 cups water
1 pint (2 cups) ripe blackberries, picked over and rinsed, or 14–16 ounces frozen blackberries, thawed (reserve the juices)
1 golf-ball-sized lump fresh masa or ½ cup masa harina (see page 51) mixed with ¼ cup cold water
½ cup sugar, or to taste
   Pinch of salt (optional)

IN a medium saucepan, bring 8 cups of the water to a boil. While it is heating, puree the blackberries in a blender with the masa and the remaining 1 cup water.

WITH a wooden spoon or pusher, force the puree through a medium-mesh sieve into the boiling water. Stir in the sugar; taste for sweetness and add more, if desired, along with the optional pinch of salt. Reduce the heat to maintain a low rolling boil and cook for 30 minutes, or until the mixture is thickened to the consistency of a thin cream soup. If it is lumpy, strain through a sieve into a heatproof pitcher. Serve hot, in mugs or breakfast cups, and caution people not to scald themselves! (It retains the heat much longer than you expect.)

Menyul

MINT JULEP

THEORIES ABOUND AS TO HOW THE IDEA OF A MINT JULEP migrated to the city of Córdoba in Veracruz. It is a favorite cocktail of the state generally, but Córdobans regard it with special pride. Most people agree that it got to Veracruz from the southern United States, and indeed the resemblance to a Kentucky mint julep seems too close to be a coincidence. But I might not dare say that out loud to a Kentuckian, considering what's in an authentic Veracruzan *menyul*. It does start out with bruised mint and sugar, but from there it goes on to become an amazing mixture of brandy or whiskey, sweet sherry, sweet vermouth, and Campari, with or without other refinements. Some places even add Coca-Cola! Yes, it does take some mental readjustment, but the following version, based on the *menyules* served by Bertha Bernal de Ríos at El Tabachín in Córdoba, should happily convert skeptics.

Makes about 1 cup
(2 servings)

24	mint leaves, plus 2 sprigs for garnish
2–4	teaspoons sugar
1	ounce brandy (any kind)
1½	ounces sweet sherry
1½	ounces sweet vermouth
1½	ounces Campari
6	drops Angostura bitters, or to taste
1	cup crushed ice

USING a bar spoon or pestle, bruise the mint leaves with the sugar in a cocktail shaker or martini pitcher. Add the remaining ingredients and shake or stir vigorously. Serve in martini or old-fashioned glasses, garnished with sprigs of mint.

Toritos de Cacahuate

MILK PUNCH WITH PEANUTS

Makes 2½ quarts

(serves 8–10)

TORITOS ARE ONE OF THE BEST-LOVED OF ALL Veracruzan institutions. I would describe them as sweet, heavy aperitifs made with the local cane liquor, or *aguardiente*.

Everywhere we went in Sotavento, people offered us a version of *toritos* like this rich milk punch made with peanuts or peanut butter. It is suave, very sweet, and unexpectedly potent. There are also *toritos* made (with or without the milk base) from an array of tropical fruits including guava, soursop, and mango. But I think the one with peanuts will be the easiest to duplicate in this country. If possible, look for Latin American liquor stores selling plain unflavored *aguardiente* (cane liquor). Otherwise, unflavored grain alcohol and vodka are good substitutes. Try it as an aperitif if you wish to be authentic, an after-dinner liqueur if you don't like sweet drinks before meals. It makes a great dessert sauce — I love it with Peanut Ice (page 351).

The peanut *toritos* I've tasted in Veracruz have usually been made with the commercial peanut butter found in all supermarkets. You can use the so-called natural (unhomogenized) peanut butter, but the texture will be a little gritty unless you strain the mixture after blending. The one thing you want to avoid is anything labeled "chunky."

2 12-ounce cans evaporated milk
1 14-ounce can condensed milk
½–¾ cup peanut butter (see above)
½ teaspoon pure vanilla extract, preferably Mexican
8 ounces (1 cup) cane liquor or 96-proof grain alcohol or vodka

PLACE all the ingredients in a blender and process to combine smoothly. If necessary, blend it in batches, or mix in a large bowl. Pour into bottles, seal tightly, and store in the refrigerator. It will keep for up to 1 month.

VARIATIONS

For *Toritos de Mango* (Mango Milk Punch), substitute 1½–2 cups peeled and cubed mango flesh for the peanut butter. (Mangoes vary a lot in size, but about 2 pounds should be enough.)

Rompope

MEXICAN EGGNOG

WHEN I WAS GROWING UP, MY PARENTS WOULD ALLOW US to have a small glass of *rompope* at Christmas, and to me it still has the aura of a special treat. Bottled versions are widely sold in Mexico (in fact, I think that was what my family used). But in many homes, it is made fresh. Señora Rosaura Reyes de Pardiño, the matriarch of the family with eponymous restaurants in Mexico City and Boca del Río, shared her recipe with me.

Please note that there is no substitute for the condensed milk.

Makes about 3³/₄ quarts

2 quarts milk

1 4-inch *canela* stick (see page 44)

1 14-ounce can condensed milk

2 teaspoons pure vanilla extract, preferably Mexican

5 large egg yolks, lightly beaten

8 ounces (1 cup) *aguardiente* (cane liquor) or 96-proof grain alcohol or vodka

5 drops yellow food coloring (optional)

POUR the fresh milk into a medium heavy saucepan, add the *canela*, and bring to a boil over medium heat, watching to keep it from boiling over. (Sticking a spoon in it sometimes seems to do the trick.) Reduce the heat to low and simmer for 5 minutes. Remove from the heat and let cool to room temperature.

REMOVE and discard the *canela*. Add the condensed milk, vanilla extract, and egg yolks; whisk to combine thoroughly. Add the liquor now if you want a milder *rompope* (or if you want to use it for Mexican Eggnog Mousse, page 339). If desired, whisk in the food coloring; *rompope* is supposed to be a rich yellow.

SET the pan over medium-low heat. Stirring constantly, heat it to just below the boil and cook until it thickens to the consistency of a thin cream soup, 3–5 minutes. Watch carefully, because it will curdle if allowed to reach a full boil. (For the sake of caution, you can cook it in a double boiler over simmering water, but it will take forever to thicken.) Remove from the heat and let cool somewhat, stirring occasionally. For *rompope* with a kick, stir in the liquor at this point. Strain into a punch bowl or serving pitcher; serve chilled.

MAIL-ORDER SOURCES

CALIFORNIA

CARLSON FOOD EQUIPMENT, 50 Mendell, #12, San Francisco, CA 94124. (415) 648-2601. Sausages and sausage-making equipment.

FRIEDA'S BY MAIL, 4465 Corporate Center Drive, Los Alamitos, CA 90720. (800) 421-9477. Web site: www.friedas.com. Wide spectrum of fresh and dried chiles, including chipotles and habaneros.

HERBS OF MEXICO, 3903 Whittier Boulevard, Los Angeles, CA 90023. (323) 261-2521. Wide assortment of dried herbs and spices such as epazote.

TIERRA VEGETABLES, 13684 Chalk Hill Road, Healdsburg, CA 95448. (707) 837-8366; fax (888) 784-3772. Web site: www. tierravegetables.com. Locally grown, dried, and smoked chiles.

FLORIDA

BURNS FARMS, 1345 Bay Lake Loop, Groveland, FL 34736. (352) 429-4048. Fresh *hoja santa*.

MASSACHUSETTS

MARÍA AND RICARDO'S TORTILLA FAC-
TORY, 25 Broad Street, Quincy, MA 02169.
(617) 769-0023; fax (617) 769-0400. Fresh
or frozen tortillas and masa.

MICHIGAN

ZINGERMAN'S, 610 Phoenix Drive, Ann Arbor,
MI 48104. (888) 636-8162; fax (734) 769-
1620. Web site: www.zingermans.com.
Great Spanish olive oils and Mexican vanilla
beans.

NEW JERSEY

CHILE TODAY-HOT TAMALE, INC., 31 Rich-
boynton Road, Dover, NJ 07801. (800) 468-
7377; fax (973) 537-2917. Web site:
www.chiletoday.com. Chipotle, dried ancho,
and guajillo chiles.

THE CMC COMPANY, P.O. Drawer 322,
Avalon, NJ 08202. (800) CMC-2780; fax
(609) 861-3065. Web site: www.thecmc-
company.com. Large selection of Mexican
ingredients and equipment, though at high
prices. Carries cast-aluminum tortilla
presses, dried avocado leaves, *canela*, epazote, and Mexican oregano.

NEW YORK

KITCHEN MARKET, 218 Eighth Avenue, New
York, NY 10011. (212) 243-4433; message,
fax, and ordering (888) HOT-4433. Web site:
www.kitchenmarket.com. Wide assortment
of Mexican ingredients, including *canela*,
Mexican oregano, and avocado leaves.

THE SAUSAGE MAKER, 1500 Clinton Street,
Buffalo, NY 14206. (716) 824-6510. Sausage
casings and sausage-making equipment.

OHIO

COMPANION PLANTS, 7247 North Coolville
Ridge Road, Athens, OH 45701. (740) 592-
4643; fax: (614) 593-3092. Epazote seeds,
Mexican oregano plants, and tomatillo
seeds.

LEHMANS NON-ELECTRIC CATALOG, One
Lehman Circle, P.O. Box 41, Kidron, OH
44636. (330) 857-5757; fax (330) 857-5785.
Web site: www.lehmans.com. Hand corn
grinder.

TEXAS

GENERATION FARMS, 1109 North McKinney,
Rice, TX 75155. (903) 326-4263; fax (903)
326-6511. Web site: www.generationfarms.
com. Fresh epazote and *hoja santa*
($1/2$ pound regular minimum, but $1/4$ pound
if you order several herbs).

IT'S ABOUT THYME, 11726 Manchaca Road,
Austin, TX 78748. (512) 280-1192; fax (512)
280-6356. Web site: www.itsaboutthyme.
com. *Hoja santa* and epazote plants.

THE MOZZARELLA CO., 2944 Elm Street,
Dallas, TX 75226. (214) 741-4072 and
(800) 798-2954; fax (214) 741-4076. Web
site: www.mozzco.com. *Queso blanco* and
queso fresco.

PENDERY'S, 304 E. Belknap Street, Fort Worth,
TX 76102. (800) 533-1870; fax (214) 741-
1966. Web site: www.penderys.com.
Smoked chipotle chiles, dried avocado
leaves, epazote, and Mexican oregano.

WISCONSIN

PENZEYS LTD., P.O. Box 933, Muskego, WI
53150. (800) 741-7787; fax (262) 679-7878.
Web site: www.penzeys.com. *Canela* (ask for
Ceylon or soft-stick cinnamon), dried epa-
zote, Mexican oregano, chipotle chiles, and
Mexican vanilla.

SHOPPING SOURCES

CALIFORNIA

Los Angeles Area

LA GUELAGUETZA, 3337 ½ West 8th Street, Los Angeles, CA
90005. (213) 427-0601. E-mail: oaxusa@pacbell.net. Fresh *hoja
santa*, dried chiles, many dried herbs, and *queso fresco*. If you
don't see something you want on display, ask for it — they almost surely have it in the storeroom.

VALLEY FOOD WAREHOUSE, 14530 Nordhoff, Panorama City, CA
91402. (818) 891-9939; fax (818) 891-1781. Avocado leaves, epazote, and banana leaves, as well as other Mexican and Central
American ingredients.

San Francisco

CASA LUCAS MARKET, 2934 24th Street, San Francisco, CA 94110. (415) 826-4334. Dried epazote and avocado leaves; Mexican seasonings and chiles.

LA PALMA MEXICATESSEN, 2884 24th Street, San Francisco, CA 94110. 415-647-1500. Mexican seasonings and chiles.

TIERRA VEGETABLES. A branch of the Healdsburg company (see Mail-Order Sources) is open at the Ferry Plaza Farmers' Market on El Embarcadero on Saturday and Sunday mornings.

ILLINOIS

JIMÉNEZ ENTERPRISES, INC., 2140 North Western and 3850 W. Fullerton, Chicago, IL.

SUPERMERCADOS CÁRDENAS, 3922 N. Sheridan and 2153 W. Roscoe, Chicago, IL. Mexican seasonings and ingredients, including epazote, chiles, and *hoja santa*.

NEW JERSEY

MI BANDERA SUPERMARKET, 518 32nd Street, Union City, NJ 07087. (201) 348-3660. Wide assortment of Latin American ingredients, including Mexican-style cheeses.

NEW YORK AREA

KITCHEN MARKET (see Mail-Order Sources).

PLAZA PIAXTLA, 898 Flushing Avenue, Brooklyn, NY 11206. (718) 386-2626. Good source for Mexican ingredients, including fresh epazote and dried *hoja santa*, and equipment.

STOP 1 SUPERMARKET, 210 W. 94th Street, New York, NY 10025. (212) 864-9456. Large selection of Mexican chiles and seasonings, including dried avocado leaves, dried *hoja santa*, epazote, and *canela*.

INDEX

A

L

M